✠✠✠✠✠✠✠✠✠✠✠✠✠✠✠✠✠✠✠✠

THE HUTH LIBRARY.

—

LIFE AND WORKS

OF

ROBERT GREENE, M.A.

VOL. XIV.—PLAYS.

A LOOKING-GLASSE FOR LONDON AND ENGLAND.
GEORGE A GREENE, THE PINNER OF WAKEFIELD.
SELIMUS, EMPEROUR OF THE TURKES.

AND

A MAIDENS DREAME.

1591—1599.

✠✠✠✠✠✠✠✠✠✠✠✠✠✠✠✠✠✠✠

Look on them all
As the rough metal for a mighty bell
That shall one day have the full ring of heaven,
Wherein each grain by the one tone divine
Is thrilled, which each contributes of itself
With the sweet silvery sound of the whole bell !
LEOPOLD SCHEFER.

The Huth Library.

THE

LIFE AND COMPLETE WORKS

IN

PROSE AND VERSE

OF

ROBERT GREENE, M.A.

CAMBRIDGE AND OXFORD.

IN FIFTEEN VOLUMES

FOR THE FIRST TIME COLLECTED AND EDITED,
WITH NOTES AND ILLUSTRATIONS, ETC.,

BY THE REV.
ALEXANDER B. GROSART, D.D., LL.D. (EDIN.), F.S.A. (SCOT.),
St. George's, Blackburn, Lancashire.

VOL. XIV.—PLAYS.

A LOOKING-GLASSE FOR LONDON AND ENGLAND.
GEORGE A GREENE, THE PINNER OF WAKEFIELD.
SELIMUS, EMPEROUR OF THE TURKES.
AND
A MAIDENS DREAME.

1591—1599.

New York
RUSSELL & RUSSELL

1964

Reissued in 1964 by Russell & Russell, Inc.,
in an Edition Limited to 400 Sets
L. C. Catalog Card No: 64-23465

828.3
G811l

v. 14

PRINTED IN THE UNITED STATES OF AMERICA

A
PLEASANT
CONCEYTED CO-
medie of *George a Greene*, the Pinner
of *VVakefield.* ɛ

*Written by .... a minister, who
ɛ pinned yet in it himself. Test W. Shakespea*

As it was sundry times acted by the seruants of the right
Honourable the Earle of Suſſex.

Ed. July sayth yʳ lyf p ley wey recd by R v Grein

Imprinted at London by Simon Stafford,
for Cuthbert Burby : And are to be ſold at his ſhop
neere the Royall Exchange. 1599:

ERRATA ET CORRIGENDA.

Page 11, l. 104, 'either'—qy. 'eather' = more easily?

,, 20, l. 318, reference to note, for [2] read [1], and l. 325 for [3] read [2].

,, 34, last l., 'goods'—qy. 'gods'?

,, 54, l. 1174, read 'fhepheard's.'

,, 93, l. 2136, 'bombafted' = bumbasted = beaten.

CONTENTS.

*** Fac-simile to face title-page of 'George a Greene' at page 117, In the Note (page 190) I promised the fac-simile only in large paper; but finding that by cutting to the edge, exactly as in the original, it could be given in all the sizes, it is given.

Why, Rome was naked once, a bastard smudge,
Tumbled on straw, the den-fellow of whelps,
Fattened on roots, and, when a-thirst for milk,
He crept beneath and drank the swagging udder
Of Tyber's brave she-wolf ; and Heaven's Judea
Was folded in a pannier.

THOMAS LOVELL BEDDOES.

v.

A LOOKING GLASSE FOR LONDON AND ENGLAND.

1594.

NOTE.

For my text I am again indebted to his Grace the Duke of Devon-shire, whose exemplar of the 1594 4to is only slightly defective in three leaves (Sig. B 2 and 3). (These broken bits Kemble had not observed, as he marks on title-page " Collated and Perfect.—J. P. K."). Besides this, I have had the advantage of the use of the 1598, 1602 and 1617 4tos. Another (apparently), without title-page, in the possession of F. Locker, Esq., kindly sent me by him. I note here a few con-temporary MS. notings on it. At the opening there is written "fflorifh," and so several times onward ; and after the first line-speech of K. of Paph. 'heere enter' (*i.e.* Rasni). 'Clownes' are changed to '1. Ruff.', '2. Ruff.' (*i.e.* ruffian) ; and instead of '*Exeunt*' is repeatedly written 'Clear.' In Rasni's first great speech of penitence, in margin is written 'that all the fubiects of o^r foueraigntie' a variant for 'That man and beaft, the woman and her child.' At the close are written these un-printed lines—

> " Thou famous Citty London cheif of all
> Theis bleft vnited nations do containe,
> More finne in thee, then in nin'vay remaines."

Opposite is the title-page of 1594. This edition is much the more accurate, but shares with all a number of flagrant misprints—indicated in their places.   G.

A
Looking Glaſse for
LONDON AND
England.

Made by *Thomas Lodge* Gentleman, and
Robert Greene,

In Artibus Magiſter.

LONDON
Printed by Thomas Creede, and are to be
ſold by William Barley, at his ſhop
in Gratious ſtreete.
1594.

[Dramatis Personæ.[1]

—++—

RASNI, *King of Nineveh.*
KING OF CILICIA.
KING OF CRETE.
KING OF PAPHLAGONIA.
THRASYBULUS, *a young gentleman, reduced to pouerty.*
ALCON, *a poor man.*
RADAGON, } *his fons.*
CLESIPHON, }
Vfurer.
Iudge.
Lawyer.

[1] Accepted from Dyce, who annotates here, "Occasionally throughout the 4tos *Rasni, Cilicia, Remilia, Alvida,* are printed *Rasin, Cicilia.
Remilias,* and *Alvia*"; and again, "'In like manner,' says Malone
(in his note about anagrams,—*Shakespeare* by Boswell, vol. ii., p. 221),
'in the "Looking Glaſſe for London and England," written by Thomas
Lodge and Robert Greene, the cruel and brutal son who treats his
parents, Alcon and Samia, with neglect and contempt, and refuses them
any succour in their utmost need, is called *Radagon,* by metathesis, from
a dragon.' It had perhaps escaped Malone's notice that a very un-
exceptionable personage, called *Radagon,* figures in the Host's Tale,
in Greene's 'Never Too Late,' Part II." The misprints 'Raſin' for
'Raſni,' 'Cicilia' for 'Cilicia,' 'Remilias' for 'Remilia,' and 'Alvia'
for 'Alvida,' are put right throughout.   G.

Smith.
Adam, *his man.*
Clown.
Firſt Ruffian.
Second Ruffian.
Gouernor of Ioppa.
Maſter of a ſhip.
Firſt Searcher.
Second Searcher.
A Man in deuil's attire.
Magi, Merchants, Sailors, Lords, Attendants, &c.

Remilia, *ſiſter to Raſni.*
Alvida, *wife to the King of Paphlagonia.*
Samia, *wife to Alcon.*
Smith's Wife.
Ladies.

An Angel.
An Euil Angel.
Oseas.
Ionas.]

A LOOKING-GLASSE
FOR LONDON AND ENGLAND.

Enters Rafni King of *Niniuie with three* Kings
of Cilicia, Creete, *and* Paphlagonia, *from the
ouerthrow of Ieroboam, King of Ierufalem.*

[*Rafni.*]

O pace ye on, tryumphant war-
   riours;
   Make Venus' Lemmon, armd in
   al his pomp,
   Bafh at the brightneffe of your
   hardy lookes,
For you the Viceroyes are,[1] the Caualires,   10
That wait on Rafnis royall mightineffe:
Boaft, pettie kings, and glory in your fates,
That ftars haue made your fortunes clime fo high,
To giue attend on Rafnis excellence.[2]

---

[1] The 4tos 1594 and '98 'and.' [2] The 4to of '98 'excellencie.'

Am I not he that rules great Niniuie,
Rounded with Lycus'[1] filuer flowing ftreams?
Whofe Citie large Diametri containes,
Euen three daies iournies length from wall to wall;
Two hundreth gates carued out of burnifht braffe,
As glorious as the portoyle of the Sunne ;   20
And for to decke heauens battlements with pride,
Six hundreth Towers that toplefle touch the cloudes:
This Citie is the footeftoole of your King;
A hundreth Lords do honour at my feete ;
My fcepter ftraineth both the paralels:[2]
And now t'enlarge the highneffe of my power,
I haue made Iudeas Monarch flee the field,
And beat proud Ieroboam from his holds,
Winning from Cades to Samaria.
Great / Iewries God, that foilde ftout Benhadad,[3]   30
Could not rebate the ftrength that Rafni brought ;
For be he God in heauen, yet, Viceroyes, know
Rafni is God on earth, and none but he.
    Cilicia. If louely fhape, feature by natures fkill
Paffing in beautie fair Endymions,
That Luna wrapt within her fnowy brefts,
Or that fweet boy that wrought bright Venus bane,
Transformde vnto a purple Hiacynth ;
If beautie Nunpareile in excellence,
May make a King match with the Gods in gree ;   40
Rafni is God on earth, and none but hee.

---

[1] 4tos 'Lycas.'   [2] *Ibid.* 'poralels.'   [3] *Ibid.* 'Benhadab.'

Creet. If martial lookes, wrapt in a cloud of wars,
More fierce than Mavors[1] lightneth frō his eyes,
Sparkling reuenge and dyre difparagement :
If doughtie deeds more haughtie[2] then any done,
Seald with the fmile of Fortune and of Fate,
Matchleffe to manage Lance and Curtelex[3] ;
If fuch high actions, grac'd with victories,
May make a King match with the Gods in gree ;
Rafni is God on earth, and none but hee.   50
    Paphlag. If Pallas wealth——
    Rafni. Viceroyes inough ; peace,[4] Paphlagon, no
See wheres my fifter, fair Remilia,   [more.
Fairer then was the virgin Dania,[5]
That waits on Venus with a golden fhow[6] ;
She that hath ftolne the wealth of Rafni's lookes,
And tide his thoughts within her louely lockes,
She that is lou'd, and loue vnto your King,
See where fhe comes to gratulate my fame.

Enters Radagon *with* Remilia *fifter to* Rafni, *Alvida* 60
    wife to Paphlagon ; *and other Ladies, bring a*
    Globe feated in a fhip.

    Remilia. Victorious Monarch, fecond vnto *Ioue,*

[1] 4tos 'Mars.' See onward, and Glossarial-Index, *s.v.*
[2] = haut, *i.e.* to be so pronounced, though printed as usual in full.
Thus *frequenter.*
[3] = curtle-axe.   [4] 'peace' dropped in '98 4to.   [5] = Danäe.
[6] Dyce annotates, "We should read, I think—
    'That *Venus wait* [*i.e.* waited] *on* with a golden *fhower*'
(Walker's *Crit. Exam. of the Text of Shakespeare,* etc., ii. 60)." Doubtful.

Mars vpon Earth, and Neptune on the Seas,
Whofe / frowne, ftrows [1] all the ocean with a calme,
Whofe fmile, drawes Flora to difplay her pride,
Whofe eye holds wanton Venus at a gaze,
Rafni, the Regent of great Niniuie;
For thou haft foyld proud Ieroboams force,
And, like the bluftering [2] breath of Æolus   70
That ouerturnes the pines of Libanon,
Haft fcattered Iury and her vpftart groomes,
Winning from Cades to Samaria ;—
Remilia greets thee with a kind falute,
And for a prefent to thy mightineffe,
Giues thee a Globe folded within a fhip,
As King on Earth and Lord of all the Seas,
With fuch a welcome vnto Nyniuie
As may thy fifters humble loue afford.

   Rafni. Sifter ? the title fits not thy degree ;   80
A higher ftate of honour fhall be thine.
The louely Trull that Mercury intrapt
Within the curious pleafure of his tongue,
And fhe that bafht the fun-god with her eyes,
Faire Semele, the choyce of Venus maides,
Were not fo beautious as Remilia.
Then fweeting, fifter fhall not ferue the turne,
But Rafni's wife, his Lemmon, and his loue :
Thou fhalt, like *Iuno*, wed thy felfe to Ioue,

---

[1] The 4tos ' ftroyes.'
[2] 4to ' muftering ' : Dyce's emendation accepted.

And fold me in the riches of thy faire ;   90
Remilia fhall be Rafni's Paramour.
For why, if I be Mars for warlike deeds,
And thou, bright Venus for thy cleare afpect,
Why fhould not from our loynes iffue a fonne
That might be Lord of royall foueraigntie,
Of twentie worlds, if twentie worlds might be ?
What faift Remilia, art thou Rafnis wife ?

   Remilia. My heart doth fwell with fauour of
              thy thoughts ;
The loue of Rafni maketh me as proud
As Iuno when fhe wore heauen's Diademe.
Thy / fifter borne was for thy wife, my [1] loue :   100
Had I the riches nature locketh vp
To decke her darling beautie when fhe fmiles,
Rafni fhould prancke him in the pride of all.

   Rafni. Remilias loue is farre more either[2] prifde,
Than Ieroboams or the world's fubdue.
Lordings, Ile haue my weddinge[3] fumptuous,
Made glorious with the treafures of the world :
Ile fetch from Albia fhelues of Margarites,
And ftrip the Indies of their Diamonds,   110
And Tyre fhall yeeld me tribute of her gold,
To make Remilias wedding glorious.
Ile fend for all the Damofell Queenes that liue

---

[1] The 4to of 1602 'my' accepted for '94 and '98 ' by.'

[2] Dyce annotates, " May be right : but qy. (according to the phrafeo-
logy of the time) ' more *richer* ' ? "

[3] 4tos ' weddings.'

Within the reach of Rafnis gouernment,
To wait as handmaides on [1] Remilia ;
That her attendant traine may paffe the troupe
That gloried Venus at her wedding day.

   Creet. Oh my Lord, not [thy] fifter to thy loue !
Tis inceft, and too fowle a fact for Kings ;
Nature allowes no limits to fuch luft.   [thy Lord, 120

   Rada. Prefumptuous Viceroy, darft thou check
Or twit him with the lawes that nature lowes ? [2]
Is not great Rafni aboue natures reach,
God vpon earth, and all his will is law ?

   Creet. Oh flatter not, for hatefull is his choice,
And fifters loue will blemifh all his worth.

   Radag. Doth not the brightneffe of his maieftie
Shadow his deeds from being counted faults?

   Rafni. Well haft thou anfwer'd with him, [3]
            Radon ;
I like thee for thy learned Sophiftri.—   130
But thou of Creet, that countercheckft thy King,
Packe hence in exile, [giue] Radagon thy crowne [4]—
Be thou [5] Vicegerent of his royaltie ;
And faile me not in what my thoughts may pleafe,
For from a beggar haue I brought thee vp,
And gracft thee with the honour of a Crowne.—
Ye quondam [6] king, what, feed ye on delaies ?

---

[1] 4to '98 ' to.'   [2] = ' allows.'   [3] 4tos ' within Radon.'
[4] The 4to of '94—
       ' Packe hence in exile, Radagon *the* crown.'
  [5] The 4tos ' thee.'   [6] *Ibid.* ' quandam.'

Creete. Better no king then Viceroy vnder him,
That hath no vertue to maintaine his Crowne.

[*Exit.* 140

Rafni. Remilia,[1] what faire dames be thofe that
    wait
Attendant on thy[2] matchleffe royaltie ?

Remilia. Tis Alvida,[3] the faire wife to the King
Of Paphlagonia.

Rafni. Truft me, fhe is fair.[4]—T'haft Paphlagon,
    a Jewell,
To fold thee in fo bright a fweetings armes.

Rad. Like you her, my Lord ?

Rafni. What if I do, Radagon ?

Rada. Why, thē fhe is yours my Lord ; for
    mariage
Makes no exception, where Rafni doth command. 150

Paphla. Ill doeft thou counfel him to fancy
    wiues.

Rada. Wife or not wife, whatfo he likes is his.

Rafni. Well anfwered, Radagon ; thou art for me :
Feed thou mine humour, and be ftill a king.—
Lords, go in tryumph of my happie loues,
And, for to feaft vs after all our broyles,
Frolicke and reuell it in Niniuie.
What foeuer[5] befitteth your conceited thoughts,

---

[1] The 4tos ' Remilias.'
[2] 4to of '98 ' my.'
[3] Dyce suggests " ' This ' [*i.e.* This is]."
[4] 4to of '98 ' a faire.'
[4] = Whate'er—*i.e.* so to be pronounced, though printed in full, as usual.

Or good or ill, loue or not loue, my boyes,
In loue, or what may fatisfie your luft,   160
Act it my Lords, for no man dare fay no.
Diuifum imperium cum Ioue nunc teneo.[1]

                [Exeunt.

Enters, brought in by an Angel, Ofeas *the Prophet,
and let*[2] *down over the ftage in a throne.*

   Angell. Amaze not, man of God, if in the fpirit
Th'art brought from Iewry vnto Niniuie ;
So was Elias wrapt within a ftorme,
And fet vpon mount Carmell by the Lord :
For thou haft preacht long to the ftubborne Iewes, 170
Whofe flintie hearts haue felt no fweet remorfe,
But lightly valuing all the threats of God,
Haue ftill perféuerd in their wickedneffe.
Loe / I haue brought thee vnto Niniuie,
The rich and royall Citie of the world,
Pampred in wealth, and ouergrowne with pride,
As Sodom and Gomorrha full of fin.
The Lord lookes downe and cannot fee one good,
Not one that couets to obey his will ;
But wicked all, from Cradle to the Cruch.   180

  [1] "To this line, in the 4tos, is prefixed ' *Smith* '—that name having
been written here on the margin of the prompter's copy as a memoran-
dum that the performer of ' the Smith's man, *Adam* ' (see note [2], next
page) and those who played his companions muft be in readiness to
appear on the stage immediately after the exit of the Angel."—*Dyce.*
4tos misprint ' *Denefum.* '

  [2] 4tos of '94, '98, 1602 and 1617 ' fet ' : Dyce's emendation accepted.

Note, then Oſeas, all their greeuous ſinnes,
And ſee the wrath of God that paies reuenge ;
And when the ripeneſſe of their ſin is full,
And thou haſt written all their wicked through,
Ile carry thee to Iewry backe againe,
And ſeate thee in the great Ieruſalem :
There ſhalt thou publiſh in her open ſtreetes,
That God ſends downe his hatefull[1] wrath for ſin
On ſuch as neuer heard his Prophets ſpeake :
Much more will he inflict a world of plagues   190
On ſuch as heare the ſweetneſſe of his voice,
And yet obey not what his Prophets ſpeake.
Sit thee Oſeas, pondring in the ſpirit
The mightineſſe of theſe fond peoples ſinnes.

   Oſeas. The will of the Lord be done.

                            Exit Angell.

Enter the Clowne *and his crew of* Ruffians, *to go to
drinke.*

   [*Firſt*] *Ruffian.* Come on, Smyth, thou ſhalt be 200
one of the Crew, becauſe thou knowſt where the
beſt Ale in the Town is.

   Adam.[2] Come on, in faith, my colts : I haue

---

  [1] = full of hate against sin.

  [2] Dyce annotates, " The 4to of 1602, throughout the scene, ' *Smith* ' ;
so the other 4tos in part of the scene, but in part of it they do not ap-
propriate his speeches to any one. It is plain that the speaker is ' the
Smith's man, *Adam*,' by which name he is several times distinguished
in the later portion of the play."

left my M[after] ftriking of a heat, and ftole away,
becaufe I would keep you company.

Clowne. Why, what, fhall we haue this paltrie
Smith with vs?

Adam. / Paltry Smith? why, you Incarnatiue
knaue, what are you that you fpeak pettie treafon
againft the Smiths trade?

Clowne. Why flaue, I am a gentleman of Nini- 210
uie.

Adam. A Gentleman? good fir, I remember you
well, and all your progenitors: your father bare
office in our towne; an honeft man he was, and in
great difcredit in the parifh, for they beftowed two
fquiers liuings on him; the one was on working-
dayes, and then he kept the towne ftage, and on
holidays they made him the Sextens man, for he
whipt dogs out of the church. Alas fir, your
father,—why, fir, mee-thinks I fee the Gentleman 220
ftill: a proper youth he was, faith, aged fome forty
and ten[1]; his beard rats colour, halfe black, halfe
white; his nofe was in the higheft degree of nofes,
it was nofe *Autem glorificam*,[2] fo fet with rubies
that after his death it fhould haue bin nailed vp in
Copper Smiths Hall for a monument: well fir, I
was beholding to your good father, for he was the
firft man that euer inftructed me in the mifterie of
a pot of Ale.

---

[1] The 4tos '*foure* and ten.'   [2] See Glossarial-Index, *s.v.*

Second Ruffian. Well faid Smith ; that, croſſt him 230
ouer the thumbs.

Clowne. Villaine, were it not that we go to be
merry, my rapier ſhould prefently quit thy oppro-
brious termes.

Adam. O Peter, Peter, put up thy fword, I prithie
heartily, into thy fcabbard, hold in your rapier ;
for though I haue not a long reacher, I haue a
ſhort hitter.—Nay then, gentlemen, ſtay me, for my
choler begins to rife againſt him ; for marke the
words, ' a paltry fmith.' [1] Oh horrible fentence : 240
thou haſt in thefe words, I will ſtand to it, libelled
againſt all the found horfes, whole horfes, fore
horfes, Courfers, Curtalls, Jades, Cuts, Hackneies,
and Mares ; whereupon, my friend, in their defence,
I giue thee this curfe,—[thou] ſhalt not [2] be worth
a horfe of thine owne this feuen yeare.

Clowne.[3] I, prithie Smith, is your occupation fo
excellent ?

Adam. ' A paltry Smith ' ? why, Ile ſtand to it,
a Smith is Lord of the foure elements ; for our 250
yron is made of the earth, our bellowes blow out
aire, our flore holdes fire, and our forge water.
Nay fir, we reade in the Chronicles, that there
was a God of our occupation.

Clowne. I, / but he was a Cuckold.

---

[1] The 4to of '98 ' *of* a.' [2] *Ibid.*, ' not ' dropped, as ' thou ' before in '94.
In '94 4to marked ' 1.'

Adam. That was the reaſone ſir,[1] he cald your
father couſin. ' Paltry ſmith'? why, in this one word
thou haſt defaced their worſhipfull occupation.

Clowne. As how?

Adam. Marrie ſir, I will ſtand to it, that a Smith 260
in his kinde is a phiſitian, a Surgeon, and a Barber.
For let a Horſe take a cold, or be troubled with
the bots, and we ſtraight giue him a potion or a
purgation, in ſuch phiſical maner that he mends
ſtraight: if he haue outward diſeaſes, as the ſpavin,[2]
ſplent, ring-bone, wind-gall, or faſhion,[3] or, ſir, a
galled backe, we let him blood & clap a plaiſter to
him with a peſtilence, that mends him with a very
vengeance: now, if his mane grow out of order,
and he haue any rebellious haires, we ſtraight to 270
our ſheeres and trim him with what cut it pleaſe
vs, picke his eares, and make him neat.   Marrie,
indeed ſir, we are ſlouings for one thing ; we neuer
vſe any muſk-balls to waſh him with, and the reaſon
is ſir, becauſe he can woe without kiſſing.

Clowne. Well ſirrha, leaue off theſe praiſes of a
Smyth, and bring vs to the beſt Ale in the Town.

Adam. Now, ſir, I haue a feate aboue all the
Smythes in Niniuie ; for ſir, I am a Philoſopher
that can diſpute of the nature of Ale ; for marke 280

---

[1] 'ſir' not in '94 4to.
[2] The first three 4tos 'ſpuing.'   Dyce's emendation accepted.
[3] " A corruption of the French *farcin*,—farcy."—*Dyce.*

you fir, a pot of Ale confifts of foure parts,—Im-
primis the Ale, the Toaft, the Ginger, and the
Nutmeg.

Clowne. Excellent.

Adam. The Ale is a reftoratiue, bread is a binder;
marke you, fir, two excellent points in phificke:
the Ginger, Oh ware of that : the philofophers
haue written of the nature of ginger, tis expulfitiue
in two degrees ; you fhal he[a]re the fentence of
Galen :   290

> *It wil make a man belch, cough, and fart,*
> *And is a great comfort to the hart:*

a proper poefie, I promife you : but now to the
noble vertue of the Nutmeg ; it is, faith one Ballad,
(I think an Englifh Roman was the authour,) an
vnderlayer to the braines, for when the Ale giues
a buffet to the head, Oh the Nutmeg that keepes
him for [a] while in temper. Thus you fee the
defcription of the vertue of a pot of Ale. Now fir,
to / put my phifical precepts in practife, follow me: 300
but afore I ftep any further——

Clowne. Whats the matter now?

Adam. Why, feeing I haue prouided the Ale,
who is the purueyor for the wenches? for, mafters,
take this of me, a cup of Ale without a wench,
why, alaffe tis like an egge without falt, or a red
herring without muftard !

Clown. Lead vs to the Ale : weele haue wenches inough, I warrant thee.   [*Exeunt.*

Oseas. Iniquitie feekes out companions ftill,   310
And mortall men are armed to do ill :
London looke on, this matter nips thee neere :
Leaue off thy ryot, pride, and fumptuous cheere ;
Spend leffe at boord, and fpare not at the doore,
But aide the infant, and releeue the poore ;
Elfe feeking mercy, being mercileffe,
Thou be adiudged to endleffe heauineffe.

Enters the Vfurer, Thrafybulus, *and* Alcon.[2]

Vfurer. Come on, I am euery day troubled with
thefe needie companions : what newes with you ? 320
what wind brings you hither ?

Thras. Sir, I hope, how far foeuer you make it
off, you remember, too well for me, that this is the
day wherein I fhould pay you mony that I took vp
of you alate in a commoditie.[3]

Alc. And fir, fir-reuerence of your manhood
and genterie, I haue brought home fuch mony as
you lent me.

Vfurer. You, yoong Gentleman, is my mony
readie ?   330

Thras. Truly fir, this time was fo fhort, the
commoditie fo bad, and the promife of friends fo

---

[1] Throughout the first two scenes where these personages appear,
the 4tos designate them '*a yoong Gentleman and a poore Man.*'
[2] See Glossarial-Index, *s.v.*

broken, that I could not prouide it againſt the
day, wherefore I am come to intreat you to ſtand
my friend, and to fauour me with a longer time,
and I wil make you ſufficient conſideration.

Vſurer. Is the winde in that doore? If thou
haſt my mony, ſo it is : I will not defer a day,
an houre, a minute, but take the forfeyt of / the
bond.   340

Thras. I pray you ſir, conſider that my loſſe
was great by the commoditie I tooke vp : you
knowe ſir, I borrowed of you fortie pounds,
whereof I had ten pounds in money, and thirty
pounds in lute-ſtrings,[1] which when I came to ſell
againe, I could get but fiue pounds for them, ſo
had I, ſir, but fifteene poundes for my fortie. In
conſideration of this ill bargaine, I pray you, ſir,
giue me a month longer.

Vſurer. I anſwered thee afore, not a minute : 350
what haue I to do how thy bargain proued? I
haue thy hand ſet to my booke that thou
receiuedſt fortie pounds of me in mony.

Thras. I, ſir, it was your deuiſe that, to colour
the Statute, but your conſcience knowes what I
had.

Alc. Friend, thou ſpeakeſt Hebrew to him
when thou talkeſt to him of conſcience ; for he
hath as much conſcience about the forfeyt of an

---

[1] See Glossarial-Index, *s.v.* ; also the same to Nashe, *s.v.*

Obligation as my blinde Mare, God bleffe her, 360
hath ouer a manger of Oates.

Thras. Then there is no fauour fir ?

Vfurer. Come to-morrow to mee, and fee how
I will vfe thee.

Thras. No, couetous Caterpillar, know that I
haue made extreame fhift rather then I would fall
into the hands of fuch a rauening panthar : and
therefore here is thy mony, and deliuer me the
recognifance of my lands.

Vfurer. [*afide.*] What a fpight is this,—hath 370
fped of his Crownes ? if he had mift but one halfe
houre, what a goodly Farme had I gotten for
fortie pounds ! well, tis my curfed fortune. Oh
haue I no fhift to make him forfeit his recognifance.

Thras. Come fir, will you difpatch and tell your
mony ?   *Strikes 4 a clocke.*

Vfurer [*afide*]. Stay, what is this a clocke? foure :
—let me fee,—'to be paid between the houres of
three and foure in the afternoone ' : this goes right 380
for me.—You fir, heare you not the clocke, and
haue you not a counterpaine of your Obligation ?
The houre is paft, it was to be paid betweene
three and foure; and now the clock hath ftrooken
foure. / I will receiue none, Ile ftand to the forfeyt
of the recognifance.

Thras. Why fir, I hope you do but ieft : why,

tis but foure, and will you for a minute take
forfeyt of my bond?   If it were fo fir, I was here
before foure.   390

Vfurer. Why didft thou not tender thy mony,
then? if I offer thee iniury, take the law of me,
complaine to the Judge : I will receiue no mony.

Alc. Well fir, I hope you will ftand my good
maifter for my Cow.   I borrowed thirtie fhillings
on her, and for that I haue paid you 18 pence a
weeke, and for her meate you haue had her milke,
and I tell you fir, fhe giues a goodly foape ²: now
fir, here is your mony.

Vfurer. Hang beggarly knaue ! commeft to me 400
for a Cow? did I not bind her bought and fold
for a peny, and was not thy day to haue paid
yefterday?   Thou getft no Cow at my hand.

Alc. No Cow fir? alaffe that word 'no cow'
goes as cold to my heart as a draught of fmall
drinke in a froftie morning ! 'No Cow,' fir? why,
alaffe, alaffe, M[after] Vfurer, what fhall become
of me, my wife, and my poore childe?

Vfurer. Thou getft no Cow of me, knaue: I
cannot ftand prating with you, I muft be gone.   410

Alc. Nay, but heare you M[after] Vfurer : 'no
Cow'? why fir, heres your thirtie fhillings : I haue
paid you 18 pence a weeke, & therefore there is
reafon I fhould haue my Cow.

¹ = sup.

Vſurer. What prateſt thou ? haue I not anſwered thee, thy day is broken ?

Alc. Why ſir, alaſſe my Cow is a Commonwealth
to me : for firſt ſir, ſhe allowes me, my wife and
ſonne, for to banket ourſelues withal, Butter,
Cheeſe, Whay, Curds, Creame, ſodmilk, raw-milke, 420
ſower-milke, ſweete-milk, and butter milke: beſides,
ſir, ſhe ſaued me euery year a peny in Almanackes,
for ſhe was as good to me as a Prognoſtication ;
if ſhe had but ſet vp her tayle and haue gallopt
about the meade, my litle boy was able to ſay,
' Oh father, there will be a ſtorme ' ; her verie
taile was a Kalender to me: & now to looſe
my cow, alas, M[aſter] Vſurer, take pittie vpō
me.

Vſurer. / I haue other matters to talke on : far- 430
well, fellowes.

Thras. Why, but thou couetous churle, wilt
thou not receiue thy mony, and deliuer me my
recogniſance?

Vſurer. Ile deliuer thee none: if I haue wronged
thee, ſeeke thy mends at the law.   [*Exit.*

Thras. And ſo I will, inſatiable peſant.

Alc. And ſir, rather then I will put vp this
word ' no Cow,' I will laie my wiues beſt gowne
to pawne. I tell you ſir, when the ſlaue vttered 440
this word ' no Cow,' it ſtrooke to my heart, for
my wife ſhall neuer haue one ſo fit for her turne

againe, for, indeed fir, fhe is a woman that hath
her twidling ftrings broke.

Thras. What meaneft thou by that fellow ?

A¹c. Marry fir, fir-reuerence of your manhood,
fhe breakes winde behinde : and indeed fir, when
fhe fat milking of her Cow[s] and let a fart, my
other Cowes would ftart at the noyfe, and kick
downe the milke, and away ; but this Cow fir, 450
the gentleft Cow : my wife might blow whilft fhe
burft : and hauing fuch good conditions, fhall the
Vfurer come vpon me with ' no Cow ' ? Nay
fir, before I pocket vp this word 'no Cow,' my
wiues gowne goes to the Lawier : why, alaffe fir,
tis as ill a word to me as ' no Crowne' to a King.

Thras. Well fellow, go with me, and Ile helpe
thee to a Lawyer.

Alc. Marry, and I will fir.   No cow ? well, the
world goes hard.   *Exeunt.* 460

Ofeas. Where hateful vfurie
Is counted hufbandrie ;
Where mercileffe men rob the poore.
And the needie are thruft out of doore ;
Where gaine is held for confcience,
And mens pleafures is¹ all on pence ;
Where yong Gentlemen forfeit their lands,
Through riot, into the Vfurers hands :

¹ Dyce finically corrects by ' are,' but this is modern, not Elizabethan
grammar.

Where pouertie is defpifde & pity banifhed,
And mercy indeed vtterly vanifhed :   470
Where / men efteeme more of mony then of God ;
Let that land looke to feele his wrathfull rod :
For there is no fin more odious in his fight
Then where vfurie defraudes the poore of his right.
London, take heed, thefe finnes abound in thee ;
The poore complaine, the widowes wronged bee ;
The Gentlemen by fubtiltie are fpoilde ;
The plough-men loofe the crop for which they
      toild :
Sin raignes in thee, ô London, euery houre ;
Repent, and tempt not thus the heauenly power.   480

Enters Remilia [*with* Alvida] *with a traine of*
      Ladies, *in all royaltie.*

Remilia. Faire Queenes,[1] yet handmaids vnto
      Rafnis loue,
Tell me, is not my ftate as[2] glorious
As Iunoes pomp, when tyred with heauens defpoile,
Clad in her veftments fpotted all with ftarres,
She croft the filuer path vnto her Ioue ?
Is not Remilia far more beautious,
Richt[3] with the pride of natures excellence,[4]
Then Venus in the brighteft of her fhine ?   490
My haires, furpaffe they not Apollos locks ?

---

[1] Dyce mis-alters into 'Queen' and 'handmaid.'
[2] 4to '98 ' fo.'   [3] ' Rich ' '98 4to.   [4] *Ibid.* ' excellencie.'

Are not my Treffes curled with fuch art
As Loue delights to hide him in their faire ?
Doth not mine eyne fhine like the morning lampe
That tels Aurora when her loue will come ?
Haue I not ftolne the beautie of the heauens,
And plac't it on the feature of my face ?
Can any Goddeffe make compare with me ?
Or match her with the faire Remilia ?

   Aluida. The beauties that proud Paris faw 'fore[1]
       Troy,   500
Muftring in Ida for the golden ball,
Were not fo gorgious as Remilia.

   Remilia. I haue trickt my tramels vp with
       richeft balme,
And made my perfumes of the pureft myrrh[2]:
The pretious drugs that Ægypts wealth affoords,
The / coftly paintings[3] fetcht fro curious Tyre,
Haue mended in my face what nature mift.
Am I not the earths wonder in my lookes ?

   Alui. The wonder of the earth, & pride of
      heauen.

   Remilia. Looke Aluida, a haire ftands not amiffe ; 510
For womens locks are tramels of conceit,
Which do intangle Loue for all his wiles.

   Aluid. Madam, vnleffe you coy it, trick and trim,
And play the ciuill[4] wanton ere you yeeld,

---

[1] 4tos 'fro.' Dyce's emendation accepted.   [2] 4tos 'Myre.'
[3] '98 4to ' painting.'   [4] See Glossarial-Index, *s.v.*

Smiting difdaine of pleafures with your tongue,
Patting your princely Rafni on the cheeke
When he prefumes to kiffe without confent;
You marre the market: beautie nought auailes:
You muft be proud; for pleafures hardly got
Are fweete if once attainde.   520

    Remilia.   Faire Aluida,
Thy counfell makes Remilia paffing wife.
Suppofe that thou weart Rafnis mightineffe,
And I Remilia, Prince of excellence.

    Aluida. I would be maifter then of Loue and
        thee.

    Remil. 'Of Loue and me'?   Proud & difdainful
Dar'ft thou prefume to touch a Deitie,   [king,
Before fhe grace thee with a yeelding fmile?

    Aluida. Tut, my Remilia, be not thou fo coy;
Say nay, and take it.   530

    Remil.   Careleffe and vnkinde:
Talkes Rafni to Remilia in fuch fort,
As if I[1] did enioy a humane forme?
Look on thy Loue, behold mine eyes diuine,
And dar'ft thou twit me with a womans fault?
Ah Rafni, thou art rafh to iudge of me:
I tell thee Flora oft hath woode my lips
To lend a Rofe to beautifie her Spring;
The fea-Nymphs fetch their lillies from my cheeks:
Then thou vnkind :—and hereon would I weepe.

          [1] 4tos '98 and 1602 and 1617 'he.'

Aluida. And here would Aluida refigne her 540
    charge :
For / were I but in thought th'Affirian King,
I needs muft quite thy teares with kiffes fweete,
And craue a pardon with a friendly touch :
You know it Madam, though I teach it not,
The touch I meane, you fmile whenas you think it.[1]
  Remi. How am I pleaf'd to hear thy pritty prate,
According to the humor of my minde ?
Ah Nymphs, who fairer then Remilia ?
The gentle winds haue woode me with their fighes,
The frowning aire hath cleerde when I did fmile ; 550
And when I trac't vpon the tender[2] grafs,
Loue, that makes warme the center of the earth,
Lift vp his creft to kiffe Remilia's foote ;
Iuno ftill entertaines her amorous Ioue
With newe delights, for feare he looke on me ;
The Phœnix feathers are become my Fanne,
For I am beauties Phœnix in this world.
Shut clofe thefe Curtaines ftraight, and fhadow me,
For feare Apollo fpie me in his walkes,
And fcorne all eyes, to fee Remilias eyes. 560
Nymphes, eunuchs,[3] fing, for Mauors draweth
    nigh ;
Hide me in Clofure, let him long to looke :
For were a Goddeffe fairer then am I,

[1] '94 'il.'   [2] dropped in '98 4to.
[3] The 4tos 'Knancks'—Dyce's emendation accepted. See Glossarial-
Index, *s.v.*

Ile ſcale[1] the heauens to pull her from the place.

They draw the Curtaines, and Muſicke plaies.

Aluida. Beleeue me, tho ſhe ſay that ſhe is faireſt,
I thinke my peny ſiluer by her leaue.

Enter Raſni, [*with* Radagon *and*] *his* Lords *in
pomp, who make a ward about him ; with him
the* Magi *in great pompe.*   570

Raſni. Magi, for loue of Raſni, by your[2] Art,
By Magicke frame an Arbour out of hand,
For faire Remilia to deſport her in.
Meane-while on further pomp I will bethinke me.[3]

Exit.

The Magi *with their rods beate the ground, and
from vnder the ſame riſeth a braue Arbour :
the* King *returneth in another ſute, while the
Trumpettes ſounde.*

Raſni. Bleſt be ye, men[4] of Art, that grace me 580
And bleſſed be this day where Himen hies   [thus,
To ioyne in vnion, pride of heauen and earth.

Lightning and thunder, wherewith Remilia
is ſtrooken.

What wondrous threatning noyſe is this I heare ?
What flaſhing lightnings trouble our delights ?

---

[1] See Glossarial-Index, under ' Will.'   [2] '98 4to ' our.'
[3] Dyce's emendation of metre accepted : in the 4tos ' Meanwhile I
will bethinke me on further pompe ' : in '98 ' furth, a.'
[4] 4tos '94, '98, and 1602 ' man.'

When I draw neare Remilias royall Tent,
I waking dreame of forrow and[1] mifhap.

　Rada. Dread not O King, at ordinary chance;
Thefe are but common exalations,　　　　　　590
Drawne from the earth, in fubftance hote and drie,
Or moift and thicke, or Meteors combuft ;
Matters and caufes incident to time,
Inkindled[2] in the fierie region firft.
Tut, be not now a Romane augurer[3] :
Approach the Tent, looke on Remilia.

　Rafni. Thou haft confirmd my doubts, kinde
　　　　　Radagon.—
Now ope ye foldes, where Queene of fauour fits,
Carrying a Net within her curled locks,
Wherein the Graces are entangled oft :　　　　600
Ope like th'imperiall gates where Phœbus fits,
When as he meanes to wooe his Clitia.
Nocturnal[4] Cares, ye blemifhers of bliffe,
Cloud not mine eyes, whilft I behold her face.—
Remilia, my delight:—fhe anfwereth not.

　　He drawes the Curtaines, and findes her ftroken
　　　　　with thunder, blacke.

How pale ? as if bereau'd in fatall meedes,
The balmy breath hath left her bofome quite :
My / Hefperus by cloudie Death is blent.[5]—　　610

---

[1] '98 4to ' or.'
[2] The 4to of '98 ' In kindling.'
[3] '94 ' Angurer.'
[4] *Ibid.* ' Necternal.'
[5] " *i.e.* destroyed, polluted,—from the verb ' blend,' which in its original
sense means to mingle, confound. The 4to of '98 ' bent.' "—*Dyce.*

Villaines away, fetch Sirropes of the Inde,
Fetch Balſamo, the kind preſerue of life,
Fetch wine of Greece, fetch oiles, fetch herbes, fetch
To fetch her life, or I will faint and die.   [all,
>   *They bring in all theſe, and offer : nought*
>   *preuailes.*

Herbes, Oyles of Inde, alaſſe, there nought preuailes.
Shut are the day-bright eyes, that made me ſee,
Lockt are the Iems of ioy in dens of Death ;
Yet triumph I on fate, and he on her :   620
Malicious miſtreſſe of inconſtancie,
Damd be thy name, that haſt[1] obſcur'd my ioy.—
Kings, Viceroyes,[2] Princes, reare a royall tombe
For my Remilia ; beare her from my ſight,
Whilſt I in teares weepe for Remilia.

>   *They beare her out.*

Rada. What maketh Raſni moodie?   Loſſe of
As if no more were left ſo faire as ſhe ?   [one,
Behold a daintie minion for the nonce,—
Faire Aluida, the Paphlagonian Queene :   630
Wooe her, and leaue this weeping for the dead.

  Ras. What, wooe my ſubiects wife that honoreth
            me !   [know :
  Rada. Tut, Kings this *meum tuum*, ſhould not
Is ſhe not faire ? is not her huſband hence ?
Hold, take her at the hands of Radagon ;
A prittie peate to driue your mourne away.

---

[1] The 4to of '98 'hath.'   [2] *Ibid.* 'viceroy.'

Rafni. She fmiles on me, I fee fhe is mine owne.—
Wilt thou be Rafnis royall Paramour?   [difpute :
Rad. She blufhing yeelds concent : make no
The King is fad, and muft be gladded ftraight ;
Let Paphlagonian King go mourne meane-while.   640
      He thruft[s] the King out, and fo they exeunt.
Ofeas. Pride hath his iudgement : London, looke
Tis not inough in fhow to be deuout.   [about ;
A Furie now from heauen to lands vnknowne,
Hath made the prophet fpeake, not to his owne.
Flie / wantons,[1] flie this pride and vaine attire,
The feales to fet your tender hearts on fire :
Be faithfull in the promife you haue paft,
Elfe God will plague and punifh at the laft.
When luft is hid in fhroude of wretched life,   650
When craft doth dwell in bed of married wife,
Marke but the prophets, we that fhortly fhowes,
After death expect for many woes.[2]

Enter Alcon *and* Thrafybulus, *with the* Lawier.[3]

   Thras. I need not fir, difcourfe vnto you the
dutie of Lawiers in tendering the right caufe of
their Clients, nor the confcience you are tied vnto
by higher command.   Therefore fuffice, the Vfurer
hath done me wrong ; you know the Cafe ; and

---

[1] The 4to of '98 ' wanton.'
[2] Dyce annotates, " Some corruption in this couplet."
[3] The 4tos 'Enters the poore man and the Gentleman, with their Lawier.'

good fir, I haue ftrained my felfe to giue you your 660 fees.

Lawier. Sir, if I fhould any way neglect fo manifeft a truth, I were to be accufed of open periury, for the cafe is euident.

Alc. And truly fir, for my cafe, if you helpe me not for my matter, why fir, I and my wife are quite vndone ; I want my meafe[1] of milk when I goe to my worke, and my boy his bread and butter, when he goes to fchoole.   M[after] Lawier, pitie me, for furely fir, I was faine to laie my wiues beft gowne 670 to pawne for your fees : when I lookt vpon it fir, and faw how hanfomly it was dawbed with ftatute lace, and what a faire mockado Cape it had, and then thought how hanfomely it became my wife, —truly fir, my heart is made of butter, it melts at the leaft perfecution,—I fell on weeping ; but when I thought on the words the Vfurer gaue me, ' no Cow,' then fir, I would haue ftript her into her fmocke, but I would make him deliuer my Cow, ere I had done : therefore, good M[after] Lawier, 680 ftand my friend.

Lawier. Truft me father, I will do for thee as much as for my felfe.

Alc. Are you married fir ?

Lawier. I marry, am I, father.

Alc. Then goods Benifon light on you & your

---

[1] "An old form of ' mess.' "—*Dyce.*

good wife, and / fend her that fhe be neuer troubled
with my wiues difeafe.

Lawier. Why, what's thy wiues difeafe ?

Alc. Truly fir, fhe hath two open faults, and 690
one priuie fault. Sir, the firft is, fhe is too eloquēt
for a poore man, and hath her words of Art ; for
fhe will call me Rafcall, Rogue, Runnagate, Varlet,
Vagabond, Slaue, Knaue. Why, alaffe fir, and thefe
be but holi-day tearmes, but if you heard her
working-day words, in faith fir, they be ratlers
like thunder fir ; for after the dewe follows a
ftorme, for then am I fure either to be well
buffeted, my face fcratcht, or my head broken :
and therefore, good M[after] Lawier, on my knees 700
I afke it, let me not go home again to my wife with
this word 'No Cow'; for then fhee will exercife
her two faults vpon me with all extremitie.

Lawier. Feare not, man. But what is thy wiues
priuy fault ?

Alc. Truly fir, thats a thing of nothing ; alaffe
fhe indeed fir-reuerence of your mafterfhip, doth
vfe to breake winde in her fleepe.—Oh fir, here
comes the Judge, and the old Caitife the Ufurer.

Enters the Iudge, *the* Vfurer, *and his* attendants. 710

Vfurer. Sir, here is fortie angels for you, and
if at any time you want a hundreth pound or two,
tis readie at your command, or the feeding of three

or foure fat bullocks : whereas thefe needie flaues
can reward with nothing but a cap and a knee ;
and therfore I pray you, fir, fauour my cafe.

Iudge. Feare not fir, Ile do what I can for you.

Vfurer. What, Maifter Lawier, what make you
here ? mine aduerfary for thefe Clients?   720

Lawier. So it chanceth now fir.

Vfurer. I know you know the old Prouerbe,
' He is not wife that is not wife for himfelfe ' : I
would not be difgracft in this action; therefore
here is twentie angels; fay nothing in the matter,
or [1] what you fay, fay to no purpofe, for the Iudge
is my friend.

Lawier. Let me alone, Ile fit your purpofe.

Iudge. Come, where are thefe fellowes that are
the plaintifes? what can they fay againft this honeft 730
Citizen our neighbour, a man of good report
amongft all men?

Alc. / Truly, M[after] Judge, he is a man much
fpoken off; marry, euery mans cries are againft
him, and efpecially we ; and therefore I thinke we
haue brought our Lawier to touch him with as
much law as will fetch his landes and my Cowe,
with a peftilence.

Thras. Sir, I am the other plaintife, and this is
my Councellour : I befeech your honour be fauour- 740
able to me in equitie.

---

[1] The 4tos ' and.'

Iudge. Oh Signor Mizaldo, what can you fay in this Gentleman's behalfe ?

Lawier. Faith fir, as yet little good.—Sir, tell you your owne cafe to the Iudge, for I haue fo many matters in my head, that I haue almoft forgotten it.

Thras. Is the winde in that doore ? Why then, my Lord, thus. I tooke vp of this curfed Vfurer, for fo I may well tearme him, a commoditie of 750 fortie poundes, whereof I receiued ten pounde in mony, & thirtie pound in Lute-ftrings, whereof I could by great friendfhip make but fiue pounds : for the affurance of this badde commoditie I bound him my land in recognifance ; I came at my day, and tendred him his mony, and he would not take it : for the redreffe of my open wrong, I craue but iuftice.

Iudge. What fay you to this fir ?

Vfurer. That firft he had no Lute-ftrings of me ; 760 for looke you, fir, I haue his owne hand to my book for ẏ receit of fortie pound.

Thras. That was fir but a deuife of him to colour the Statute.

Iudge. Well, he hath thine owne hand, and we can craue no more in law.—But now fir, he faies his mony was tendered at the day and houre.

Vfurer. This is manifeft contrary fir, and on that I will depofe ; for here is the obligation, 'to

be paide betweene three & foure in the after-noone,' 770
and the Clocke ſtrooke foure before he offered it,
and the words be 'betweene three and foure,'
therefore to be tendred before foure.

Thras. Sir, I was there before foure, & he held
me with brabling till the Clock ſtrooke, and then
for the breach of a minute he refuſed my money,
and kept[1] the recogniſance of my land for ſo
ſmall / a trifle.—Good Signor Mizaldo, ſpeak what
is law; you haue your fee, you haue heard what
the caſe is, and therefore do me iuſtice and right : 780
I am a yoong Gentleman, and ſpeake for my
patrimony.

Lawier. Faith ſir, the Caſe is altered; you told
me it before in an other manner: the law goes
quite againſt you, and therfore you muſt pleade
to the Iudge for fauour.

Thras. O execrable bribery.

Alc. Faith Sir Judge, I pray you let me be the
Gentlemans Counſellour, for I can ſay thus much
in his defence, that the Uſurers Clocke is the 790
ſwifteſt Clock in all the Towne: 'tis ſir, like a
womans tongue, it goes euer halfe an houre before
the time; for when we were gone from him, other
Clocks in the Town ſtrooke foure.

Iudge. Hold thy prating, fellow :—and you,
yoong Gentleman, this is my ward : looke better

---

[1] The first three 4tos 'keepe.'

another time both to your bargains and to the
paiments; for I muſt giue flat ſentence againſt
you, that for default of tendering the mony
betweene the houres, you haue forfeited your 800
recogniſance, and he to haue the land.

Thras. O inſpeakeable iniuſtice!

Alc. O monſtrous, miſerable, moth-eaten Judge!

Iudge. Now you, fellow, what haue you to ſay
for your matter?

Alc. Maiſter Lawier, I laid my wiues gowne to
pawne for your fees : I pray you, to this geere.[1]

Lawier. Alaſſe poore man, thy matter is out
of my head, and therefore, I pray thee, tell it
thy ſelfe. 810

Alc. I hold my Cap to a noble[2] that the Uſurer
hath giuen him ſome gold, and he, chawing it in
his mouth, hath got $\tilde{y}$ toothache that he cannot
ſpeake.

Iudge. Well ſirrha, I muſt be ſhort, and therefore
ſay on.

Alc. Maiſter Judge, I borrowed of this man
thirtie ſhillings, for which I left him in pawne my
good Cow ; the bargaine was, he ſhould haue
eighteene pence a weeke, and the Cows milk for 820
vſurie : Now ſir, aſſoone as I had gotten the mony,
I brought it him, and broke but a day, and for
that he refuſed his mony, and keepes / my Cow ſir.

---

[1] ═ business.   [2] See Glossarial-Index, *s.v.*

Iudge. Why, thou haſt giuen ſentence againſt thy ſelfe, for in breaking thy day thou haſt loſt thy Cow.

Alc. Maſter Lawier, now for my ten ſhillings.

Lawier. Faith poore man, thy Caſe is ſo bad, I ſhall but ſpeak againſt thee.

Alc. Twere good, thē, I ſhuld haue my ten 830 ſhillings again.

Lawier. Tis my fee, fellow, for comming: wouldſt thou haue me come for nothing?

Alc. Why then, am I like to goe home, not onely with no Cow, but no gowne: this geere goes hard.

Iudge. Well, you haue heard what fauour I can ſhew you: I muſt do iuſtice.—Come M[after] Mizaldo,—and you, ſir, go home with me to dinner.   840

Alc. Why but M[after] Iudge, no Cow?—&,
    M[after] Lawier, no gowne?
Then muſt I cleane run out of the Towne.

[*Exeunt* Judge *attended,* Lawyer, *and* Vſurer.
How cheere you, gentleman? you crie 'no lands' too; the Judge hath made you a knight for a gentleman, haʒh dubd you ſir John Lack-land.

Thras. O miſerable time, wherein gold is aboue God.

Alc. Feare not, man; I haue yet a fetch to get 850 thy landes and my Cow againe, for I haue a ſonne

in the Court, that is either a king or a kings fellow,
and to him will I go & complaine on the Judge
and the Uſurer both.

Thras. And I will go with thee, and intreat him
for my Caſe.

Alc. But how ſhall I go home to my wife, when
I ſhall haue nothing to ſay vnto her but ' no Cow'?
alaſſe ſir, my wiues faults will fall vpon me.

Thras. Feare not ; lets go ; Ile quiet her, ſhalt 860
ſee.   [*Exeunt.*

Oſeas. Flie Iudges, flie corruption in your Court ;
The Iudge of truth, hath made your iudgement
Looke ſo to iudge, that at the latter day   [ſhort.
Ye be not iudg'd with thoſe that wend aſtray.
Who paſſeth iudgement for his priuate gain,
He well may iudge he is adiudg'd to paine.

Enters / the Clowne and all his crew drunke.

Adam. Farewell, gentle Tapſter.—Maiſters, as
good Ale as euer was tapt ; looke to your feete, 870
for the Ale is ſtrong.—Well, farwell, gentle Tapſter.

Firſt Ruf. [*to Second Ruf.*] Why ſirrha ſlaue, by
heauens maker, thinkeſt thou the wench loues[1]
thee beſt becauſe ſhe laught on thee ? giue me but
ſuch an other word and I will throw the pot at
thy head.

Adam. Spill no drinke, ſpill no drinke, the Ale

[1] The 4tos of '94 and '98 ' loue.

is good : Ile tell you what, Ale is Ale, & fo Ile
commend me to you with heartie commendations.
—Farewell, gentle Tapſter.   880

Second Ruf. Why, wherfore peaſant, ſcornſt thou
that the wench ſhould loue me ? looke but on her
& Ile thruſt my daggar in thy boſome.

Firſt Ruf. Well, ſirrha, well, th'art as th'art,
and fo Ile take thee.

Second Ruf. Why, what am I ?

Firſt Ruf. Why, what thou wilt : a ſlaue.

Second Ruf. Then take that villaine, and learne
how thou[1] vſe me another time. [*Stabs* Firſt Ruf.

Firſt Ruf. Oh I am ſlaine.   [*Dies.* 890

Second Ruf. Thats all one to me, I care not :
now will I in to my wench, and call for a freſh pot.

[*Exit : and then exeunt all except* Adam.

Adam. Nay, but heare ye, take me with ye, for
the Ale is Ale.—Cut a freſh toaſt Tapſter, fil me
a pot ; here is mony, I am no beggar, Ile follow
thee as long as the Ale laſts.—A peſtilence on the
blocks for me, for I might haue had a fall : wel,
if we ſhal haue no Ale, Ile fit me downe : and fo
farwell, gentle Tapſter.   900

[*Here he fals ouer the dead man.*

Enter the King, Aluida, *the* Kings of Cilicia, *and of*
Paphlagonia, *with* Lords *and other* attendant[s].

---

[1] The 4to of '98 ' to.'

Raſni. What ſlaughtred wretch lies bleeding
      here his laſt,
So neare the royall palace of the King ?
Search out if any one be hiding[1] nie,
That can diſcourſe the maner of his death.—
Seate thee, faire Aluida, the faire of faires ;
Let not this obiect[2] once offend thine eyes.

Firſt Lord. Heres one ſits here aſleepe my Lord. 910
Raſni. Wake him, and make enquiry of this
      thing.
Firſt Lord. / Sirrha you, heareſt thou fellow ?
Adam. If you will fill a freſh pot, heres a peny,
or elſe farewell, gentle Tapſter.
Firſt Lord. He is drunke, my Lord.   [laugh.
Raſni. Weele ſport with him, that Aluida may
Firſt Lord. Sirrha, thou fellow, thou muſt come
to the King.
Adam. I wil not do a ſtroke of work to day,
for the Ale is good Ale, and you can aſke but a
peny for a pot, no more by the ſtatute.
Firſt Lord. Villaine, heres the King ; thou muſt 920
come to him.
Adam. The king come to an Ale-houſe ?—
Tapſter, fil me three pots.—Wheres the King ?
is this he ?—Giue me your hand ſir : as good Ale
as euer was tapt ; you ſhall drinke while your ſkin
cracke.

---

[1] The 4tos misprint ' biding.'   [2] The first three 4tos ' the *otrict.*'

Rafni. But heareft thou fellow, who kild this man?

Adam. Ile tell you fir,—if you did tafte of the Ale,—all Niniuie hath not fuch a cup of Ale, it 930 floures in the cup fir; by my troth, I fpent eleuen pence, befides three rafes of ginger—

Rafni. Anfwer me, knaue, to my queftion, how came this man flaine?

Adam. Slain? why, [the] Ale is ftrong Ale, tis hufcap; I warrant you, twill make a man well.— Tapfter, ho, for the King a cup of ale and a frefh toaft; heres two rafes more.

Alvi. Why, good fellow, the King talkes not of drinke; he would haue thee tell him how this man 940 came dead.

Adam. Dead? nay, I thinke I am aliue yet, and wil drink a ful pot ere night: but hear[1] ye, if ye be the wench that fild vs drink, why fo do your office, & giue vs a frefh pot; or if you be the Tapfters wife, why fo wafh the glaffe cleane.

Aluida. He is fo drunke my Lord, theres no talking with him.

Adam. Drunke? nay then wench, I am not drunke: th'art a fhitten queane to call me drunke; 950 I tell thee I am not drunke, I am a Smith, I.[2]

Enter the Smith, *the Clownes Maifter.*

---

[1] 4tos 'here.'   [2] Not in the 4to of '98.

Firſt Lord. Sir, here comes one perhaps that can tell.

Smith. God ſaue you, maſter.   [came dead ?

Raſni. / Smith, canſt thou tell me how this man

Smith. May it pleaſe your highneſſe, my man here and a crue of them went to the Ale-houſe, and came out ſo drunke that one of them kild another : and now ſir, I am faine to leaue my 960 ſhop, and come to fetch him home.

Raſni. Some of you carry away the dead bodie ; drunken men muſt haue their fits ; and, ſirrha Smith, hence with thy man.

Smith. Sirrha you, riſe, come go with me.

Adam. If we ſhall haue a pot of Ale, lets haue it, heres mony ; hold Tapſter, take my purſe.

Smith. Come then with me, the pot ſtands full in the houſe.

Adam. I am for you, lets go, th'art an honeſt 970 Tapſter : weele drinke ſixe pots ere we part. *Exeunt.*

Raſni. Beautious, more bright then beautie in
              mine eyes,
Tell me faire ſweeting, wants thou any thing
Conteind within the threefold circle of the world,[1]
That may make Aluida liue full content ?

[1] Dyce queries
    " ' Tell me, fair ſweeting, want'ſt thou *aught* contaln'd
      Within the threfold circle of the world,' etc. ? "
These alterations make more 'smooth,' but smoothness was no char-
acteristic of the period.

Aluida. Nothing my Lord; for all my thoughts
        are pleafde
When as mine eye furfets with Rafnis fight.

Enter the King of Paphlagonia *malecontent.*

Rafni. Looke how thy hufband haunts our
        royall Courte,
How ftill his fight breeds melancholy ftormes.   980
Oh Aluida, I am paffing[1] paffionate,
And vext with wrath and anger, to the death:
Mars, when he held faire Venus on his knee,
And faw the limping Smith come from his forge,
Had not more deeper furrowes[2] in his brow
Than Rafni hath to fee this Paphlagon.
    Alui. Content thee fweet, Ile falue thy forow
        ftraight ;
Reft but the eafe of all thy thoughts on me,
And if I make not Rafni blyth againe,
Then fay that womens fancies haue no fhifts.   990
    Paphla. Shamft thou not Rafni, though thou
        beeft a King.
To fhroude adultry in thy royall feate ?
Art thou arch-ruler of great Niniuie,
Who / fhouldft excell in vertue as in ftate,
And wrongft thy friend by keeping backe his wife ?
Haue I not battail'd in thy troupes full oft,
Gainft Aegypt, Iury, and proud Babylon,

---

[1] The 4to of '94 'paffion.'   [2] The 4to of '98 'forrowes in.'

Spending my blood to purchafe thy renowne,
And is the guerdon of my chiualrie
Ended in this abufing of my wife ?   1000
Reftore her me, or I will from thy Courts,
And make difcourfe of thy adulterous deeds.

    Ras. Why, take her, Paphlagon, exclaime not
        man ;
For I do prife mine honour more then loue.—
Faire Aluida, go with thy hufband home,

    Alui. How dare I go, fham'd with fo deep mis-
        deed ?
Reuenge will broile within my hufbands breft,
And when he hath me in the Court at home,
Then Aluida fhall feele reuenge for all.   [this ?

    Rafni. What faift thou, king of Paphlagon to 1010
Thou heareft the doubt thy wife doth ftand vpon.
If fhe hath[1] done amiffe, it is my fault ;
I prithie pardon and forget [it] all.

    Paphla. If that I meant not Rafni, to forgiue,
And quite forget the follies that are paft,
I would not vouch[2] her prefence in my Courts ;
But fhe fhall be my Queene, my loue, my life,
And Aluida vnto her Paphlagon,
And lou'd, and more beloued then before.

    Rafni. What faift thou, Aluida, to this?   1020
    Alui. That, will he fweare it to my Lord the
And in a full caroufe of Greekifh wine   [king,

---

[1] The 4to of '98 ' haue.'   [2] *Ibid,* ' vouchfafe.'

Drinke down the malice of his deepe reuenge,
I will go home, and loue him new againe.

Raſni. What anſweres Paphlagon?

Paphla. That what ſhe hath requeſted, I will do.

Alui. Go damoſell [and] fetch me that ſweete
wine

That ſtands within my[1] Cloſet on the ſhelfe :
Powre it into a ſtanding bowle of gold,
But, / on thy life, taſte not before the king :   1030
Make haſt.   [*Exit* Female Attendant.
Why is great Raſni melancholy thus?
If promiſe be not kept, hate all for me.

            [*Wine brought in by* Female Attendant.
Here is the wine, my Lord: firſt make him ſweare.

Paphla. By Niniues great gods, and Niniues
great king,

My thoughts ſhall neuer be to wrong my wife:
And thereon heres a full carouſe to her. [*Drinks.*

Alui. And thereon, Raſni, heres a kiſſe for thee ;
Now maiſt thou freely fold thine Aluida.   1040

Paphla. Oh I am dead! obſtructions of my
breath ;

The poiſon is of wondrous ſharpe effect :
Curſed be all adultrous queenes,[2] ſay I :
And curſing ſo, poore Paphlagon doth die. [*Dies.*

Alui. Now, haue I not ſalued the ſorrowes of
my Lord?

---

[1] The 4to of '98 'thy.'   [2] Dyce misprints 'queans.'

Haue I not rid a riuall of thy loues?
What faift thou, Rafni, to thy Paramour?
    Rafni. That for this deed Ile decke my Aluida
In Sendall, and in coftly Suffapine,
Bordred with Pearle and India Diamond ;   1050
Ile caufe great Æol perfume all his windes
With richeft myrrh[1] and curious Ambergreece.
Come, louely minion, paragon for fair,
Come follow me, fweet goddeffe of mine eye,
And tafte the pleafures Rafni will prouide.
                                            Exeunt.
    Ofeas. Where whordom raines, there murther
                   followes faft,
As falling leaues before the winter blaft.
A wicked life, trainde vp in endleffe crime,
Hath no regard[2] vnto the latter time,   1060
When Letchers fhall be punifht for their luft
When Princes plagu'd becaufe they are vniuft.
Forefee in time, the warning bell doth towle;
Subdue the flefh, by praier to faue the foule :
London, behold the caufe of others wracke,
And fee[3] the fword of iuftice at thy backe :
Deferre not off, to-morrow is too late ;
By night he comes perhaps to iudge thy ftate.

        Enter / Ionas, *folus.*   [foule
    Ionas. From forth the depth of my imprifoned 1070

---

[1] As before, spelled 'myre.'   [2] The 4to of '98 'reward.'   [3] *Ibid.* 'fet.'

Steale you, my fighes, [to] teftifie my paine ;
Conuey on wings of mine immortall tone
My zealous praiers, vnto the ftarrie throne.
Ah mercifull and iuft, thou dreadfull God,
Where is thine arme to lay reuengeful ftroakes
Upon the heads of our rebellious race ?
Loe Ifraell, once that flourifht like the vine,
Is barraine laide ; the beautifull encreafe
Is wholly blent, and irreligious zeale
Incampeth there where vertue was inthron'd :   1080
Ah-laffe the while, the widow wants reliefe,
The fatherleffe is wrongd by naked need,
Deuotion fleepes in finders of Contempt,
Hypocrifie infects the holie Prieft ;
Aye me, for this, woe me, for thefe mifdeeds :
Alone I walke to thinke vpon the world,
And figh to fee thy Prophets fo contemn'd,
Ah-laffe contemn'd by curfed Ifraell :
Yet Ionas, reft content, tis Ifraels finne,
That caufeth this ; then mufe no more thereon,   1090
But pray amends, and mend thy owne amiffe.

An Angel *appeareth to* Ionas.

Angel. Amittais[1] fonne, I charge thee mufe no
        more :
(I AM) hath power to pardon and correct ;
To thee pertains to do the Lords command.

----

[1] 4tos 'Amithais.'

Go girt thy loines, and haft thee quickly hence,
To Niniuie, that mightie citie wend,
And fay this meffage from the Lord of hoafts :
Preach vnto them thefe tidings from thy God ;—
'Behold, thy wickedneffe hath tempted me,   1100
And pierced through the ninefold orbes of heauen :
Repent, or elfe thy iudgement is at hand.'

       This | faid, the Angell *vanifheth.*

Ionas. Proftrate I lye before the Lord of hoftes,
With humble eares intending his beheft :
Ah honoured be Iehouahs great command :
Then Ionas muft to Niniuie repaire,
Commanded as the Prophet of the Lord.
Great dangers on this iourney do await,
But dangers none where heauens direct the courfe. 1110
What fhould I deeme ?   I fee, yea, fighing fee,
How Ifraell finne[s], yet knowes[1] the way of truth,
And thereby growes the by-word of the world.
How then, fhould God in iudgement be fo ftrict
Gainft thofe who neuer heard or knew his power,
To threaten vtter ruine of them all ?
Should I report this iudgement of my God,
I fhould incite them more to follow finne,
And publifh to the world my countries blame :
It may not be, my confcience tels me no.   1120

---

[1] The 4to of '98 ' to.'

[2] " Had it not been for the words 'knows' and 'grows,' the old
reading ' fin' might have stood ;—' they made peace with Ifrael, and
served them' (2 Samuel x. 19."—*Dyce.*

Ah Ionas, wilt thou proue rebellious then ?
Confider ere thou fall,[1] what errour is.
My minde mifgiues : to Ioppa will I flee,[2]
And for a while to Tharfus fhape my courfe,
Vntill the Lord vnfret his angry browes.

Enter certaine Merchants *of* Tharfus, *a* Maifter,
and fome Sailers.

M[*as*]. Come on,[3] braue merchants; now the
      wind doth ferue,
And fweetly blowes a gale at Weft Southweft,
Our yardes a croffe, our anchors on the pike ;   1130
What, fhall we hence, and take this merry gale ?
      [*Firft*] *Mer*. Sailers, conuey our budgets ftrait
           aboord,
And we will recompenfe your paines at laft :
If once in fafetie we may Tharfus fee,
M[after], weele feaft thefe merry mates, and thee.
      M[*as*]. Mean-while content yourfelues with filly
           cates ;
Our beds are boordes, our feafts are full of mirth,
We / vfe no pompe, we are the Lords of fea[4];
When Princes fwet in care, we fwinke of glee.
Orions[5] fhoulders and the Pointers ferue   1140

---

[1] The 4to of '94 'fall.'
[2] *Sic* all the 4tos, and the usual spelling then.
[3] 4tos 'one,' which is rather misleading.
[4] *Ibid*. 'fee,' which again, as misleading, I alter.
[5] 4tos 'Orious.'

To be our load-ftars in the lingering night;
The beauties of Arcturus we behold ;
And though the Sailer is no booke-man held,
He knowes more Art then euer booke-men read.
    Sailer. By heauens, well faid, in honour of our
          trade ;
Let's fee the proudeft fcholler fteer[1] his courfe,
Or fhift his tides, as filly failers do ;
Then wil we yeeld them praife, elfe neuer none.
    Mer. Well fpoken fellow, in thine owne behalfe ;
But let vs hence, wind tarries none, you wot,   1150
And tide and time let flip is hardly got.
    M[as]. March to the hauen, merchants, I follow
          you.   *Exeunt* Merchants.
    Ionas. [afide.] Now doth occafion further my
          defires ;
I finde companions fit to aide my flight.—
Staie fir, I pray, and heare a word or two.
    M[as]. Say on good friend, but briefly, if you
          pleafe,
My paffengers by this time are aboord.   [felues?
    Ionas. Whether pretend you to imbarke your-
    M[as]. To Tharfus fir, and here in Ioppa hauen 1160
Our fhip is preft, and readie to depart.
    Ionas. May I haue paffage for my mony then ?
    M[as]. What not for mony ? pay ten filuerlings :
You are a welcome gueft, if fo you pleafe.

                [1] The 4tos ' ftir.'

Ionas [*giuing money*]. Hold, take thine hire, I
   follow thee, my friend.   [fir.
M[*as*]. Where is your budget? let me beare it
Ionas. To one in peace, who faile[s] as I do now,
Put truft in him who fuccoureth euery want.
         Exeunt.

Ofe. When Prophets, new infpirde, prefume to 1170
   force
And tie the power of heauen to their conceits;
When feare, promotion, pride, or fimony,
Ambition, fubtill craft, their thoughts difguife,
Woe to the flocke whereas the fhepheards foule;[1]
For, / lo, the Lord at vnawares fhall plague
The careleffe guide, becaufe his flocks do ftray.
The axe alreadie to the tree is fet;
Beware to tempt the Lord, ye men of art.

 Enter Alcon, Thrafybulus, Samia, *and* Clefiphon
    a lad.   1180

 Cles. Mother, fome meat, or elfe I die for want.
 Samia. Ah litle boy, how glad thy mother would
Supply thy wants, but naked need denies:
Thy fathers flender portion in this world
By vfury and falfe deceit is loft;
No charitie within this Citie bides,
All for themfelues, and none to helpe the poore.
 Cles. Father, fhall Clefiphon haue no reliefe?

---

[1] The 4to of '98 'fold.'

Alcon. Faith, my boy, I muſt be flat with thee,
we muſt feed vpon prouerbes now, as 'Neceſſitie 1190
hath no law,' 'A churles feaſt is better then none
at all' : for other remedies haue we none, except
thy brother Radagon helpe vs.

Samia. Is this thy ſlender care to helpe our
         childe ?
Hath nature armde thee to no more remorſe ?
Ah cruell man, vnkind and pittileſſe :
Come Cleſiphon my boy, Ile beg for thee.

Cles. Oh how my mothers mourning moueth
         me !

Alcon. Nay, you ſhall paie mee intereſt for get-
ting the boye (wife) before you carry him hence : 1200
Ah-laſſe, woman, what can Alcon do more ? Ile
plucke the belly out of my heart for thee : ſweete
Samia, be not ſo waſpiſh.

Samia. Ah ſilly man, I know thy want is great,
And fooliſh I to[1] craue where nothing is.
Haſte Alcon, haſte, make haſte vnto our ſonne ;
Who, ſince he is in fauour of the King,
May helpe this hapleſſe Gentleman and vs,
For to regaine our goods from tyrants hands.

Thra. Haue patience Samia, waight your weale 1210
         from heauen :
The [2] Gods haue raiſde your ſonne, I hope, for this,
To / ſuccour innocents in their diſtreſſe.

---

[1] The 4to of '98 '*fooliſhly* I *do.*'   [2] *Ibid.* '94 ' Tho.'

Enter Radagon, *folus.*[1]

Lo, where he comes from the imperiall Court;
Go let vs proſtrate vs before his feete.

Alcon. Nay, by my troth, Ile neuer aſke my
ſonnes bleſſing ; che.trow, cha,[2] taught him his
leſſon to know his father.   What, ſonne Radagon ?
y'faith boy, how doeſt thee?

Rada. Villaine diſturbe me not, I cannot ſtay.   1220

Alcon. Tut ſonne, Ile help you of that diſeaſe
quickly, for I can hold thee: aſke thy mother,
knaue, what cunning I haue to eaſe a woman
when a qualme of kindneſſe come[s] too neare her
ſtomacke.   Let me but claſpe mine armes about
her bodie, and ſaie my prayers in her boſome, and
ſhe ſhall be healed preſently.

Rada. Traitor vnto my Princely Maieſtie,
How dar'ſt thou laie thy hands vpon a King ?

Samia. No Traitor Radagon, but true is he :   1230
What, hath promotion bleared thus thine eye,
To ſcorne thy father when he viſits thee?
Ah-laſſe, my ſonne, behold with ruthfull eyes
Thy parents robd of all their worldly weale,
By ſubtile meanes of vſurie and guile :

---

[1] Dyce annotates, "But that Radagon does not enter here *folus* is
shown by his presently ſaying, ' Marſhal, why whip you not,' etc., and
' Slaues, fetch out tortures,' etc."   Of course, but he first enters ' folus.'
Dyce misplaces six lines on.

[2] "*i.e.* I trow, I have.   Why the author gives us here a sudden touch
of rustic dialect, it would be difficult to say."—*Dyce.*

The Judges eares are deaffe and fhut vp clofe;
All mercie fleepes: then be thou in thefe plundges
A patron to thy mother in[1] her paines :
Behold thy brother almoft dead for foode :
Oh fuccour vs, that firft did fuccour thee. [avant ; 1240

    Rada. What, fuccour me? falfe callet, hence,
Old dotard, pack ; moue not my patience ;
I know you not ; kings neuer look fo low.

    Samia. You know vs not? O Radagon, you know
That, knowing vs, you know your parents then ;
Thou knowft this wombe firft brought thee forth
    to light:
I know thefe paps did fofter thee, my fonne.

    Alcon. And I know he hath had many a piece of
bread & cheefe at my hands, as proud as he is;
that know I.   1250

    Thras. I waight no hope of fuccours in this place,
Where / children hold their fathers in difgrace.

    Rada. Dare you enforce the furrowes of reuenge
Within the browes of royall Radagon ?
Villaine auant : hence beggers, with your brats.—
Marfhall, why whip you[2] not thefe rogues away,
That thus difturbe our royall Maieftie ?

    Clefiphon. Mother, I fee it is a wondrous thing,
From bafe eftate for to become a King ;
For why, meethinke my brother in thefe fits   1260
Hath got a kingdome, and hath loft his wits.

---

    [1] The 4to of '98 ' to.'   [2] *Ibid.* '*ye* you.'

Rada. Yet more contempt before my royaltie?
Slaues, fetch out tortures worfe then Titius plagues,
And teare their toongs from their blafphemous
  heads.
    Thras. Ile get me gone, tho woe begon with griefe:
No hope remaines :—come Alcon, let vs wend.
    Ra. Twere beft you did, for feare you catch
          your bane.   [*Exit* Thrafybulus.
    Samia. Nay Traitor, I wil haunt thee to the
Ungratious fonne, vntoward and peruerfe, [death: 1270
Ile fill the heauens with ecchoes of thy pride,
And ring in euery eare thy fmall regard,
That doeft defpife thy parents in their wants;
And breathing forth my foule before thy feete,
My curfes ftill fhall haunt thy hatefull head,
And being dead, my ghoft fhall thee purfue.

  Enter Rafni, *King of Affiria, attended on by his*
        Sooth-fayers *and* Kings.

    Rafni. How now ? what meane thefe outcries in
          our Court,
Where nought fhould found but harmonies of 1280
  heauen?
What maketh Radagon fo paffionate?
    Samia. Juftice O King, iuftice againft my fonne.
    Rafni. Thy fonne? what fonne?
    Samia. This curfed Radagon.
    Rada. Dread Monarch, this is but a lunacie,

Which griefe and want hath brought the woman
    to.—
What, doth this paffion hold you euerie Moone?
  Samia. / Oh polliticke in finne and wickedneffe,
Too impudent for to delude thy Prince—
Oh Rafni, this fame wombe firft[1] brought him foorth: 1290
This is his father, worne with care and age,
This is his brother, poore vnhappie lad,
And I his mother, though contemn'd by him.
With tedious toyle we got our litle good,
And brought him vp to fchoole with mickle charge:
Lord, how we ioy'd to fee his towardneffe ;
And to our felues we oft in filence faid,
This youth when we are old may fuccour vs.
But now preferd and lifted vp by thee,
We quite deftroyd by curfed vfurie,   1300
He fcorneth me, his father, and this childe.
  Cles. He plaies the Serpent right, defcrib'd in
        Æfopes tale.   [life.
That fought the Fofters death, that lately gaue him
  Alc. Nay, and pleafe your Maiefti-fhip, for proofe
he was my childe, fearch the parifh booke : the
Clarke will fweare it, his godfathers and godmothers
can witneffe it : it coft me fortie pence in ale and
cakes on the wiues at his chriftning.—Hence,
proud King, thou fhalt neuer more haue my
bleffing.   1310

---

[1] ' firft ' not in the 4to of '98.

He takes him apart.

Rafni. Say footh in fecret, Radagon,
Is this thy father?
Rada.   Mightie King, he is;
I blufhing, tell it to your Maieftie.
Rafni. Why[1] doft thou then, contemne him &
    his friends?
Rada. Becaufe he is a bafe and abiect fwaine,
My mother and her brat both beggarly,
Unmeete to be allied vnto a King:
Should I, that looke on Rafnis countenance,   1320
And march amidft his royall equipage,
Embafe my felfe to fpeake to fuch as they?
Twere impious fo to impaire the loue
That mightie Rafni beares to Radagon
I would your grace would quit them from your fight,
That / dare prefume to looke on Ioue's compare.
Rafni. I like thy pride, I praife thy pollicie;
Such fhould they be that wait vpon my Court:
Let me alone to anfwere (Radagon).—
Villaines,[2] feditious traitors, as you be,   1330
That fcandalize the honour of a King,
Depart my Court you ftales of impudence,
Unleffe you would be parted from your limmes!
So bafe for to intitle father-hood
To Rafnis friend, to Rafnis fauourite.

[1] The 4to of '94 'Thy.'   [2] The 4to of '98 'Villaine.'

Rada. Hence, begging ſcold, hence caitiue, clogd
　　　with yeares !
On paine of death, reuiſit not the Court.
Was I conceiu'd by ſuch a ſcuruie trull,
Or brought to light by ſuch a lump of dirt?
Go, Loſſell, trot it to the cart and ſpade ;　　　1340
Thou art vnmeete to looke vpon a King,
Much leſſe to be the father of a King.

Alcon. You may ſee wife, what a goodly peece of
worke you haue made : haue I tought you *Ar'metry*,
as *additiori multiplicarum*, the rule of three, and all
for the begetting of a boy, and to be baniſhed for
my labour? O pittiful hearing. Come, Cleſiphon,
follow me.

Cles. Brother, beware : I oft haue heard it told,
That ſonnes who do their fathers ſcorne, ſhall beg 1350
　　　when they be old.

Radagon. Hence, baſtard boy, for feare you taſte
　　　the whip.

　　　　　　[*Exeunt* Alcon *and* Cleſiphon.
Samia. Oh all you heauens, and you eternall
　　　powers
That ſway the ſword of iuſtice in your hands,
(If mothers curſes for[1] her ſon's contempt
May fill the balance of your furie full,)
Powre downe the tempeſt of your direful plagues
Vpon the head of curſed Radagon.

　　　　　[1] The 4to of '98 'of.'

Vpon this prayer fhe departeth, and a flame of fire 1360
appeareth from beneath, and Radagon *is fwallowed.*
So you are iuft: now triumph Samia. [*Exit Samia.*
    Rafni. What exorcifing charme, or hatefull hag,
Hath rauifhed the pride of my delight?
What tortuous planets, or maleuolent
Confpiring power, repining deftenie,
Hath made the concaue of the earth vnclofe,
And fhut in ruptures louely Radagon?
If I be Lord-commander of the cloudes,
King of the earth, and Soueraigne of the feas,   1370
What daring Saturne, from his fierie denne,
Doth dart thefe furious flames amidft my Court?
I am not chiefe, there is more great then I:
What, greater than th'Affyrian Satrapos?
It may not be, and yet I feare there is,
That hath bereft me of my Radagon.
    Soothfayer. Monarch and Potentate of all our
                    Prouinces,
Mufe not fo much vpon this accident,
Which is indeed nothing miraculous.
The hill of Sicely, dread Soueraigne,   1380
Sometime on fodaine doth euacuate
Whole flakes of fire, and fpues out from below
The fmoakie brands that Vulcans[1] bellowes driue:
Whether by windes inclofed in the earth,
Or fracture of the earth by riuers force,

---

[1] 4tos 'Vulneus.'

Such chances as was this, are often feene ;
Whole Cities funcke, whole Countries drowned quite :
Then mufe not at the loffe of Radagon,
But frolicke with the dalliance of your loue.
Let cloathes of purple, fet with ftuddes of gold,   1390
Embellifhed with all the pride of earth,
Be fpred for Aluida to fit vpon :
Then thou, like Mars courting the queene of loue,
Maift driue away this melancholy fit.

   Rafni. The proofe is good and philofophicall ;
And more, thy counfaile plaufible and fweete.—
Come Lords, though Rafni wants his Radagon,
Earth will repaie him many Radagons,
And / Aluida with pleafant lookes reuiue
The heart that droupes for want of Radagon.| 1400

                      Exeunt.

   Ofeas. When difobedience raigneth in the childe,
And Princes eares by flattery be beguilde ;
When lawes do paffe by fauour, not by truth,
When falfhood fwarmeth both in old and youth ;
When gold is made a god to wrong the poore,
And charitie exilde from rich mens doore ;
When men by wit do labour to difproue
The plagues for finne fent downe by God aboue ;
When[1] great mens eares are ftopt[2] to good aduice, 1410
And apt to heare thofe tales that feed their vice ;
Woe to the land : for from the Eaft fhall rife

---

  [1] The 4tos ' Where.'   [2] *Ibid.* ' ftop.'

A Lambe of peace, the fcourge of vanities,
The iudge of truth, the patron of the iuft :
Who foone will laie prefumption in the duft,
And giue the humble poore their hearts defire,
And doome the worldlings to eternall fire :
Repent all you that heare for feare of plagues.
O London, this and more doth fwarme in thee ;
Repent, repent, for why the Lord doth fee :   1420
With trembling pray, and mend what is amiffe,
The fwoord of iuftice drawne alreadie is.

Enter Adam *and the* Smiths Wife.

Adam. Why, but heare you miftreffe : you
know a womans eies are like a pair of pattens, fit
to faue fhoo leather in fommer, and to keepe away
the cold in winter ; fo you may like your hufband
with the one eye becaufe you are married, and me
with the other, becaufe I am your man. Alaffe,
alaffe, think miftreffe, what a thing loue is : why, 1430
it is like to an oftry faggot, that, once fet on fire,
is as hardly quenched as the bird Crocodill driuen
out of her neaft.

Wife. Why,[1] Adam, cannot a woman winke
but fhe muft fleep, and can fhe not loue but fhe
muft crie it out at the Croffe ?   Know Adam, / I
loue thee as my felfe, now that we are together in
fecret.

[1] Again the 4to of '94 ' Thy.'

Adam. Mif[treffe] thefe words of yours are like
a Fox taile placed in a gentlewomans Fanne, which, 1440
as it is light, fo it giueth life : Oh thefe words are
as fweete as a lilly; whereupon offering a borachio
of kiffes to your vnfeemly perfonage, I entertaine
you vpon further acquaintance.

Wife. Alaffe, my hufband comes !

Adam. Strike vp the drum,
And fay no words but mum.

[*Enter the* Smith.]

Smith. Sirrha you, and you, hufwife, well taken
togither: I haue long fufpected you, and now I 1450
am glad I haue found you togither.

Adam. Truly fir, and I am glad that I may do
you any way pleafure, either in helping you or my
miftreffe.

Smith. Boy here, and knaue, you fhall know it
ftraight ; I will haue you both before the Magis-
trate, and there haue you furely punifhed.

Adam. Why then, maifter, you are iealous ?

Smith. Jelous, knaue? how can I be but iealous,
to fee you euer fo familiar togither ? Thou art 1460
not only content to drinke away my goods, but to
abufe my wife.

Adam. Two good quallities, drunkenneffe and
leachery : but maifter, are you iealous ?

Smith. I, knaue, and thou fhalt know it ere I

paſſe, for I will beſwindge thee while this roape
will hold.

Wife. My good huſband, abuſe him not, for he
neuer proffered you any wrong.

Smith. Nay whore, thy part ſhall not be behinde. 1470

Adam. Why, ſuppoſe, maiſter, I haue offended
you, is it[1] lawful for the maiſter to beate the ſeruant
for all offences ?

Smith. I, marry, is it, knaue.

Adam. Then maiſter, will I proue by logicke,
that ſeeing all ſinnes are to receiue correction, the
maiſter is to be corrected of the man. And ſir,
I pray you, what greater ſinne is then iealouſie?
tis like a mad dog that for anger bites himſelfe.
Therefore that I may doe my dutie to you, good 1480
maiſter, and to make a white ſonne[2] / of you, I will
ſo[3] beſwinge iealouſie out of you, as you ſhall loue
me the better while you liue.

Smith. What, beate thy maiſter, knaue ?

Adam. What, beat thy man, knaue? and I,
maiſter, and double beate you, becauſe you are a
man of credite, and therfore haue at you the faireſt
for[4] fortie pence !   [*Beats the* Smith.

Smith. Alaſſe wife, help, helpe, my man kils me.

Wife. Nay, euen as you haue baked, ſo brue :
iealouſie muſt be driuen out by extremities.   1490

The 4to of '98 'it is.'   [3] ' ſo ' not in '98 4to.
See Gloſſarial-Index, *.v.*   [4] '98 4to ' of.'

Adam. And that will I do, miſtreſſe.

Smith. Hold thy hand, Adam ; and not only I forgiue and forget all, but I will giue thee a good Farme to liue on.

Adam. Be gone Peaſant, out of the compaſſe of my further wrath, for I am a correƈtor of vice ; and at night I will bring home my miſtreſſe.

Smith. Euen when you pleaſe, good Adam.

Adam. When I pleaſe,—marke the[1] words,—tis 1500 a leaſe paroll to haue and to hold. Thou ſhalt be mine for euer : and ſo lets go to the Ale-houſe.

[*Exeunt.*

Oſeas. Where ſeruants [a]gainſt maiſters do
    rebell,
The Common-weale may be accounted hell ;
For if the feete the head ſhall hold in ſcorne,
The Cities ſtate will fall and be forlorne.
This error, London, waiteth on thy ſtate :
Seruants amend, and maiſters, leaue to hate ;
Let loue abound, and vertue raign in all ;   1510
So God will hold his hand, that threatneth thrall.

Enter the Merchants *of Tharſus, the* M[aſter] o̅f̅ *the ſhip,* [and] *ſome* Sailers, *wet from the ſea ; with them the* Gouernour *of* Ioppa.

Gouer. Iop. What ſtrange encounters met you
    on the ſea,

---

[1] The 4to of '98 ' thy.'

That thus your Barke is batter'd by the flouds,
And you return thus fea-wreckt as I fee ?

    Mer. / Moft mightie gouernor, the chance is
        ftrange,
The tidings full of wonder and amaze,
Which, better then we, our M[after] can report.   1520

    Gouer. M[after] difcourfe vs all the accident.

    M[as]. The faire Triones with their glimmering
        light
Smil'd at the foote of clear Bootes' waine,[1]
And in the north,[2] diftinguifhing the houres,
The Load-ftarre of our courfe difpearft his cleare ;
When to the feas with blithfull wefterne blafts
We faild amaine, and let the bowling flie.
Scarce had we gone ten leagues from fight of land,
But lo an hoaft of blacke and fable cloudes
Gan to eclips Lucinas filuer face ;   1530
And, with a hurling noyfe from foorth the South,
A guft of winde did reare[3] the billowes vp.
Then fcantled we our failes with fpeedie hands,
And tooke our drablers from our bonnets ftraight,
And feuered our bonnets from our[4] courfes :
Our topfailes vp, we truffe our fpritfailes in ;
But vainly ftriue they that refift the heauens.
For loe the waues incence them more and more,
Mounting with hideous roarings from the depth ;

---

[1] The 4tos ' Rootes a raine.'   [2] The 4to of '98 ' raife.'
[3] *Ibid.* (except '94) ' wrath.'   [4] The 4to of '94 ' the.'

Our Barke is battered by incountering ſtormes,   1540
And wel ny ſtemd by breaking of the flouds.
The ſteers-man pale, and carefull, holds his helme,
Wherein the truſt of life and ſafetie laie ;
Till all at once (a mortall tale to tell)
Our ſailes were ſplit by Biſa's[1] bitter blaſt,
Our rudder broke, and we bereft of hope.
There might you ſee, with pale and gaſtly lookes,
The dead in thought, and dolefull merchants lift[2]
Their eyes and hands vnto their Countries Gods.
The goods we caſt in bowels of the ſea,   1550
A ſacrifice to ſwage proud Neptunes ire.
Onely alone a man of Iſraell,
A paſſenger, did vnder hatches lie,
And / ſlept ſecure, when we for ſuccour praide :
Him I awooke, and ſaid, ' Why ſlumbereſt thou ?
Ariſe, and pray, and call vpon thy God ;
He will perhaps in pitie looke on vs.'
Then caſt we lots to know by whoſe amiſſe
Our miſchiefe came,[3] according to the guiſe ;
And loe the lot did vnto Ionas fall,   1560
The Iſraelite of whom I told you laſt.
Then queſtion we his Country and his name ;
Who anſwered vs, ' I am a Hebrue borne,
Who feare the Lord of heauen, who made the ſea,
And fled from him ; for which we all are plagu'd :

---

[1] See Glossarial-Index, *s.v.*   [2] 4tos ' lifts.'
[3] 4tos of '94, '98, 1602 and 1617, ' come.'

So, to affwage the furie of my God,
Take me and caft my carkaffe in the fea ;
Then fhall this ftormy winde and billow ceafe.'
The heauens they know, the Hebrues God can tell,
How loath we were to execute his will :   1570
But when no Oares nor labour might fuffice,
We heaued the hapleffe Ionas ouer-boord.
So ceaft the ftorme, and calmed all the fea,
And we by ftrength of oares recouered fhoare.

   Gouer. A wonderous chance of mighty confe-
         quence.   [fame ;
   Mer. Ah honored be the God that wrought the
For we haue vowd, that faw his wonderous workes,
To caft away profaned Paganifme,
And count the Hebrues God, the onely God :
To him this offering of the pureft gold,   1580
This mirrhe and Cafcia, freely I do yeeld.

   M[after.] And on his altars fume[1] thefe Turkie
This gaffampine[2] and gold, Ile facrifice.   [clothes,
   Sailer. To him my heart and thoughts I will
Then fuffer vs, moft mightie Gouernour,   [addict.
Within your Temples to do facrifice.

   Gouer. You men of Tharfus, follow me,
Who facrifice vnto the[3] God of heauen ;
And welcome friends, to Ioppais Gouernor.
             [*Exeunt. A facrifice.* 1590

---

[1] The 4tos 'perfume.'   [2] See Glossarial-Index, *s.v.*
[3] "The 4to of '98 'your.' This speech seems to be somewhat imperfect."—*Dyce.*

Ofeas. / If warned once, the Ethniks thus repent,
And at the firft their errour do lament,
What fenfelefs beafts, devoured in their finne,
Are they whom long perfwations cannot winne.
Beware, ye wefterne Cities ;—where the word
Is daily preached, both at church and boord ;
Where maieftie the Gofpell doth maintaine,
Where Preachers, for your good, themfelues do
      paine,—
To dally long and ftill protract the time ;
The Lord is iuft, and you but duft and flime :   1600
Prefume not far, delaie not to amend ;
Who fuffereth long, will punifh in the end.
Caft thy account ô London, in this cafe,
Then iudge what caufe thou haft to call for grace.

Ionas *the Prophet caft out of the Whales belly*
vpon the Stage.

Ionas. Lord of the light, thou maker of the world,
Behold, thy hands of mercy reares me vp ;
Loe from the hidious bowels of this fifh   1610
Thou haft returnd me to the wifhed aire ;
Loe here, apparant witneffe of thy power,
The proud Leuiathan that fcoures the feas,
And from his nofthrils fhowres out ftormy flouds,
Whofe backe refifts the tempeft of the winde,
Whofe prefence makes the fcaly troopes to fhake

With fimple ftretche[1] of his broad opened chappes,
Hath lent me harbour in the raging flouds.
Thus, though my fin hath drawne me down to death,
Thy mercy hath reftored me to life.   1620
Bow ye, my knees, and you, my bafhful eyes,
Weepe fo for griefe, as you to water would.
In trouble Lord, I called vnto thee,
Out of the belly of the deepeft hell ;
I cride, and thou didft heare my voice O God :
Tis / thou hadft caft me downe into the deepe,
The feas and flouds did compaffe me about ;
I thought I had bene caft from out thy fight ;
The weeds were wrapt about my [2] wretched head ;
I went vnto the bottome of the hilles :
But thou, O Lord my God, haft brought me vp ;   1630
On thee I thought when as my foul did faint ;
My prayers did preafe before thy mercy feate.
Then will I paie my vowes vnto the Lord,
For why faluation commeth from his throane.

The Angell *appeareth.*

Angell. Ionas arife, get thee to Niniuie,
And preach to them the preachings that I bad ;
Hafte thee to fee the will of heauen perform'd.

                                        Depart Angell. 1640
Ionas. Iehouah, I am preft [3] to do thy will.—

---

[1] The 4tos 'humble ftreffe': I emend by 'fimple,' and accept Dyce's
of 'ftretch.'
[2] The 4to of '98 'thy.'   [3] 4tos 'Prieft.'

What coaft is this, and where am I arriu'd ?
Behold fweete Lycus[1] ftreaming in his boundes,
Bearing the walles of haughtie Niniuie,
Whereas three hundered towers[2] do tempt the
Faire are thy[3] walles, pride of[4] Affiria;   [heauen.
But lo, thy finnes haue pierced through the cloudes.
Here will I enter boldly, fince I know
My God commands, whofe power no power refifts.
                                             [*Exit.*
    Ofeas. You Prophets, learne by Ionas how to liue;   1650
Repent your finnes, whilft he doth warning giue.
Who knowes his maifters will, and doth it not,
Shall fuffer many ftripes, full well I wot.

    Enter Aluida *in rich attire, with the* King of
            Cilicia, [*and*] her Ladies.

    Aluida. Ladies, go fit you downe amidft this
And let the Euniches plaie you all a fleepe : [bowre,
Put garlands made of Rofes on your heads,
And / plaie the wantons, whilft I talke a while.
    Lady. Thou beautifull of all the world, we will. 1660
                    [Ladies] *enter the bowers.*
    Aluid. King of Cilicia, kind and curtious,
Like to thy felfe, becaufe a louely King,
Come, laie thee downe vpon thy miftreffe knee,
And I will fing and talke of loue to thee.

---

[1] 4tos 'Licas.'   [2] The 4tos of '94, '98, 1602, and 1617, 'towns.'
[3] The 4tos 'the.'   [4] The 4to of 1602 'of proud.'

K. of Cili.[1] Moſt gratious Paragon of excellence,
It fits not ſuch an abiect Prince as I,
To talke with Raſnis Paramour and loue.

 Al. To talke ſweet friend? who would not talke
  with thee?

Oh be not coy, art thou not only faire?   167
Come, twine thine armes about this ſnow white neck,
A loue-neſt for the great Aſſirian King:
Bluſhing I tell thee, faire Cilician Prince,
None but thy ſelfe can merit ſuch a grace.

 K. of Cil. Madam, I hope you mean not for to
  mock me.

 Al. No, king, faire king, my meaning is to
  yoke thee.

Heare me but ſing of loue, then by my ſighes,
My teares, my glauncing lookes, my changed cheare,
Thou ſhalt perceiue how I do hold thee deare.

 K. of Cil. Sing Madam, if you pleaſe, but loue 168
  in ieſt.

 Aluid. Nay, I will loue, and ſigh at euery reſt.

            [Sings.

    Song.

 Beautie alaſſe, where waſt thou borne,
 Thus to hold thy ſelfe in ſcorne?
 When as Beautie kiſt to wooe thee,
 Thou by Beautie doſt vndo mee:
   Heigho, deſpiſe me not.

   [1] 4tos 'King Cili' and 'K. Ci.'

I and thou, in footh are one,
Faireft thou,[1] I fairer none ;　　　　　1690
Wanton thou, and wilt thou wanton,
Yeeld a cruell heart to pant [2] on ?
Do me right, and do me reafon,
Crueltie is curfed treafon :
　　Heigho, I loue, heigho, I loue !
　　Heigho ; and yet he eies me not.

K./of Cil. Madam, your fong is paffing paffionate.
Alv. And wilt thou not then, pitie my eftate ?
K. of Cil. Afke loue of them who pitie may
　　　　impart.
Alv. I afke of thee, fweet; thou haft ftole my hart. 1700
K. of Cil. Your loue is fixed on a greater King.
Alv. Tut, womens loue, it is a fickle thing.
I loue my Rafni for my [3] dignitie,
I loue Cilician King for his fweete eye ;
I loue my Rafni fince he rules the world,
But more I loue this kingly little world.
　　　　　　　　　Embrace him.
How fweete he lookes! Oh were I Cinthia's Pheere,
And thou Endimion, I fhould hold thee deere :
Thus fhould mine armes be fpred about thy necke" 1710
　　　　　　　　　Embrace his neck.

[1] " Should it be ' *Faireft* thou ' ? (Walker's *Crit. Exam. of the Text of Shakespeare*, etc., i. 59)."—*Dyce.* Accepted for ' Fairer.'
[2] 4to ' plant ' : I venture to change to ' pant.'
[3] Dyce misreads ' his.'

Thus would I kiſſe my loue at euery becke ; *Kiſſe.*
Thus would I ſigh to ſee thee ſweetly ſleepe ;
And if thou wakeſt not ſoone, thus would I weepe ;
And thus, and thus, and thus, thus much I loue
    thee.   *Kiſſe him.*
  K. of Cil. For all theſe vowes, beſhrow me, if I
      proue you :[1]
My faith vnto my King ſhall not be falc'd.
  Alui. Good Lord, how men are coy when they
      are crau'd !
  K. of Cil. Madam, behold our King approacheth   1720
      nie.
  Alui. Thou art Endimion, then, no more :
      heigho, for him I die.
      [*Faints : point at the* king of Cilicia.

Enter Raſni, *with his* Kings *and* Lords
      [*and* Magi].

  [*Raſni.*] What ailes the Center of my happineſſe,
Whereon depends the heauen of my delight ?
Thine eyes, the motors to command my world,
Thy hands, the axier to maintaine my world,
Thy ſmiles, the prime and ſpring-tide of my world,
Thy frownes, the winter to afflict my[2] world ;   1730
Thou Queene of me, I King of all the world.

  [1] " The 4tos ' you ' : but here a rhyme was intended."—*Dyce.* And
ſo he prints ' ye.'
  [2] The 4tos ' the.'

Alui. Ah feeble eyes, lift vp, and looke on him !
            [*She rifeth as out of a traunce.*
Is Rafni here ? then droupe no more, poore
    hart.—
Oh / how I fainted when I wanted thee !
                [*Embrace him.*
How faine am I, now I may looke on thee !
How glorious is my Rafni, how diuine !—
Eunukes, play himmes to praife his deitie :
He is my Ioue, and I his Iuno am.   1740
    Rafni. Sun-bright as is the eye of fommers day
When as he futes his pennons [1] all in gold
To wooe his Leda in a fwanlike fhape ;
Seemely as Galatea [2] for thy white ;
Rofe-coloured lilly, louely, wanton, kinde,
Be thou the laborinth to tangle loue,
Whilft I command the crowne from Venus creft,
And pull Orion's [3] girdle from his loines,
Enchaft with Carbunckles and diamonds,
To beautifie faire Aluida, my loue.—   1750
Play, Eunukes, fing in honour of her name :
Yet look not, flaues, upon her woing eyne,
For fhe is faire Lucina to your king,
But fierce Medufa to your bafer eie.
    Alui. What if I flept, where fhould my pillow be?

---

[1] " The correction of the Rev. J. Mitford, *Gent. Mag.* for March,
1833, p. 216. The 4tos ' Spenori.' "—*Dyce.*
[2] The 4tos ' Galbocia.'   [4] *Ibid.* ' Onoris.'

Rafni. Within my bofome, nimph, not on my
Sleepe like the fmiling puritie of heauen,   [knee:
When mildeft wind is loath to blend the peace ;
Meane-while thy[1] balme[2] fhall from thy breath
     arife ;
And while thefe clofures of thy lampes be fhut,   1760
My foule may haue his peace from fancies warre—
This is my Morn,[3] and I her Cephalus :—
Wake not too foon, fweete Nimph, my loue is
     wonne—   [me?
Caitiffs[4] why ftaie your ftraines? why tempt you

Enter the Prieft[s] *of the funne, with the miters on
     their heads, carrying fire in their hands.*
Prieft. All haile vnto th'Affyrian deitie.
Rafni. Priefts, why prefume you to difturbe my
     peace ?
Prieft. Rafni, the deftinies difturbe thy peace.
Behold, / amidft the adyts[5] of our Gods,   1770
Our mightie Gods, the patrons of our warre,
The ghoft[s] of dead men howling walke about,
Crying '*Væ, væ,* wo to this Citie, woe !'[6]
The ftatutes of our gods are throwne downe,
And ftreames of blood our altars do diftaine.

---

[1] The whole of the 4tos 'thy,' and Dyce's 'my' doubtful. Cf. 'thy
lampes.'
     [2] The 4to of '98 'blame.'   [3] The 4tos 'Morane.'   [4] *Ibid.* 'Catnies.'
     [5] The 4tos 'addittes' and 'addites': from the Latin *adytum,* the
innermoft part of a temple.
     [6] The 4tos 'Ve, Ve.'

Aluida. [*ſhe ſtarteth.*] Ah-laſſe, my Lord, what
        tidings do I hear?
Shall I be ſlaine ?
  Raſni.   Who tempteth Aluida?
Go, breake me vp the brazen doores [1] of dreames,
And binde me curſed Morpheus in a chaine,   1780
And fetter all the fancies of the night,
Becauſe they do diſturbe my Aluida.
     A hand from out a cloud threatneth with a
      burning ſword.
  K. of Cil. Behold, dread Prince, a burning ſword
       from heauen,
Which by a threatning arme is brandiſhed !
  Raſni. What, am I threatned then, amidſt my
       throane ?
Sages, you Magi, ſpeake ; what meaneth this?
  Sages. Theſe are but clammy exhalations,
Or retrograde coniunctions of the ſtarres,   1790
Or oppoſitions of the greater lights,
Or radiations [2] finding matter fit,
That in the ſtarrie Spheare kindled be ;
Matters betokening dangers to thy foes,
But peace and honour to my Lord the King.
  Raſni. Then frolicke Viceroies, Kings, & poten-
      tates ;
Driue all vaine fancies from your feeble mindes.
Prieſts, go and pray, whilſt I prepare my feaſt,

  [1] The 4to of '98 ' walles.'   [2] The 4tos ' radiatrous.'

Where Aluida and I, in pearle and gold,
Will quaffe vnto our Nobles, richeſt wine   180
In ſpight of fortune, fate, or deſtinie.   *Exeunt.*

Oſeas. Woe to the traines of womens fooliſh luſt,
In wedlocke rites that yeeld but litle truſt,
That / vow to one, yet common be to all :
Take warning, wantons, pride will haue a fall.
Woe to the land, where warnings profit nought,
Who ſay that Nature Gods decrees hath wrought ;
Who build on[1] fate, and leaue the corner-ſtone,
The God of Gods, ſweete Chriſt, the onely one.
If ſuch eſcapes, ô London, raigne in thee,   181
Repent, for why each ſin ſhall puniſht bee :
Repent, amend, repent, the houre is nie ;
Defer not time ; who knowes when he ſhall die ?

Enters one clad in diuels attire alone.

Longer liues a merry man then a ſad ; and becauſe I meane to make myſelfe pleaſant this night,
I haue put myſelfe into this attire, to make a Clowne
afraid that paſſeth this way : for of late there haue
appeared many ſtrange apparitions, to the great
fear and terror of the Citizens.—Oh here my yoong 182
maiſter comes.

Enters Adam *and his miſtreſſe.*

Adam. Feare not, miſtreſſe, Ile bring you ſafe
home : if my maiſter frowne, then will I ſtampe

----

[1] Again 4tos ' one.'

and ftare; and if all be not well then, why then
to-morrow morne put out mine eyes cleane with
fortie pound.

Wife. Oh but Adam, I am afraid to walke fo late,
becaufe of the fpirits that appeare in the Citie.   1830

Adam. What, are you afraid of fpirits? Armde
as I am, with Ale and Nutmegs, turne me loofe to
all the diuels in hell.

Wife. Alaffe Adam, Adam, the diuell, the
diuell.

Adam. The diuell, miftreffe : flie you for your
fafeguard; [*Exit* S. Wife.] let me alone; the diuell
and I will deale well inough, if he haue any honeftie
at all in him : Ile either win him with a fmooth
tale, or elfe with a tofte and a cup of Ale.

The Diuell fings here.   1840

Diuell. Oh, Oh, Oh, Oh, faine would I bee,
  If that my kingdome fulfilled I might fee :
    Oh, Oh, Oh, Oh !

Adam. Surely, this is a merry diuell, and I beleeue he is one / of Lucifers Minftrels; hath a
fweete voice ; now furely, furely, he may fing to a
paire of Tongs and a Bag-pipe.

Diuell. Oh thou art he that I feeke for.

Adam. Spritus fantus !—Away from me, Satan !
I haue nothing to do with thee.   1850

Diuell. Oh villaine, thou art mine !

Adam. *Nominus patrus !*—I bleſſe me from thee, and I coniure thee to tell me who thou art.

Diuell. I am the ſpirit of the dead man that was ſlaine in thy company when we were drunke to-gither at the Ale.[1]

Adam. By my troth ſir, I cry you mercy ; your face is so changed that I had quite forgotten you : well, maiſter diuell, we haue toſt ouer many a pot of Ale togither.   1860

Diuell. And therefore muſt thou go with me to hell.

Adam. [*aſide.*] I haue a pollicie to ſhift him, for I know he comes out of a hote place, and I know my ſelfe the Smith, and the diuel, hath a drie tooth in his head ; therefore will I leaue him a ſleepe, and runne my way.

Diuell. Come, art thou readie ?

Adam. Faith ſir, my old friend, and now good-man diuell, you know you and I haue been toſſing 1870 many a good cup of Ale : your noſe is growne verie rich : what ſay you, will you take a pot of Ale now at my hands ? Hell is like a Smiths forge, full of water, and yet euer athruſt.

Diuell. No Ale, villaine, ſpirits cannot drinke : come, get vpon my backe, that I may carrie thee.

Adam. You know I am a Smith, ſir : let me looke whether you be well ſhod or no ; for if you

---

[1] See Glossarial-Index, *s.v.*

want a fhoe, a remoue, or the clinching of a naile,
I am at your command.   1880

Diuell. Thou haft neuer a fhoe fit for me.

Adam. Why fir, we fhooe horned beafts, as well
as you.—[*Afide.*] Oh good Lord, let me fit downe
and laugh ; hath neuer a clouen foote : a diuell,
quoth he, Ile vfe *Spritus fantus* nor *Nominus patrus*
no more to him, I warrant you ; Ile do more good
vpon him with my cudgell : now will I fit me
downe and become Iuftice of peace to the diuell.

Diuell. / Come, art thou readie?

Adam. I am readie ; and with this cudgell I will 1890
coniure thee.   [*Beats him.*

Diuell. Oh hold thy hand, thou kilft me, thou
kilft me.   [*Exit.*

Adam. Then may I count my felfe, I thinke, a
tall man, that am able to kill a diuell : now who
dare deale with me in the parifh ? or what wench
in Niniuie will not loue me, when they fay, ' There
goes he that beate the diuell '?   [*Exeunt.*

Enter Thrafibulus.

Thrafi. Loathd is the life that now inforc'd I 1900
But fince neceffitie will haue it fo,   [leade ;
(Neceffity that[1] doth command the Gods,)
Through euerie coaft and corner now I prie,
To pilfer what I can to buy me meate.

---

[1] 4tos ' it ': Dyce queries ' that ' (the MS. having had ' y^t ')?—
accepted.

Here haue I got a cloake, not ouer old,
Which will affoord fome litle fuftenance ;
Now will I to the broaking Ufurer,
To make exchange of ware for readie coine.

[*Enter* Alcon, Samia, *and* Clefiphon.]

Alcon. Wife, bid the trumpets found, a prize, a 1910
prize : mark the pofie : I cut this from a new-
married wife, by the helpe of a horne thombe and
a knife,—fixe fhillings, foure pence.

Samia. The better lucke ours ; but what haue we
here, caft apparell ?   Come away, man, the Ufurer
is neare : this is dead ware, let it not bide on our
hands.

Thrafi. [*afide.*] Here are my partners in my
Inforc'd to feeke their fortunes as I do : [pouertie,
Alaffe that fewe men fhould poffeffe the wealth,   1920
And many foules be forc'd to beg or fteale.—
Alcon, well met.

Alcon. Fellow begger, whither now ?

Thrafi. To the Ufurer, to get gold on commoditie.

Alcon. And I to the fame place, to get a vent
for my villany.   See where the olde cruft comes :
let vs falute him.

[*Enter* Vfurer.]

God fpeede fir : may a man abufe your patience 1930
vpon a pawne ?

Vſurer.[1] Friend, let me ſee it.

Alcon. Ecce ſignum ! a faire doublet and hoſe, new bought out of the pilferers ſhop, [and] a hanſome cloake.

Vſurer. How were they gotten ?

Thraſi. How catch the fiſher-men fiſh? M[aſter,] take them as you thinke them worth : we leaue all to your conſcience.

Vſurer. Honeſt men, toward men, good men, 1940 my friends, like to proue good members, vſe me, command me ; I will maintaine your credits. There's mony : now ſpend not your time in idle-neſſe ; bring me commoditie, I haue crownes for you : there is two ſhillings for thee, and ſix ſhillings for thee.   [*Gives money.*

Alcon. A bargaine—Now, Samia, haue at it for a new ſmocke.—Come, let vs to the ſpring of the beſt liquor, whileſt this laſtes, tril-lill.

Vſurer. Good fellowes, propper fellowes, my 1950 companions, farwell : I haue a pot for you.

Samia. [*aſide.*] If he could ſpare it.

Enters to them, Ionas.

[*Ionas.*] Repent, ye men of Niniuie, repent !
The day of horror and of torment[2] comes :
When greedie hearts ſhall glutted be with fire,
When as corruptions vailde, ſhall be vnmaſkt,

---

[1] 4tos catch-word ' Diuell.'   [2] The 4to of '98 ' iudgment.'

When briberies fhall be repaide with bane,
When whoredoms fhall be recompenc'd in hell,
When riot fhall with rigor be rewarded,   196o
When as negleĉt of truth, contempt of God,
Difdaine of poore men, fatherleffe, and ficke,
Shall be rewarded with a bitter plague.
Repent, ye men of Niniuie, repent,
The Lord hath fpoke, and I do crie it out;
There are as yet but fortie daies remaining,
And then fhall Niniuie be ouerthrowne.
Repent, ye men of Niniuie, repent:
There are as yet but fortie daies remaining,
And then fhall Niniuie be ouerthrowne.   [*Exit.*[1] 197

   Vfur. Confuf'd in thought, Oh whither fhall I
      wend ?   [*Exit.*
   Thrafi. My confcience cries, that I haue done
      amiffe.   [*Exit.*
   Alcon. Oh God of heauen, gainft thee haue I
      offended.   [*Exit.*
   Samia. Afham'd of my mifdeeds, where fhal I
      hide me ?   [*Exit.*
   Clefi. Father, methinks this word 'repent' is
      good :
He that [doth] punifh difobedience
Doth hold a fcourge for euery priuie fault. [*Exit.*
   Ofeas. Looke London, look, with inward eies
What leffons the euents do here vnfold.   [behold

---

[1] Here and often spelled ' Exet.'

Sinne growne to pride, to mifery is thrall,   1980
The warning bell is rung, beware to fall.
Ye worldly men, whom wealth doth lift on hie,
Beware and feare, for worldly men muft die.
The time fhall come, where leaft fufpect remaines,
The fword fhall light vpon the wifeft braines ;
The head that deemes to ouer-top the fkie,
Shall perifh in his humaine pollicie.
Lo, I haue faid, when I haue faid the truth,
When will is law, when folly guideth youth,
When fhew of zeale is prankt in robes of zeale,   1990
When Ministers powle the pride of common-weale,
When law is made a laborinth of ftrife,
When honour yeelds him friend to wicked life,
When Princes heare by others ears their follie,
When vfury is moft accounted holie;
If thefe fhall[1] hap, as would to God they might not,
The plague is neare : I fpeake, although I write not.

Enters the Angell.

Angell. Ofeas.
Ofeas. Lord.   [fins, 2000
An. Now hath thine eies peruf'd thefe hainous
Hatefull vnto the mightie Lord of hoftes.
The time is come, their finnes are waxen ripe,
And though the Lord forewarnes, yet they repent
     not ;

---

[1] The 4to of '98 ' fhould.'

Cuftome / of finne hath hardned all their hearts.
Now comes reuenge, armed with mightie plagues,
To punifh all that liue in Niniuie ;
For God is iuft as he is mercifull,
And doubtleffe plagues all fuch as fcorne repent.
Thou fhalt not fee the defolation   201
That falles vnto thefe curfed Niniuites,
But fhalt returne to great Ierufalem,
And preach vnto the people of thy God,
What mightie plagues are incident to finne,
Unleffe repentance mittigate his ire :
Wrapt in the fpirit, as thou wert hither brought,
Ile feate thee in Iudeas prouinces.
Feare not Ofeas then, to preach the word.
    Ofeas. The will of the Lord be done !
                                Ofeas *taken away.* 202

Enters Rafni *with his* Viceroyes; Aluida *and her*
            Ladies ; *to a banquet.*

Rafni. So Viceroyes, you haue pleafde me paffing
            well ;
Thefe curious cates are gratious in mine eye,
But thefe Borachious of the richeft wine,
Make me to thinke how blythfome we will be.—
Seate thee, faire Iuno, in the royall throne,
And I will ferue thee [but] to fee thy face ;
That, feeding on the beautie of thy lookes,
My ftomacke and mine eyes may both be fild.—   20

Come, Lordings, feate you, fellow-mates at feaft,
And frolicke wags, this is a day of glee ;
This banquet is for brightfome Aluida.
Ile haue them fkinck my ftanding bowles with wine,
And no man drinke but quaffe a whole[1] caroufe
Vnto the health of beautious Aluida :
For who fo rifeth from this feaft not drunke,
As I am Rafni, Niniuies great King,
Shall die the death as traitor to my felfe,
For / that he fcornes the health of Aluida.   2040

    K. of Cil. That will I neuer do, my L[ord]
Therefore with fauour, fortune to your grace,
Carowfe vnto the health of Aluida.

    Rafni. Gramercy Lording, here I take thy
           pledge :—
And, Creete, to thee a bowle of Greekifh wine,
Here to the health of [heauenly] Aluida.[2]

    K. of Crete. Let come, my Lord.—Jack fkincker,
          fil it full ;
A[3] pledge vnto the health of Aluida.

    Rafni. Vaffals attendant on our royall feafts,
Drinke you, I fay, vnto my louers health ;   2050
Let none that is in Rafnis royall court
Go this night fafe and fober to his bed.[4]

   [1] The 4to of '98 ' full.'
   [2] " Qy. ' *heauenly* Aluida ' ? and omit that epithet in the next speech ?
[accepted].   Did the author forget here that the King of Crete had
been banished by Rafni ? "—*Dyce.*   But Rafni recalled the sentence.
   [3] The 4to of '98 ' I.'   [4] See Glossarial-Index, *s.v.*

Enters Adam [*the Clowne*].

Adam. This way he is, and here will I fpeake
with him.

Lord. Fellow, whither preffeft thou ?

Adam. I prefs no bodie fir ; I am going to fpeake
with a friend of mine.

Lord. Why flaue, here is none but the King
and his Viceroyes.   206c

Adam. The King ? marry fir, he is the man I
would fpeake withall.

Lord. Why, calft him a friend of thine ?

Adam. I marry do I fir ; for if he be not my
friend, Ile make him my friend, ere he and I paffe.

Lord. Away, vaffaile, be gone, thou fpeake vnto
the King !

Adam. I, marry, will I fir ; and if he were a
king of veluet, I will talke to him.

Rafni. Whats the matter there ? what noyce is 207c
        that ?

Adam. A boone, my Liege, a boone, my Liege !

Rafni. What is it that great Rafni will not
        graunt,
This day, vnto the meaneft of his land,
In honour of his beautious Aluida ?
Come hither, fwaine ; what is it that thou craueft ?

Adam. Faith fir, nothing, but to fpeake a fewe
fentences to your worfhip.

Rafni. / Say, what is it ?

Adam. I am fure, fir, you haue heard of the
fpirits that walke in the Citie here.   2080

Rafni. I, what of that?

Adam. Truly fir, I haue an oration to tel you of
one of them ; and this it is.

Alui. Why goeft not forward with thy tale ?

Adam. Faith miftreffe, I feele an imperfection
in my voyce, a difeafe that often troubles me ;
but, alaffe, eafily mended ; a cup of Ale or a cup
of wine, will ferue the turne.

Alui. Fill him a bowle, and let him want no
drinke.   2090

Adam. Oh what a pretious word was that,
'And let him want no drinke.' [*Drink given to*
Adam.] Well fir, now Ile tell you forth my tale :
Sir, as I was comming alongft the port-royal[1] of
Niniuie, there appeared to me a great diuell, and
as hard fauoured a diuell as euer I faw ; nay fir,
he was a cuckoldly diuell, for he had hornes on
his head. This diuell, marke you now, preffeth
vpon me, and fir, indeed I charged him with my
pike ftaffe ; but when ȝ would not ferue, I came 2100
vpon him with *Spritus fantus,*—why, it had beene
able to haue put Lucifer out of his wits : when I
faw my charme would not ferue, I was in fuch a
perplexitie, that fixe peny-worth of Juniper would
not haue made the place fweete againe.

[1] The 4tos 'port *ryuale,*' and 'port *ryualt.*'

Alui. Why, fellow, weart thou fo afraid?

Adam. Oh miftreffe, had you bene there and
feene, his verie fight had made you fhift a cleane
fmocke, I promife you ; though I were a man, and
counted a tall fellow, yet my Landreffe calde me 211c
flouenly knaue the next day.

Rafni. A pleafaunt flaue.—Forward, firrha, on
with thy tale.

Adam. Faith fir, but I remember a word that
my miftreffe your bed-fellow fpoake.

Rafni. What was that, fellow?

Adam. Oh fir, a word of comfort, a pretious
word—' And let him want no drinke.'

Rafni. Her word is lawe ; and thou fhalt want
no drinke.   [*Drink giuen to* Adam. 212c

Adam. / Then fir, this diuell came vpon me,
and would not be perfwaded, but he would needs
carry me to hell. I proffered him a cup of Ale,
thinking, becaufe he came out of [1] fo hotte a place,
that he was thirftie ; but the diuell was not drie,
and therfore the more forrie was I. Well, there
was no remedie, but I muft with him to hell :
and at laft I caft mine eye afide ; if you knew
what I fpied, you would laugh, fir ; I lookt from
top to toe, and he had no clouen feete. Then I 213c
ruffled vp my haire, and fet my cap on the one
fide, & fir, grew to be a Juftice of peace to the

---

[1] The 4to of '98 ' from.'

diuel. At laſt in a great fume, as I am very
choloricke, and ſometime ſo hotte in my fuſtian[1]
fumes, that no man can abide within twentie yards
of me, I ſtart vp, and ſo bombaſted the diuell, that
ſir, he cried out and ranne away.

    Alui. This pleaſant knaue hath made me laugh
          my fill.

Raſni, now Aluida begins her quaffe,
And drinkes a full carouſe vnto her King.   2140

    Raſni. A[2] pledge, my loue, as heartie[3] as great
          Ioue

Drunke when his Iuno heau'd a bowle to him.—
Frolicke my Lords ;[4] let all the ſtanderds walke ;[5]
Ply it, till euery man hath tane his load.—
How now ſirrha, what cheere ?[6] we haue no words
of you.

    Adam. Truly ſir, I was in a broune ſtudy about
my miſtreſſe.

    Alui. About me ? for what ?

    Adam. Truly miſtreſſe, to thinke what a golden   2150
ſentence you did ſpeake : all the philoſophers in
the world could not haue ſaid more ;—' What,
come, let him want no drinke.' Oh wiſe ſpeech.

    Alui. Villaines, why ſkinck you not vnto this
          fellow ?

---

[1] The 4to of '94 ' faſtin ' ; the other 4tos ' fuſtin.'
[2] The 4to of '98 · I.'   [3] The 4to of '94 ' hardie.'
[4] The 4tos ' lord.'   [5] " *i.e.* the standing-bowls go round."—*Dyce.*
[6] The 4to of '94 ' how.'

He makes me blyth and merry in my thoughts:
Heard you not that the King hath giuen command,
That all be drunke this day within his Court,
In quaffing to the health of Aluida ?

[*Drink given to* Adam.

Enter Ionas.   2160

Ionas. Repent,[1] ye men of Niniuie, repent ;
The Lord hath fpoke,[2] and I do crie it out,]
There are as yet but fortie daies remaining,
And then fhall Niniuie be ouerthrowne :
Repent, / ye men of Niniuie, repent.

Rafni. What fellow is this, that thus difturbes
                our feafts
With outcries and alarams to repent ?

Adam. Oh fir, tis one goodman Ionas, that is
come from Iericho ; and furely I thinke he hath
feene fome fpirit by the way, and is fallen out of 2170
his wits, for he neuer leaues crying night nor day.
My maifter heard him, and he fhut vp his fhop,
gaue me my Indenture, and he and his wife do
nothing but faft and pray.

Ionas. Repent, ye men of Niniuie, repent.

Rafni. Come hither, fellow ; what art, & from
whence commeft thou ?

Ionas. Rafni, I am a Prophet of the Lord,

---

[1] The 4tos ' Repent, *repent.*'

[2] " The 4tos ' fpoken ' : but see the repetition of the line in Jonas's
second speech after this."—*Dyce.* Accepted.

Sent hither by the mightie God of hoftes
To cry deftruction to the Niniuites.   2180
O Niniuie, thou harlot of the world,
I raife thy neighbours round about thy boundes,
To come and fee thy filthineffe and finne.
Thus faith the Lord, the mightie God of hoftes :[1]
Your King loues chambering and wantonneffe,
Whoredom and murther do diftaine his Court,
He fauoureth couetous and drunken men.
Behold, therefore, all like a ftrumpet foule,
Thou fhalt be iudg'd, and punifht for thy crime ;
The foe fhall pierce the gates with iron rampes,   2190
The fire fhall quite confume thee from aboue,
The houfes fhall be burnt, the Infants flaine,
And women fhall behold their hufbands die.
Thine eldeft fifter is Gomorrah,[2]
And Sodome on thy right hand feated is.
Repent, ye men of Niniuie, repent,
The Lord hath fpoke, and I do crie it out,
There are as yet but fortie daies remaining,
And then fhall Niniuie be ouerthrowne.
                                    Exit offered. 2200

Rafni. Staie, Prophet, ftaie.

Ionas. Difturbe not him that fent me ;
Let me performe the meffage of the Lord.   *Exit.*

[1] The 4tos ' hofte.'
[2] Dyce annotates, " Some corruption here," in respect of ' Lamana,'
but has made no suggestion. I have unhesitatingly printed ' Gomorrah,'
which was probably written (nearer the Greek) ' Gomorra.'

Raſni. / My ſoule is buried in the hell of
        thoughts.——
Ah Aluida, I looke on thee with ſhame.——
My Lords on ſodeine fixe their eyes on ground,
As if diſmayd to looke vpon the heauens.——
Hence Magi, who haue flattered me in ſinne,

                          Exeunt his Sages.

Horror of minde, diſturbance of my ſoule,   2210
Make me agaſt for Niniuies miſhap.
Lords, ſee proclaim'd, yea, ſee it ſtraight proclaim'd,
That man and beaſt, the woman and her childe,
For fortie days in ſacke and aſhes faſt ;
Perhaps the Lord will yeeld, and pittie vs.——
Beare hence theſe wretched blandiſhments of ſinne.

          [Taking off his crown and robe.

And bring me ſackcloth to attire your King :
Away with pompe, my ſoule is full of woe.——
In pittie looke on Niniuie, O God.   2220

        [Exeunt all except Aluida *and Ladies.*[1]

Alui. Aſſaild with ſhame, with horror ouerborne,
To ſorrowe ſold, all guiltie of our ſinne,
Come Ladies come, let vs prepare to pray.
Ah-laſſe, how dare we looke on heauenly light,
That haue diſpiſde the maker of the ſame?
How may we hope for mercie from aboue,
That ſtill deſpiſ[d]e the warnings from aboue?

              [1] 4tos ' Exet. A man.'

Woes me, my confcience is a heauie foe.   2230
O patron of the poore, oppreft with finne,
Looke, looke on me, that now for pittie craue :
Affaild with fhame, with horror ouerborne,
To forrow fold, all guiltie of our finne :
Come Ladies, come, let vs prepare to pray.

                       Exeunt.

Enter the Vfurer *folus with a halter in one hand,*
        a dagger in the other.

  Vfurer. Groning in confcience, burdened with my
            crimes,
The hell of forrow hauntes me vp and downe.
Tread / where I lift, mee-thinkes the bleeding ghoftes 2240
Of thofe whom my corruption brought to noughts,
Do ferue for ftumbling blocks before my fteppes ;
The fatherleffe and widow wrongd by me,
The poore, oppreffed by my vfurie ;
Mee-thinkes I fee their hands reard vp to heauen,
To crie for vengeance of my couetoufneffe.
Where fo I walke, all[1] figh and fhunne my way ;
Thus am I made a monfter of the world ;
Hell gapes for me, heauen will not hold my foule. 2250
You mountaines, fhroud me from the God of truth :
Mee-thinkes I fee him fit to iudge the earth ;
See how he blots me out o' the booke of life :
Oh burthen, more then Ætna,[2] that I beare.

---

  [1] The 4tos ' Ile.'   [2] 4tos ' Atna.'

Couer me hilles, and fhroude me from the Lord;
Swallow me, Lycus,[1] fhield me from the Lord.
In life no peace; each murmuring that I heare,
Mee-thinkes, the fentence of damnation foundes,
' Die reprobate, and hie thee hence to hell.'   2260

The Euill Angel *tempteth him, offering the knife
and rope.*

What fiend is this that temptes me to the death?
What, is my death the harbour of my reft?
Then let me die :—what fecond charge is this?
Methinks[2] I hear a voice amidft mine eares,
That bids me ftaie, and tels me that the Lord
Is mercifull to thofe that do repent.
May I repent?   Oh thou, my doubtfull foule,
Thou maift repent, the Judge is mercifull.
Hence, tooles of wrath, ftales of temptation,   2270
For I will pray and figh vnto the Lord;
In fackcloth will I figh, and fafting pray :
O Lord, in rigor looke not on my finnes.

*He fits downe in fack-cloathes, his hands and eyes
reared to heauen.*

Enter | Aluida *with her* Ladies, *with difperfed
locks,*[3] [*and in fackcloth.*]

Alui. Come, mournfull dames, laie off your
brodred locks,

---

[1] 4tos 'Licas,' as before.
[2] The 4to of '94 ' Mee-things,' and of '98 ' Methinke.'
[3] 4tos 'difpiearfed lookes.'

And on your fhoulders fpred difperfed[1] haires :
Let voice of muficke ceafe, where forrow dwels :
Cloathed in fackcloaths, figh your finnes with me ; 2280
Bemone your pride, bewaile your lawleffe lufts ;
With fafting mortifie your pampered loines ;
Oh thinke vpon the horrour of your finnes,
Think, think with me, the burthen of your blames.
Woe to thy pompe, falfe[2] beautie, fading floure,
Blafted by age, by fickneffe, and by death.
Woe to our painted cheekes, our curious oyles,
Our rich array, that foftered vs in finne :
Woe to our idle thoughts, that wound our foules.
Oh would to God all nations might receiue   2290
A good example by our greeuous fall.

  Ladies. You that are planted there where plea-
    fure dwels,
And thinkes[3] your pompe as great as Niniuies,
May fall for finne as Niniuie doth now.

  Alui. Mourne, mourne, let moane be all your
    melodie,
And pray with me, and I will pray for all :—
O[4] Lord of heauen, forgiue vs our mifdeeds !

  Ladies. O Lord of heauen, forgiue vs our mis-
            [deeds.

---

[1] So 4tos here ' difpiearfed.'
[2] The 4to of '98 'fal, e '; the other 4tos 'fall,' and 'falls.'
[3] 4to 'thinkes,' and fo by the nearer nominative 'pleafure.' Hence
retained, not altered, as by Dyce, to 'think.'
[4] In 4tos 'Lord ' is put before this line, not as spoken by 'a Lord,'
as Dyce states, but by inadvertently repeating the divine name.

Vſurer. O Lord of light, forgiue me my mis-
     deeds.

Enters Raſni, *the King*[1] *of Aſſiria, with his nobles* 2300
     in ſackcloath.

K. of Cil. Be not ſo ouercome with griefe, O
          King,
Leaſt you endanger life by ſorrowing ſo.
     Raſni. King of Cilicia, ſhould I ceaſe my griefe,
Where as my ſwarming ſinnes afflict my ſoule?
Vaine man, know this, my burthen greater is
Then euery priuate ſubiect['s] in my land :
My life hath been a loadſtarre vnto them,
To guide them in the laborinth of blame :
Thus I haue taught them for to do amiſſe ;   2310
Then / muſt I weepe, my friend, for their amiſſe.
The fall of Niniuie is wrought by me,
I haue maintaind this Citie in her ſhame,
I haue contemnd the warnings from aboue,
I haue vpholden inceſt, rape, and ſpoyle :
Tis I that wrought the[2] ſinne muſt weepe the ſinne.
Oh had I teares, like to the ſiluer ſtreames,
That from the Alpine Mountains ſweetly ſtreame,[3]

[1] 4tos misprint 'Kings'; for although other kings also enter with
him, they do so as his 'nobles' (being subject to him).

[2] '98 4to 'thy' (*bis*).

[3] " Qy. 'flow' ('ſtream' having been repeated by mistake from the
preceding line) ? "—*Dyce.*   Not at all.

Or had I fighes, the treafures of remorfe,   2320
As plentifull as Æolus hath blafts,
I then would tempt the heauens with my laments,
And pierce the throane of mercy by my fighes.

 K. of Cil. Heauens are propitious[1] vnto faithful
    praiers.

 Rafni. But after our repent, we muft lament,
Leaft that a worfer mifchiefe doth befall.
Oh pray ; perhaps the Lord will pitie vs.—
Oh God of truth, both mercifull and iuft,
Behold repentant men, with pitious eyes !
We waile the life that we haue led before :
O pardon Lord, O pitie Niniuie.   2330

 Omnes. O pardon Lord, O pitie Niniuie.

 Rafni. Let not the Infants, dallying on the
    teat,[2]
For fathers finnes in iudgement be oppreft.

 K. of Cil. Let not the painfull mothers big with
    childe,
The innocents, be punifht for our finne.

 Rafni. O pardon Lord, O pitie Niniuie.

 Omnes. O pardon Lord, O pitie Niniuie.

 Rafni. O Lord of heauen, the virgins weepe to
The couetous man forrie[3] for his finne, [thee !
The Prince and poore, all pray before thy throane ; 2340
And wilt thou, then, be wroth with Niniuie ?

---

[1] 4tos spell ' prepitions.' [2] The 4tos of '94, '98, 1602 and 1617 ' tent.'
    [3] The 4to of '94 '*forie* forie.'

K. of Cil. Giue truce to praiers, O king, and
rest a space.

Rafni. Giue truce to praiers, when times require
no truce !

No, Princes, no.   Let all our fubiects hie
Unto our temples,[1] where, on humbled knees,
I will exfpect fome mercy from aboue.

Enter the temple omnes.

Enters Ionas, *folus.*

Ionas. This is the day wherein the Lord hath
said

That / Niniuie fhall quite be ouerthrowne ;   2350
This is the day of horror and mifhap,
Fatall vnto the curfed Niniuites.
Thefe ftately Towers fhall in thy watery bounds,
Swift flowing Lycus,[2] find their burials ;
Thefe pallaces, the pride of Affurs kings,
Shall be the bowers of defolation ;
Whereas the folitary bird fhall fing,
And Tygers traine their young ones to their neft.
O all ye nations bounded by the Weft,
Ye happy Iles, where Prophets do abound,   2360
Ye Cities famous in the wefterne world,
Make Niniuie a prefident for you.

---

[1] " Qy. ' temple ' (as in the stage-direction which follows) ?   But
compare onward."—*Dyce* (altered).

[2] 4tos ' Licas,' as before.

Leaue leaud defires, leaue couetous delights,
Flie vfurie, let whoredom be exilde,
Leaft you with Niniuie be ouerthrowne.
Loe, how the funnes inflamed torch preuailes,
Scorching the parched furrowes of the earth.
Here will I fit me downe, and fixe mine eye
Vpon the ruines of yon wretched towne :
And lo, a pleafant fhade, a fpreading vine,   2370
To fhelter Ionas in this funny heate.
What meanes my God ? the day is done and fpent :
Lord, fhall my Prophecie be brought to nought ?
When falles the fire ? when will the iudge be wroth ?
I pray thee Lord, remember what I faid,
When I was yet within my country land :
Iehouah is too mercifull, I feare,
O let me flie, before a Prophet fault ;
For thou art merciful, the Lord my God,
Full of compaffion, and of[1] fufferance,   2380
And doeft repent in taking punifhment.
Why ftaies thy hand ? O Lord, firft take my life,
Before my Prophefie be brought to noughts[2]
Ah, he is wroth, behold, the gladfome vine,
That did defend me from the funny heate,
Is witherd quite, and fwallowed by a Serpent :
                    A ferpent deuoureth the vine.

[1] 'of' not in the 4to of '98.
[2] "The 4tos here (as before, p. 97, l. 2241) 'to *noughts*' : but in
the present speech we have just had 'to nought.'—*Dyce.* No reason
why the text should be made finically uniform.

Now / furious Phlegon triumphs on my browes,
And heate preuailes, and I am faint in heart.

Enters the Angell.   2390

 Angell. Art thou fo angry Ionas? tell me why.
 Ionas. Iehouah, I with burning heate am plungde,
And fhadowed only by a filly vine ;
Behold, a Serpent hath deuoured it !
And lo, the funne incenft by Eafterne winde,
Afflicts me with canicular[1] afpect.
Would God that I might die, for, well I wot,
Twere better I were dead then reft aliue.
 Angell. Ionas, art thou fo angry for the vine ?
 Ionas. Yea, I am angry to the death, my God. 2400
 Angell. Thou haft compaffion Ionas, on a vine,
On which thou neuer labour didft beftow ;
Thou neuer gaueft it life or power to grow,
But fodeinly it fprung, and fodeinly dide :
And fhould not I haue great compaffion
On Niniuie, the Citie of the world,[2]
Wherein there are a hundred thoufand foules,
And twentie thoufand infants that ne wot
The right hand from the left, befide[3] much cattle ?
O Ionas, looke into their Temples now,   2410
And fee the true contrition of their King,
The fubiects teares, the finners true remorfe ;

<hr>

[1] The 4tos ' cariculer.'   [2] The 4to of '98 'Lord.'
   [3] The 4to of '98 ' befides.'

Then from the Lord proclaime a mercie day,
For he is pitifull as he is iuſt.

    Ionas. I go, my God, to finiſh thy command,
                        [*Exit* Angelus.[1]
Oh who can tell the wonders of my God,
Or talke his praiſes with a feruent tong ?
He bringeth downe to hell, and lifts to heauen ;
He drawes the yoake of bondage from the iuſt,   2420
And lookes vpon the Heathen with pitious eyes ;
To him all praiſe and honour be aſcribed.
Oh who can tell the wonders of my God ?
He makes the infant to proclaime his truth,
The / Aſſe to ſpeake, to ſaue the Prophets life,
The earth and ſea to yeeld increaſe for man.
Who can deſcribe the compaſſe of his power ?
Or teſtifie in termes his endleſſe might ?
My rauiſht ſpright, oh whither doeſt thou wend ?
Go and proclaime the mercy of my God ;   2430
Relieue the carefull hearted Niniuites ;
And, as thou weart the meſſenger of death,
Go bring glad tydings of recouered grace. [*Exit.*

Enters Adam *ſolus, with a bottle of beere in one
ſlop, and a great peece of beefe in an other.*[2]

[*Adam.*] Well, goodman Ionas, I would you had
neuer come from Iury to this Country ; you haue

---

[1] 4tos place this a line above.
[2] Dyce reduces all this to ' Enter Adam.'

made me looke like a leane rib of roaſt beefe, or
like the picture of Lent painted vpon a red-herrings
cob. Alaſſe, maiſters, we are commanded by the 2440
proclamation to faſt and pray : by my troth, I
could prettely ſo, ſo, away with praying ; but for
faſting, why, tis ſo contrary to my nature, that I
had rather ſuffer a ſhort hanging then a long faſting. Marke me, the words be theſe, ' Thou ſhalt
take no maner of foode for ſo many daies.' I had
as leeue he ſhould haue ſaid, ' Thou ſhalt hang thy
ſelfe for ſo many daies.' And yet, in faith, I need
not find fault with the proclamation, for I haue a
buttry and a pantry, and a kitchen about me ; for 2450
proofe *Ecce ſignum*. This right ſlop is my pantry,
behold a manchet [*Draws it out*]; this place is
my kitchin, for, loe a peece of beefe [*Draws it
out*],—Oh let me repeat that ſweet word againe :
For loe a peece of beefe. This is my buttry, for,
ſee, ſee, my friends, to my great ioy, a bottle of
beere [*Draws it out*]. Thus, alaſſe I make ſhift
to weare out this faſting ; I driue away the time.
But there go Searchers about to ſeeke if any man
breakes the Kings command. Oh here they be ; 2460
in with your victuals, Adam.

[*Puts them back into his ſlops.*

Enters two Searchers.

1 *Searcher.* How duly the men of Niniuie keep

the proclamation; how are they armde to repentance ! We haue fearcht through the whole Citie,
& haue not as yet found one that breaks the faft.

2 *Sear.* The figne of the more grace :—but
ftaie, here fits one, mee-thinkes, at his praiers, let
vs fee who it is.   2470

1 *Sear.* Tis Adam, the Smithes man.—How
now, Adam !

Adam. Trouble me not ; ' Thou fhalt take no
maner of foode, but faft / and pray.'

1 *Sear.* How devoutly he fits at his oryfons ; but
ftaie, mee-thinks I feele a fmell of fome meate or
bread about him.

2 *Sear.* So thinkes me too.—You, firrha, what
victuals haue you about you ?

Adam. Victuals? O horrible blafphemie? Hin- 2480
der me not of my praier, nor driue me not into
a chollor. Victuals ! why hardft thou not the
fentence, ' Thou fhalt take no foode, but faft and
pray ' ?

2 *Sear.* Truth, fo it fhould be ; but, methinkes,
I fmell meate about thee.

Adam. About me, my friends ? thefe words are
actions in the Cafe. About me ? No, no : hang
thofe gluttons that cannot faft and pray.

1 *Sear.* Well, for all your words, we muft 2490
fearch you.

Adam. Search me ? take heed what you do ;

my hofe are my caftles, tis burglary if you breake
ope a flop : no officer muft lift vp an iron hatch ;
take heede my flops are iron.

[*They fearch* Adam.

    2 *Sear*. Oh villaine, fee how he hath gotten
victuailes, bread, beefe, and beere, where the King
commanded vpon paine of death none fhould eate
for fo many daies, no, not the fucking infant.   2500

    Adam. Alaffe, fir, this is nothing but a *modicum
non nocet*[1] *vt medicus daret*; why, fir, a bit to comfort my ftomacke.

    1 *Sear*. Villaine, thou fhalt be hangd for it.

    Adam. Thefe are your words, 'I fhall be hangd
for it;' but firft anfwer me to this queftion, how
many daies haue we to faft ftil?

    2 *Sear*. Fiue daies.

    Adam. Fiue daies: a long time: then I muft be
hangd?   2510

    1 *Sear*. I, marry, muft thou.

    Adam. I am your man, I am for you fir; for
I had rather be hangd thē abide fo long a faft.
What, fiue days ? Come, Ile vntruffe. Is your
halter, and the gallowes, the ladder, and all fuch
furniture in readineffe ?

    1 *Sear*. I warrant, thee fhalt want none of thefe.

    Adam. But heare you, muft I be hangd?

    1 *Sear*. I, marry.

[1] 4tos misprint 'necet.'

Adam. And for eating of meate. Then, friends, 2520
know ye by thefe prefents, I will eate vp all my
meate, and drink vp all my drink, for it fhall
neuer be faid, I was hangd with an emptie
ftomacke.

1 *Sear.* / Come away knaue : wilt thou ftand
feeding now ?

Adam. If you be fo[1] haftie, hang your felfe an
houre, while I come to you, for furely I will eate
vp my meate.

2. *Sear.* Come, lets draw him away perforce.

Adam. You fay there is fiue daies yet to faft, 2530
thefe are your words.

2 *Sear.* I, fir.

Adam. I am for you : come, lets away, and yet
let me be put in the Chronicles.   *Exeunt.*

Enters Ionas, Rafni, Aluida, *King*[2] *of Cilicia* [*and*]
        others royally attended.

Ionas. Come, carefull King, caft off thy mourn-
                full weedes,
Exchange thy cloudie lookes to fmoothed fmiles ;
Thy teares haue pierc'd the pitious throane of grace,
Thy fighes, like incenfe[3] pleafing to the Lord,   2540
Haue been peace-offerings for thy former pride :
Reioyce, and praife his name that gaue thee peace.
And you, faire Nymphs, ye louely Niniuites,

---

[1] fo ' not in '98 4to.   [2] 4tos ' kings.'   [3] The 4tos ' imence.'

Since you haue wept and fafted fore[1] the Lord
He gratioufly hath[2] temperd his reuenge.
Beware hencefoorth to tempt him any more ;
Let not the niceneffe of your beautious lookes
Ingraft in you a high-prefuming minde ;
For thofe that clime, he cafteth to the ground,
And they that humble be, he lifts aloft.   2550

   Rafni. Lowly I bend, with awfull bent of eye,
Before the dread Iehouah, God of hofts,[3]
Defpifing all profane deuice of man.
Thofe luftfull lures, that whilome led awry
My wanton eyes, fhall wound my heart no more ;
And fhe, whofe youth in dalliance I abuf'd,
Shall now at laft become my wedlocke mate.—
Faire Aluida, looke not fo woe begone ;
If for thy finne thy forrow do exceed,
Bleffed be thou : come, with a[4] holy band   2560
Lets knit a knot to falue our former fhame.

   Alui. With blufhing lookes, betokening my
I lowly yeeld, my King, to thy beheft,   [remorfe,
So as this man of God fhall thinke it good.

   Ionas. Woman, amends may neuer come too late ;
A[5] / will to practife good is vertuous :[6]

---

[1] 4tos misprint 'for the.'   [2] The 4tos 'haue.'
[3] *Ibid.* 'hofte,' as before.   [4] The 4to of '98 'thy.'
[5] The catch-word in 4tos is ' The.'
[6] The 4to of '94—
      ' A will to practise *gooduoffe* vertuous.'
The other 4tos—
      ' *I* will *thou* practife *goodneffe and vertuoufneffe.*'

The God of heauen, when finners do repent,
Doth more reioyce then in ten thoufand iuft.
  Rafni. Then witneffe holy Prophet, our accord.
  Alui. Plight in the prefence of the Lord thy 2570
        God.   [fheaues
  Ionas. Bleft may you be, like to the flouring
That plaie with gentle windes in fommer tide;
Like Oliue branches let your children fpred,
And as the Pines in loftie Libanon,
Or as the Kids that feede on Lepher[1] plains,
So be the feede and offpring [2] of your loines!

    Enters the Vfurer, Thrafybulus, *and* Alcon.

  Vfurer. Come foorth, my friends, whom wit-
      tingly I wrongd:
Before this man of God receiue your due;
Before our King I meane to make my peace.—   2580
Ionas, behold, in figne of my remorfe,
I here reftore into thefe poore mens hands
Their goods which I vniuftly haue detaind[3];
And may the heauens fo pardon my mifdeeds
As I am penitent for my offence.
  Thrafi. And what through want from others I
      purloynd,

[1] "Qy. 'Sepher'? which the Vulgate gives in Numbers, xxxiii. 23-4, while our version has 'Shapher': but 'Sepher,' or 'Shapher,' is described as a mountain.)"—*Dyce.*
[2] The 4to of '98 'offsprings.'
[3] *Ibid.* 'retain'd.'

Behold O King, I proffer fore[1] thy throane,
To be reftord to fuch as owe[2] the fame.
  Ionas. A vertuous deed, pleafing to God and
      man.
Would God, all Cities drowned in like fhame   2590
Would take example of thefe Niniuites.
  Rafni. Such be the fruites of Niniuies repent ;
And fuch for euer may our dealings be,
That he that cald vs home in height of finne
May fmile to fee our hartie penitence.—
Viceroyes, proclaime a faft vnto the Lord ;
Let Ifraels God be honoured in our land ;
Let all occafion of corruption die,
For, who fhall fault therein, fhall fuffer death :—
Beare witneffe God, of my vnfaigned zeale—   2600
Come, holie man, as thou fhalt counfaile me,
My Court and Citie fhall reformed be.
  Ionas. / Wend on in peace, and profecute this
      courfe.   *Exeunt [all except* Ionas].
You Ilanders, on whom the milder aire
Doth fweetly breathe the balme of kinde increafe ;
Whofe lands are fatned with the deaw of heauen,
And made more fruitfull then Actean plaines ;
You, whom delitious pleafures dandle foft,
Whofe eyes are blinded with fecuritie,   2610
Unmafke your felues, caft error cleane afide.
O London, mayden of the miftreffe Ile,

---

[1] The 4to of '98 ' forth.'   [2] = own.

Wrapt in the foldes and fwathing cloutes of fhame,
In thee more finnes than Niniuie containes:
Contempt of God, difpight of reuerend age,
Neglect of law, defire to wrong the poore,
Corruption, whordom, drunkenneffe, and pride.
Swolne are thy browes with impudence and fhame;
O proud adulterous glorie of the Weft,
Thy neighbors burne,[1] yet doeft thou feare no fire,   2620
Thy Preachers crie, yet doeft thou ftop thine eares,
The larum rings, yet fleepeft thou fecure.
London, awake, for feare the Lord do frowne.
I fet a looking Glaffe before thine eyes,
O turne, O turne, with weeping to the Lord,
And thinke the praiers and vertues of thy Queene,
Defers the plague which otherwife would fall.
Repent O London, leaft, for thine offence,
Thy fhepheard faile, whom mightie God preferue;
That fhe may bide the pillar of his Church   2630
Againft the ftormes of Romifh AntiChrift ;
The hand of mercy ouerfhead her head,
And let all faithfull fubiects, fay Amen.

[1] 4tos 'burnes.'

FINIS.

VI

GEORGE A GREENE,
THE PINNER OF WAKEFIELD.

1599.

NOTE.

As stated in the Introductory Note to these Plays, I am indebted to his Grace the Duke of Devonshire for his *unique* exemplar of 1599. As shown in the fac-simile of its title-page, the following contemporary MS. notes are written on it, somewhat shorn by the binder :—

"Written by . . . . a minifter, who ac[ted] th piñers pᵗ in it himfelf.   Tefte W. Shakefpea[re].

"Ed. Iuby faith that yˢ play was made by Ro. Gree[ne]."

See our annotated Biography of Greene by Storojenko in its place on these MS. notes (vol. i.).

The title-page (exclusive of fac-simile in post quarto) is given opposite. Earlier in the Play, specimens of the arbitrary printing of prose as verse and verse as prose are given ; but it has not been thought necessary to pursue the record.   Dyce took great pains in reducing all to (a kind of) verse and in returning pseudo-verse to prose, and I have entered into his labours—gratefully.   In this Play more than in most, Dyce has re-written throughout (silently) the stage-directions. The Author's own are restored, and are much pithier and more idiomatic and in harmony with the style of the Play.   G.

A
PLEASANT
CONCEYTED CO-
medie of *George a Greene*, the Pinner
of *VVakefield*.

*As it was sundry times acted by the seruants of the right
Honourable the Earle of Suffex.*

Avt nunc avt nunquam.

Imprinted at London by Simon Stafford,
for Cuthbert Burby : And are to be fold at his fhop
neere the Royall Exchange. 1599.

[DRAMATIS PERSONÆ.[1]

—‡‡—

EDWARD, *King of England.*

IAMES, *King of Scotland.*

EARL OF KENDAL.

EARL OF WARWICK.

LORD BONFIELD.

LORD HUMES.

SIR GILBERT ARMSTRONG.

SIR NICHOLAS MANNERING.

GEORGE-A-GREENE.

MUSGROVE.

CUDDY, *his fon.*

NED-A-BARLEY.

GRIME.

ROBIN HOOD.

MUCH, *the Millers fon.*

SCARLET.

[1] Accepted from Dyce.

IENKIN, *George-a-Greene's man.*

WILY, *George-a-Greene's boy.*

IOHN.

Iuſtice.

Townſmen, Shoemakers, Soldiers, Meſſengers, &c.

IANE-A-BARLEY.

BETTRIS, *daughter to Grime.*

MAID MARIAN.]

A pleasant conceyted Comedie of
George a Greene, the Pinner of Wakefield.[1]

*Enter the Earle of Kendall, with him the Lord
Bonfild, Sir Gilbert Armestrong, [Sir Nicholas
Mannering] and Iohn.*

Earle of Kendall.

Elcome to Bradford, martiall gentle-
men,
L[ord] *Bonfild*, & Sir *Gilbert
Armstrong*, both,
And all my troups, euē to my 10
basest groome,

---

[1] Dyce annotates here, " Or *Pinder ;* the keeper of the Pinfolds be-
longing to the common fields about Wakefield. Junius, in his *Etymo-
logicon*, voce *Pende*, says, ' *Pende* Includere. Ch. ab A.-S. pennan
pynðan idem significante. Hinc *pinder, pinner.* Qui pecora ultra
fines vagantia septo includit.' Mr. [George] Steevens observes, that
the figure of this rustic hero is still preserved on a sign at the bottom
of Gray's-Inn-Lane.—*Reed.*"

Courage and welcome ; for the day is ours :
Our caufe is good, it is for the lands auayle :
Then let vs fight, and dye for Englands good.
    Omnes. We will, my Lord.
    Kendall. As I am *Henrie Momford*, Kendals
          Earle,
You honour me with this affent of yours,
And here vpon my fword I make proteft
For[1] / to relieue the poore, or dye my felfe :
And know, my Lords, that *Iames*, the King of
    Scots,
Warres hard vpon the borders of this land :   20
Here is his Poft : Say, Iohn Taylour,
What newes with King Iames ?
    Iohn. Warre, my Lord, [I] tell, and good newes,
I trow : For king Iame[s] vowes to meete you the
26. of this month, God willing : marie, doth he fir.
    Kendall. My friends, you fee what we haue to
          winne.
Well, Iohn, commend me to king Iames, and tell
    him,[2]
I will meete him the 26. of this month,
And all the reft : and fo, farewell.   [*Exit* Iohn.
Bonfild, why ftandft thou as a man in dumps ?   30
Courage : for if I winne, Ile make thee Duke :
I Henry Momford will be King my felfe,

---

[1] Dyce queries ' Or '—mere finicalism.
[2] Original ' And tell,' etc., a new line.

And I will make thee Duke of Lancaſter,
And Gilbert Armeſtrong Lord of Doncaſter.

    Bonfild. Nothing, my Lord, makes me amazde
        at all,
But that our ſouldiers[1] findes our victuals ſcant:
We muſt make hauocke of thoſe countrey Swaynes:
For ſo will the reſt tremble and be afraid,
And humbly ſend prouiſion to your campe.

    Gilb. [*Armſtrong*]. My Lord Bonfild giues good
        aduice,
They make a ſcorne and ſtand vpon the King: 40
So what is brought, is ſent from them perforce ;
Aſke Mannering elſe.

    Kend.   What ſayeſt thou, Mannering ?

    Man. Whenas I ſhew'd your high commiſſion,
They / made this anſwere,
Onely to ſend prouiſion for your horſes.

    Kend. Well, hye thee to Wakefield, bid the
To ſend me all prouiſion that I want ;   [Towne
Leaſt I, like martiall Tamberlaine, lay waſte
Their bordering countries, leauing none aliue
That contradicts my Commiſſion.[2]   50

    Man. Let me alone, my Lord, Ile make them
Their plumes :   [vayle[3]

---

   [1] = plural-singular, and hence 'findes.'

   [2] Original divides 'Their . . . Countries / And leauing . . . Commiſſion.'

   [3] *Ibid.* 'Let . . . them / Vayle . . . he be, / The . . . gainſayeth /
Your . . . feare.'

For whatfoere he be, the proudeft Knight,
Iuftice, or other, that gainfayeth your word,
Ile clap him faft, to make the reft to feare.

Kend. Doe fo Nick : hye thee thither prefently
And let vs heare of thee againe to-morrowe.

Man. Will you not remooue, my Lord ?

Kend. No : I will lye at Bradford all this night,
And all the next : come, Bonfield, let vs goe,   60
And liften out fome bonny laffes here.

                    [Exeunt omnes.

*Enter the Iuftice, a Townefman,[1] George-a-Greene,
    and Sir Nicholas Mannering with his Com-
    miffion.*

    Iuftice. M[after] Mannering, ftand afide, whileft
             we conferre
What is beft to doe. Townfmen of Wakefield,[2]
The Earle of Kendal here hath fent for victuals ;
And in ayding him, we fhewe our felues no leffe
Than traytours to the King : therefore   70
Let me heare, Townfmen, what is your confents.

    [Firft] Townes. / Euen as you pleafe we are all
             content.

[1] Dyce notes here, "*i.e.*, the spokesman of the body of townsmen who are on the stage during this scene."

[2] Original divides ' What . . . doe. / Townefmen . . . Kendall / Here . . . victuals ; / And . . . ourfelues / No leffe . . . King : / Therefore . . . Townefmen, / What . . . confents.' It must be noted that whilst accepting nearly all Dyce's line-arrangements in the present Play, Greene and his contemporaries affected 5 and 6-foot lines.

Iuſtice. Then M[aſter] Mannering, we are re-
Man. As howe?   [ſolu'd.
Iuſtice. Marrie ſir, thus.
We will ſend the Earle of Kendall no victuals,
Becauſe he is a traytour to the King ;
And in ayding him we ſhewe our ſelues no leſſe.
    Man. Why, men of Wakefield, are you waxen
                madde ;
That preſent danger cannot whet your wits,   80
Wiſely to make prouiſion of your ſelues ?
The Earle is thirtie thouſand men ſtrong in power,
And what towne ſo euer him reſiſt,
He layes it flat and leuell with the ground :
Ye ſilly men, you ſeeke your owne decay :
Therefore ſend my Lord ſuch prouiſion as he
So he will ſpare your towne   [wants,[1]
And come no neerer Wakefield then he is.[2]
    Iuſtice. M[aſter] Mannering, you haue your
You may be gone.   [anſwere, 90
    Man. Well, Woodroffe, for ſo I geſſe is thy
Ile make thee curſe thy ouerthwart deniall ; [name,
And all that ſit vpon the bench this day,
Shall rue the houre they haue withſtood my Lords
Commiſſion.
    Iuſtice. Doe thy worſt, we feare thee not.

---

[1] Two 6-foot lines as one line in original. Dyce gives a line to
' Therefore.'
[2] Original divides ' So . . . neerer / Wakefield . . . is.

Man. See you thefe feales ? before you paffe the
I will haue all things my Lord doth want, [towne,
In fpite of you.

> *George | a Greene.* Proud dapper Iacke, vayle
> bonnet to the bench[1]

That reprefents the perfon of the King ;   100
Or firra, Ile lay thy head before thy feete.

Man. Why, who art thou ?

George. Why, I am George a Greene,
True liegeman to my king,
Who fcornes that men of fuch efteeme as thefe,
Should brooke the braues of any trayterous fquire:
You[2] of the bench, and you my fellowe friends,
Neighbours, we fubiects all vnto the King ;
We are Englifh borne, and therefore Edwards
    friends,
Voude vnto him euen in our mothers wombe ;   110
Our mindes to God, our hearts vnto our King,
Our wealth, our homage, and our carcafes,
Be all King Edwards : then, firra, we haue
Nothing left for traytours, but our fwordes,
Whetted to bathe them in your bloods, and dye[3]
Gainft you, before we fend you any victuals.

---

[1] ' The bench ' a line to itself in original.

[2] Dyce notes, " ' You ' seems to be a misprint for ' Yon ' : but the
whole passage is corrupted." ' Yon ' would be nonsense, and there
seems no corruption.

[3] Original divides ' Whetted . . . bloods, / And . . . victuals ' :
also misreads ' dye againft.'

Iuſtice. Well ſpoken, George a Greene.

[*Firſt*] *Townes.* Pray let George a Greene ſpeake
for vs.

George. Sirra you get no victuals here,

Not if a hoofe of beefe would ſaue your liues.　120

Man. Fellowe, I ſtand amazde at thy preſump-
tion :

Why, what art thou that dareſt gaynſay my Lord,

Knowing his mighty puiſſance and his ſtroke ?

Why, my friend, I come not barely of my ſelfe :

For ſee, I haue a large Commiſſion.

George. / Let me ſee it, ſirra.　[*Takes the Commiſſion.*]　Whoſe ſeales be theſe ?

Man. This is the Earle of Kendals ſeale at armes,

This Lord Charnel Bonfields,

And this ſir Gilbert Armeſtrongs.

George. I tell thee, ſirra, did good King Edwards
ſonne　　　　　　　　　　　　　　130

Seale a commiſſion 'gainſt the King his father,

Thus would I teare it in deſpite of him.

He teares the Commiſſion.

Being traytour to my Soueraigne.

Man. What ? haſt thou torne my Lords Commiſſion ?

Thou ſhalt rue it, and ſo ſhall all Wakefield.

George. What, are you in choler ?　I will giue
you pilles

To coole your ftomacke.   Seeft thou thefe feales ?
Now by my fathers foule,
Which was a yeoman when he was aliue,   140
Eate them, or eate my daggers poynt, proud fquire.[1]
   Man. But thou doeft but ieft, I hope.   [*part.*
   George. Sure that fhall you fee, before we two
   Man. Well, and[2] there be no remedie, fo, George :
                 [*Swallows one of the feals.*
One is gone : I pray thee, no more nowe.
   George. O, fir,[3]
If one be good, the others cannot hurt.
So, fir ;   [*Mannering* swallows the other two feals.
Nowe you may goe tell the Earle of Kendall,   150
Although I haue rent his large Commiffion,
Yet of curtefie I haue fent all his feales
Backe againe by you.
   Man. Well, fir, I will doe your arrant.   [*Exit.*
   George. / Nowe let him tell his Lord, that he
          hath fpoke[4]
With George a Greene,
Hight[5] pinner of merrie Wakefield towne,
That hath phificke for a foole,

---

   [1] The original divides 'To coole . . . ftomacke./ Seeft . . . feales?/
Now . . . yeoman/ When . . . them,/ Or . . . fquire.'   See
annotated Biography on this incident.
   [2] 'And' = An' = if.
   [3] Original divides 'O fir . . . hurt./ So, fir . . . Kendall, / Although . . . Commiffion, / Yet . . . feales.'
   [4] Original divides 'Nowe . . . hath / Spoke . . . Greene.'
   [5] *Ibid.* misprints ' Right '—Dyce's correction.

Pilles for a traytour that doeth wrong his Soueraigne.

Are you content with this that I haue done?   160

   Iuſtice. I, content, George :

For highly haſt thou honourd Wakefield towne,

In cutting of proud Mannering ſo ſhort.

Come, thou ſhalt be my welcome gheſt to day ;

For well thou haſt deſeru'd reward and fauour.

                      [Exeunt omnes.

   Enter olde Muſgroue and yong Cuddie his ſonne.

   Cuddie. Nowe gentle father liſt vnto thy ſonne,

And for my mothers loue,

That earſt was blythe and bonny in thine eye,   170

Graunt one petition that I ſhall demaund.

   Olde Muſgroue. What is that, my Cuddie ?

   Cuddie. Father, you knowe [1]

The ancient enmitie of late [2]

Between the Muſgroues and the wily Scottes,

Whereof they haue othe,

Not to leaue one aliue[3] that ſtrides a launce.

O Father,[4]

You are olde, and wayning age vnto the graue :

---

  [1] Original divides ' Father . . . late. '

  [2] Dyce queries ' enmity of late *reviv'd.'*

  [3] Dyce annotates, "*i.e.* not to leave even a child of them alive, one who *equitat in arundine longa.* [' Equitare in arundine longa.'—Horace, *Sat.* ii. 3. 248] —*Steevens.*"

  [4] Original divides ' O Father . . . graue : '

G. XIV.   9

Olde William Mufgroue, which whilome was
        thought,   180
The braueft horfeman in all Weftmerland,
Is weake, and forcft to ftay his arme vpon a ftaffe,[1]
That earft could wield a launce:
Then, / gentle Father, refigne the hold to me ;
Giue armes to youth, and honour vnto age.
  Mus. Auaunt, falfe hearted boy, my ioynts doe
        quake
Euen with anguifh of thy verie words.
Hath William Mufgroue feene an hundred yeres?
Haue I beene feard and dreaded of the Scottes,
That when they heard my name in any roade[2]   190
They fled away, and pofted thence amaine ?
And fhall I dye with fhame nowe in mine age?
No, Cuddie, no, thus refolue I,
Here haue I liu'd, and here will Mufgroue dye.
                                      Exeunt omnes.

*Enter Lord Bonfild, Sir Gilbert Armeftrong, M.
    Grime, and Bettris his daughter.*

  Bon. Now, gētle Grime, God a mercy for our
        good chere,
Our fare was royall, and our welcome great;
And fith fo kindly thou haft entertained vs,   200

----

[1] One line of two 6-foot lines.
[2] Dyce annotates, "*i.e.* inroad": but not so ; =on any of the high-
ways. See next line.

If we returne with happie victorie,
We will deale as friendly with thee in recompence.
   Grime. Your welcome was but dutie, gentle
             Lord :
For wherefore haue we giuen vs our wealth,
But to make our betters welcome when they come ?
[*Afide.*] O, this goes hard when traytours muft be
           flattered :
But life is fweete, and I cannot withftand it :
God (I hope) will reuenge the quarrell of my King.
   Gilb. [*Arm.*] What faid you, Grime ?
   Grime. I fay, fir Gilbert, looking on my daughter, 210
I curfe the houre that ere I got the girle :
For / fir, fhe may haue many wealthy futers,
And yet fhe difdaines them all,
To haue[1] poore George a Greene vnto her hufband,
   Bonfild. On that, good Grime, I am talking
         with thy Daughter ;
But fhe, in quirkes and quiddities of loue,
Sets me to fchoole, fhe is fo ouer-wife.
But, gentle girle, if thou wilt forfake the pinner[2]
And be my loue, I will aduance thee high :
To dignifie thofe haires of amber hiew,   220
Ile grace them with a chaplet made of pearle,
Set with choice rubies, fparkes,[3] and diamonds

---

[1] Original divides 'And yet . . . to haue.'
[2] *Ibid.* divides 'But . . . forfake.'
[3] Dyce queries 'ruby-fparks,'—but surely not?

Planted vpon a veluet hood, to hide that head
Wherein two fapphires burne like fparkling fire :
This will I doe, fair Bettris, and farre more,
If thou wilt loue the Lord of Doncafter.

    Bettris. Heigh ho, my heart is in a higher place,
Perhaps on the Earle, if that be he : [1]
See where he comes, or angrie, or in loue ;
For why, his colour looketh difcontent.   230

     Enter the Earle of Kendall and [Sir] Nicholas
               Mannering.[2]

    Kendall. Come, Nick, followe me.
    Bonfild. Howe nowe, my Lord ? what newes ?
    Kendall. Such newes, Bonfild, as will make thee
        laugh,
And fret thy fill, to heare how Nick was vfde :
Why, the Iuftices ftand on their termes ;
Nick, as you knowe, is hawtie in his words ;
He / layd the lawe vnto the Iuftices
With threatning braues, that one lookt on another, 240
Ready to ftoope : but that a churle came in,
One George a Greene, the pinner of the towne,
And with his dagger drawne layd hands on Nick,
And by no beggers fwore that we were traytours,
Rent our Commiffion, and vpon a braue

---

[1] Dyce asks, "Ought this line (which is imperfect) and the two following lines to be given to Bonfield ?" Certainly not.

[2] Original misplaces this after Kendall's speech, 'Come,' etc.

Made Nick to eate the feales, or brooke the
    ftabbe :   [ftraight.
Poore Mannering afraid, came pofting hither
   Bettris. O louely George, fortune be ftill thy
       friend,
And as thy thoughts be high, fo be thy minde,
In all accords, euen to thy hearts defire.   250
   Bonfild. What fayes faire Bettris ?
   Grimes. My Lord, fhe is praying for George a
       Greene :
He is the man, and fhe will none but him.
   Bonfild. But him ? why looke on me, my girle :
Thou knoweft, that yefternight I courted thee,
And fwore at my returne to wedde with thee :
Then tell me, loue, fhall I haue all thy faire ? [1]
   Bettris. I care not for Earle, nor yet for Knight,
Nor Baron that is fo bold :
For George a Greene, the merrie pinner,   260
He hath my heart in hold.
   Bonfild. Bootleffe, my Lord, are many vaine
      replies.
Let vs hye vs to Wakefield, and fend her the
      pinners head.
   Kend. It fhall be fo. Grime, gramercie,
Shut vp thy daughter, bridle her affects,
Let me not miffe her when I make returne :
Therefore / looke to her, as to thy life, good Grime.

               [1] = beauty.

Grime. I warrant you, my Lord.

[*Ex. Grime & Bettris.*[1]

Ken. And Bettris,   270
Leaue a bafe pinner, for to loue an Earle.
Faine would I fee this pinner George a Greene.
It fhall be thus :
Nick Mannering fhall leade on the battell,
And we three will goe to Wakefield in fome dis-
    guife :
But howfoeuer, Ile haue his head to day.

Exeunt omnes.

*Enter the King of Scots, Lord Humes, with fouldiers
    and Iohnie.*

King. Why, Iohnie : then the Earle of Kendall 280
    is blithe,
And hath braue men that troupe along with him.
Iohnie. I, marrie, my liege,
And hath good men that come along with him,[2]
And vowes to meete you at Scrafblefea,[3] God willing.
King. If good S[aint] Andrewe lend King Iam[i]e
    leaue,
I will be with him at the pointed day.
But, foft : whofe pretie boy art thou ?

---

[1] *Ex* = going. Dyce places after Kendall's speech 'And Bettris.
Original divides 'And . . . Earle' in one line.
[2] Original divides 'I . . . him' as one line.
[3] Dyce queries, 'Scriuelfby' or 'Scamblefby'?

Enter Iane a Barleys ſonne.

Ned. Sir, I am ſonne vnto Sir Iohn a Barley,
Eldeſt, and all that ere my mother had,   290
Edward my name.

    Iame[s]. And whither art thou going, pretie
        Ned ?

    Ned. To ſeeke ſome birdes, and kill them, if I
        can :

And now my ſcholemaſter is alſo gone :
So haue I libertie to ply my bowe ;
For / when he comes, I ſtirre not from my booke.

    Iames. Lord Humes, but marke the viſage of
        this child ;

By him I geſſe the beautie of his mother :
None but Læda could breede Helena.
Tell me, Ned, who is within with my mother ?   300

    Ned. None[1] but her ſelfe and houſhold ſeruants,
        ſir :

If you would ſpeake with her, knocke at this gate.

    Iames. Iohnie, knocke at that gate.

                Iohn knocks at the gate.

Enter Iane a Barley vpon the walles.

    Iane. O, I am betraide : what multitudes be
        theſe ?

    Iames. Feare not, faire Iane·: for all theſe men
        are mine,

           [1] Original 'Not.'

And all thy friends, if thou be friend to me :
I am thy louer, Iames the King of Scottes,
That oft haue fued and wooed with many letters,   310
Painting my outward paffions with my pen,
When as my inward foule did bleede for woe :
Little regard was giuen to my fute,
But haply thy hufbands prefence wrought it :
Therefore, fweete Iane, I fitted me to time ;
And, hearing that thy hufband was from home,
Am come to craue what long I haue defirde.

   Ned. Nay, foft you, fir, you get no entrance here,
That feeke to wrong Sir Iohn a Barley fo,
And offer fuch difhonour to my mother.   320

   Iames. Why, what difhonour, Ned?

   Ned. Though young,[1]
Yet often haue I heard my father fay,
No greater wrong than to be made cuckold.
Were / I of age, or were my bodie ftrong,
Were he ten Kings, I would fhoote him to the heart,
That fhould attempt to giue fir Iohn the horne.—
Mother, let him not come in :
I will go lie at Iockie Millers houfe.

   Iames. Stay him.   330

   Iane. I, well faid Ned, thou haft giuen the king
      his anfwere ;
For were the ghoft of Cefar on the earth,
Wrapped in the wonted glorie of his honour,

---

[1] Original divides ' Though . . . heard / My . . . fay,'.

He fhould not make me wrong my hufband fo :
But good King Iames is pleafant, as I geffe,
And meanes to trie what humour I am in ;
Elfe would he neuer haue brought an hofte of men,
To haue them witnes of his Scottifh luft.
   Iames. Iane, in faith, Iane,—
   Iane. Neuer reply : [1]   340
For I proteft by the higheft holy God,
That doometh iuft reuenge for things amiffe,
King Iames, of all men, fhall not haue my loue.
   Iames. Then lift to me, Saint Andrewe be my
           boote,
But Ile rafe thy caftle to the verie ground,
Vnleffe thou open the gate, and let me in.
   Iane. I feare thee not, King Iamie, doe thy worft :
This caftle is too ftrong for thee to fcale ;
Befides, to-morrowe will fir Iohn come home.
   Iames. Well, Iane, fince thou difdainft King 350
           Iames loue,
Ile draw thee on with fharpe and deepe extremes ;
For, / by my father's foule, this brat of thine
Shall perifh here before thine eyes,
Vnleffe thou open the gate, and let me in.
   Iane. O deepe extremes : my heart begins to
My little Ned lookes pale for feare.—   [breake ;
Cheare thee, my boy, I will doe much for thee.
   Ned. But not fo much, as to difhonour me.

---

[1] Original divides ' Neuer . . . higheft / Holy God.'

Iane. And[1] if thou dyeſt, I cannot liue, ſweete
    Ned.
Ned. Then dye with honour, mother, dying 360
Iane. I am armed :   [chaſte.
My huſbands loue, his honour, and his fame,
Ioynes[2] victorie by vertue. Nowe, King Iames,
If mothers teares cannot alay thine ire,
Then butcher him ; for I will neuer yeeld :
The ſonne ſhall dye before I wrong the father.
Iames. Why, then, he dyes.

     Allarum within : Enter a Meſſenger.

Meſſenger. My Lord, Muſgroue is at hand.
Iames. Who, Muſgroue ? The deuill he is.   370
Come, my horſe !   [*Exeunt omnes.*

  Enter Olde Muſgroue with King Iames priſoner.

Mus. Nowe, King Iames, thou art my priſoner.
Iames. Not thine, but fortunes priſoner.

         Enter Cuddie.

Cuddie. Father, the field is ours :[3]
Their colours we haue ſeyzed, and Humes is ſlayne ;
I ſlewe him hand to hand.

[1] ' And ' = an', *i.e.* if.
[2] Dyce reads ' Ioin,' and queries ' Gain ' or ' Win ' ? but text yields
a good sense, and the singular verb to successive nouns was common.
Original divides ' Ioynes . . . vertue / Nowe . . . ire.'
[3] *Ibid.* ' Father . . . we / Haue ſeyzed :/ And . . . hand.'

Mus. / God and Saint George.
Cuddie. O father, I am fore athirſt.   380
Iane. Come in, young Cuddie, come and drink
    thy fill :
Bring in King Iam[i]e with you as a gheſt;
For all this broile was caufe he could not enter.
                        Exeunt omnes.

Enter George a Greene alone.

George. The fweete content of men that liue in
    loue,
Breedes fretting humours in a reſtleſſe minde ;
And fanfie, being checkt by fortunes fpite,
Grows too impatient in her fweete defires :
Sweete to thofe men whome loue leades on to bliſſe, 390
But fowre to me, whofe happe is ſtill amiſſe.

Enter the Clowne [*Jenkin*].

Ienkin. Marie, amen fir.
George. Sir, what doe you crye Amen at ?
Ienkin. Why, did not you talke of loue ?
George. Howe doe you knowe that ?
Ienkin. Well, though I fay it that ſhould not fay
it, there are few fellowes in our parish fo netled
with loue as I haue bene of late.[1]

[1] Original divides ' Well . . . it, / There . . . pariſh / So . . . late ';
and so onward in the most absurd way, though nearly all prose.
Enough of such divisions have been recorded. The ' copy' must have
been bad and illiterate throughout.

Geor. Sirra, I thought no leſſe, when the other 400
morning, you roſe ſo earely to goe to your
wenches. Sir, I had thought you had gone about
my honeſt buſines.

Ienkin. Trow, you haue hit it ; for maſter, be it
knowne to you, there is ſome good-will betwixt
Madge the Souſewife and I : marie / ſhe hath
another louer.

George. Canſt thou brooke any riuals in thy
loue ?

Ien. A rider ? no, he is a ſow-gelder and goes 410
afoote. But Madge pointed to meete me in your
wheate-cloſe.

George. Well, did ſhe meete you there ?

Ien. Neuer make queſtion of that. And firſt
I ſaluted her with a greene gowne, and after fell
as hard a-wooing as if the Prieſt had bin at our
backs, to haue married vs.

Georg. What, did ſhe grant ?

Ien. Did ſhe graunt ?   Neuer make queſtion
of that. And ſhe gaue me a ſhirt coler, wrought 420
ouer with no counterfeit ſtuffe.

Georg. What, was it gold ?

Ien. Nay, twas better than gold.

Georg. What was it ?

Ien. Right Couentrie blew. We[1] had no ſooner
come there, but wot you who came by ?

---

[1] Original ‘Who ’—‘ We ’ Dyce's correction.

Georg. No, who ?

Ien. Clim the fow-gelder.

Georg. Came he by ?

Ien. He fpide Madge and I fit together : he 430 leapt from his horfe, laid his hand on his dagger, and began to fweare. Now I feeing he had a dagger, and I nothing but this twig in my hand, I gaue him faire words and faid nothing. He / comes to me, and takes me by the bofome : You hoorefen[1] flaue, faid he, hold my horfe, and looke he take no colde in his feet. No, marie, fhall he, fir, quoth I ; Ile lay my cloake vnderneath him. I tooke my cloake, fpread it all along, and [fet] his horfe on the midft of it. 440

Georg. Thou clowne, didft thou fet his horfe vpon thy cloake ?

Ien. I, but marke how I ferued him. Madge and he were no fooner gone downe into the ditch, but I plucked out my knife, cut foure holes in my cloake, and made his horfe ftand on the bare ground.

Geor. Twas well done. Now fir, go and furuay my fields : if you finde any cattell in the corne, to pound with them. 450

Ien. And if I finde any in the pound, I fhall turne them out. *Exit Ienkin.*

---

[1] = whore-son.

Enter the Earle of Kendal, Lord Bonfield, fir Gilbert [Armftrong], all difguifed, with a traine of men.

Kend. Now we haue put the horfes in the corne,
Let vs ftand in fome corner for to heare
What brauing tearmes the pinner will breathe
When he fpies our horfes in the corne.

               [Retires with the others.]

    [Re]enter Ienkin[1] blowing of his horn.   460

Ien. O mafter, where are you? we haue a prife.
Georg. A prife, what is it?
Ienkin. / Three goodly horfes in our wheate-clofe.
George. Three horfes in our wheat-clofe? whofe
      be they?
Ienkin. Marie thats a riddle to me; but they
are there: veluet horfes, and I neuer fawe fuch
horfes before. As my dutie was, I put off my
cappe, and faid as followeth: My mafters, what
doe you make in our clofe? One of them,
hearing me afke what he made there, held vp his 470
head and neighed, and after his maner laught as
heartily as if a mare had bene tyed to his girdle.
My mafters, faid I, it is no laughing matter; for,
if my mafter take you here, you goe as round
as a top to the pound. Another vntoward iade,
hearing me threaten him to the pound, and to

        [1] Original 'Iacke.

tell you of them, caft vp both his heeles, and let
fuch a monftrous great fart, that was as much as
in his language to fay, A fart for the pound, and a
fart for George a Greene. Nowe I, hearing this, 480
put on my cap, blewe my horne, called them all
iades, and came to tell you.

Georg. Nowe fir, goe and driue me thofe three
horfes to the pound. Doe you heare ? [1]

Ienkin. I were beft take a conftable with me.

George. Why fo ?

Ienkin. Why, they, being gentlemens horfes,
may ftand on their reputation, and will not
obey me.

George. Goe, doe as I bid you, fir. 490

Ienkin. Well, I may goe.

The Earle of Kendall, the Lord Bonfild, and fir
Gilbert Armeftrong, meete them.

Kend. / Whither away, fir ?

Ienkin. Whither away ? I am going to put the
horfes in the pound.

Kend. Sirra, thofe three horfes belong to vs, and
we put them in, and they muft tarrie there, and
eate their fill.

Ienkin. Stay, I will goe tell my mafter.—Heare 500
you mafter? we haue another prife : thofe three

---

[1] Original misassigns the question to 'Ienkin,' and so Dyce. So the
next speech 'Why they,' etc., is misassigned to George.

horfes be in your wheate-clofe ftill, and here be
three geldings more.

George. What be thefe?

Ienkin. Thefe are the mafters of the horfes.

George. Nowe gentlemen,—I knowe not your
          degrees,
But more you cannot be, 'leffe [1] you be Kings,—
Why wrong you vs of Wakefield with your horfes?
I am the pinner, and before you paffe,
You fhall make good the trefpaffe they haue done. 510

Kend. Peace, faucie mate, prate not to vs:
I tell thee, pinner, we are gentlemen.

George. Why fir,
So may I fir, although I giue no armes.

Kend. Thou? how art thou a gentleman?

Ienkin. And [2] fuch is my mafter, and he may
giue as good Armes, as euer your great grandfather
could giue.

Kend. Pray thee let me heare howe.

Ienkin. Marie, my mafter may giue for his
armes the picture of Aprill in a greene ierkin, 520
with a rooke on one fift, and an horne on the
other: but my mafter giues his armes the wrong
way; for he giues the horne on his fift; and /
your grandfather, becaufe he would not lofe his
armes, weares the horne on his owne head.

---

[1] Dyce's correction of 'vnleffe' of original.

[2] Dyce queries 'Ay'? But 'And' dexterously assumes that he
(George) was a gentleman.

Kend. Well pinner, fith our horfes be in,
In fpite of thee they now fhall feede their fill,
And eate vntil our leifures ferue to goe.

George. Now, by my fathers foule,
Were good King Edwards horfes in the corne, 530
They fhall[1] amend the fcath, or kiffe the pound ;
Much more yours fir, whatfoere you be.

Kend. Why man, thou knoweft not vs :
We do belong to Henry Momford, Earle of Kendal;
Men that, before a month be full expirde,
Will be king Edwards betters in the land. [lieft.

Georg. King Edwards better[s] : rebell, thou

George ftrikes him.

Bonfild. Villaine, what haft thou done ? thou
haft ftroke an Earle.

Geor. Why, what care I ? A poore man that is 540
Is better then an Earle, if he he falfe : [true,
Traitors reape no better fauours at my hands.

Kend. I, fo me thinks ; but thou fhalt deare aby
this blow.——
Now or neuer lay hold on the pinner.

Enter all the ambufh.

George. Stay, my Lord, let vs parlie on thefe
broiles :

---

[1] Dyce annotates, " In passages like this our old writers often prefer
' fhall' to ' fhould.' "

Not Hercules againft two, the prouerbe is,
Nor I againft fo great a multitude.—　[they did,
[*Afide.*] Had not your troupes come marching as
I would / haue ftopt your paffage vnto London :　550
But now Ile flie to fecret policie.

　　Kend. What doeft thou murmure, George?

　　George. Marie this, my Lord, I mufe,
If thou be Henrie Momford Kendals Earle,
That thou wilt doe poor G[eorge] a Greene this
Euer to match me with a troupe of men.　[wrong,

　　Kend. Why didft[1] thou ftrike me then?

　　Geor. Why my Lord, meafure me but by your-
Had you a man had feru'd you long,　　[felfe :
And heard your foe mifufe you behinde your backe, 560
And would not draw his fword in your defence,
You would cafhere him.[2]
Much more, king Edward is my king ;
And before Ile heare him fo wrong'd,
Ile die within this place,
And maintaine good whatfoeuer I haue faid.
And, if I fpeake not reafon in this cafe,
What I haue faid Ile maintaine in this place.

---

　　[1] Original 'doeft'—Dyce's correction.
　　[2] Dyce annotates here, "In Dodsley's *Old Plays* a vain attempt is
made to restore the metre of this corrupted passage by arranging it as
follows :—

　　　　'You would cashier him.　Much more,
　　　　King Edward is my king : and before I'll hear him
　　　　So wrong'd, I'll die within this place,
　　　　And maintain,' etc."

Bon. A pardon my Lord, for this pinner ;
For, truſt me he ſpeaketh like a man of worth. 570
    Kend. Well, George,
Wilt thou leaue Wakefielde and wend with me,
Ile freely put vp all and pardon thee.
    Georg. I, my Lord, conſidering[1] me one thing,
You will leaue theſe armes and follow your good
      king.
    Ken. Why George, I riſe not againſt king Edward,
But for the poore that is oppreſt by wrong ;
And / if king Edward will redreſſe the ſame,
I will not offer him diſparagement,
But otherwiſe ; and ſo let this ſuffiſe : 580
Thou hear'ſt the reaſon why I riſe in armes, [me ;
Nowe, wilt thou leaue Wakefield, and wend with
Ile make thee captaine of a hardie band,
And when I haue my will, dubbe thee a knight.
    Georg. Why, my Lord, haue you any hope to
      winne ?
    Kend. Why, there is a prophecie doeth ſay,
That King Iames and I ſhall meete at London,
And make the King vaile bonnet to vs both.
    Geo. If this were true, my Lord,
This were a mightie reaſon. 590
    Ken.   Why, it is
A miraculous prophecie, and cannot faile.

---

[1] Dyce queries 'conceding'? but see Glossarial-Index, *s.v.*

George. Well, my Lord, you haue almoſt turned
Ienkin, come hither.   [me.—

Ienkin. Sir ?

George. Goe your waies home, ſir.

And driue me thoſe three horſes home vnto my
        houſe,

And powre them downe a buſhell of good oates.

Ienkin. Well, I will.—[*Aſide.*] Muſt I giue theſe
ſcuruie horſes Oates?   [*Exit Ienkin.* 600

Geor. Will it pleaſe you to commaund your
        traine aſide ?

Kend. Stand aſide.   [*Exit the trayne.*

Georg. Nowe liſt to me :

Here in a wood, not farre from hence,

There dwels an old man in a caue alone,

That can foretell what fortunes ſhall befall you,

For he is greatly ſkilfull in magicke arte :

Goe / you three to him early in the morning,

And queſtion him : if he ſaies good,

Why, then, my Lord, I am the formoſt man   610

Who[1] will march vp with your campe to London.

Kend. George, thou honoureſt me in this :

But where ſhall we finde him out ?

George. My man ſhall conduct you to the place;

But good my Lord,[2] tell me true what the wiſe
        man ſaith.

Kend. That will I, as I am Earle of Kendal.

The original ' We.'   [2] *Ibid.* ' Lords.'

George. Why then, to honour G[eorge] a.Greene
      the more,
Vouchſafe a peece of beefe at my poore houſe ;
You ſhall haue wafer-cakes your fill,
A peece of beefe hung vp ſince Martilmas :   620
If that like you not, take what you bring, for me.
Kend. Gramercies, George.   [*Exeunt omnes.*

*Enter George a Greenes boy Wily, diſguiſed like a
woman, to M. Grime.*

Wily. O, what is loue ? it is ſome mightie power,
Elſe could it neuer conquer G[eorge] a Greene :
Here dwels a churle that keepes away his loue :
I know the worſt, and if I be eſpied,
Tis but a beating ; and if I by this meanes
Can get faire Bettris forth her fathers dore,
It is inough.   630
Venus, for me, and all goes alone,[1]
Be aiding to my wily enterprize.

     He knocks at the doore.

     Enter Grime.

Gri. How now, who knocks there ? what would
      you haue ?
From / whence came you ? where doe you dwell ?

---

[1] Dyce changes to 'Venus, for me, of all the gods alone' : Reed,
apud Dodsley's *Old Plays,* printed 'Venus be for me and ſhe alone.'
No need of tinkering of the text—'and ' = an' (*i.e.* if) yields sufficient
sense.

Wily. I am, forſooth, a ſemſters maide hard-by,
That hath brought worke home to your daughter.[1]

Grime. Nay, are you not   [Greene, 640
Some craftie queane that comes from George a
That raſcall, with ſome letters to my daughter?
I will haue you ſearcht.

Wily. Alas, ſir, it is Hebrue vnto me,
To tell me of George a Greene, or any other.
Search me, good ſir, and if you finde a letter
About me, let me haue the puniſhment that is due.

Grime. Why are you mufled? I like you the
          worſe for that.

Wily. I am not, ſir, aſham'd to ſhew my face,
Yet loth I am my cheekes ſhould take the aire :   650
Not that I am charie of my beauties hue,
But that I am troubled with the tooth-ach ſore.
                    [*Unmuffles.*

Grime. [*aſide.*] A pretie wench, of ſmiling
          countenance :
Olde men can like, although they cannot loue ;
I,
And loue, though not ſo briefe as yong men can.—
Well,—
Goe in, my wench, and ſpeake with my daughter.
        Exit [*Wily into the houſe.*] 660
I wonder much at the Earle of Kendall,

---

[1] Dyce annotates, "Here 'daughter' is a trisyllable : see Walker's *Shakespeare's Versification,* etc., p. 208."

Being a mightie man, as ftill he is,
Yet for to be a traitor to his king,
Is more then God or man will well allow :
But what a foole am I to talk of him?
My / minde is more heere of the pretie laffe :
Had fhe brought fome fortie pounds to towne[1]
I could be content to make her my wife :
Yet I haue heard it in a prouerbe faid,
He that is olde, and marries with a laffe,   670
Lies but at home, and prooues himfelfe an affe.

   Enter Bettris in Wilies apparell, to Grime.

How now, my wench, how ift? what, not a word?—
Alas, poore foule, the tooth-ach plagues her fore.—
Well, my wench, ...   *[Gives money.*
Here is an Angel for to buy thee pinnes,
And I pray thee vfe mine houfe ;
The oftner, the more welcome : farewell. *[Exit.*
  Bettris. O bleffed loue, and bleffed fortune both:
But Bettris, ftand not here to talke of loue,   680
But hye thee ftraight vnto thy George a Greene :
Neuer went Roe-bucke fwifter on the downes
Then I will trip it till I fee my George.   *[Exit.*

*Enter the Earle of Kendall, L[ord] Bonfield, fir
   Gilbert [Armftrong], and Ienkin the clowne.*

  Kend. Come away, Ienkin.

---

[1] Dyce queries 'dower' ?

Ien. Come, here is his houſe [*Knocks at the door*].
—Where be you, ho?

Georg. [*within.*] Who knocks there?

Kend. Heere are two or three poore men, father, 690
Would ſpeake with you.

    Georg. [*within.*] Pray, giue your man leaue to
        leade me forth.

Kend. Goe Ienkin, fetch him forth.

Enter George a Greene diſguiſed.

Ien. Come, olde man.

Kend. / Father,
Heere is three poore men come to queſtion thee
A word in ſecrete that concernes their liues.

    George. Say on, my ſonne.[1]

    Kend. Father, I am ſure you heare the newes, 700
        how that
The Earle of Kendal wars againſt the king.
Now father, we three are Gentlemen by birth,
But yonger brethren that want reuenues,
And for the hope we haue to be preferd,
If that we knew that we ſhall winne,
We will march with him : if not,
We will not march a foote to London more.
Therefore, good father, tell vs what ſhall happen,
Whether the King or the Earle of Kendal ſhall win.

    George. The king, my ſonne.   710

---

[1] Original 'ſonnes.'

Kend. Art thou fure of that ?

George. I, as fure as thou art Henry Momford,
The one L[ord] Bonfild, the other fir Gilbert
    [Armftrong].

Kend. Why, this is wondrous, being blinde of
    fight,
His deepe perfeuerance[1] fhould be fuch to know vs.

Gilb. Magike is mightie, and foretelleth great
    matters.——
Indeede Father, here is the Earle come to fee thee,
And therefore, good father, fable not with him.

George. Welcome is the Earle to my poore cell,
    and fo
Are you, my Lords : but let me counfell you   720
To leaue thefe warres againft your king, and liue
In quiet.

Kend. Father, we come not for aduice in warre,
But to know whether we fhall win or leefe.

George. / Lofe gentle Lords, but not by good king
A bafer man fhall giue you all the foile. [Edward:

Kend. I marie, father, what man is that ?

George. Poor George a Greene, the pinner.

Kend. What fhall he ?

George. Pull all your plumes, and fore difhonour 730

Kend. He ? as how ?   [you.

George. Nay, the end tries all; but fo it will fall
    out.

         [1] See Glossarial-Index, *s.v.*

Kend. But fo it fhall not, by my honor,[1] Chrift.
Ile raife my campe, and fire Wakefield towne,
And take that feruile pinner George a Greene,
And butcher him before king Edwards face.

George. Good my Lord, be not offended,
For I fpeake no more then arte reueales to me:
And for greater proofe,
Giue your man leaue to fetch me my ftaffe.   740

Kend. Ienkin, fetch him his walking ftaffe.

Ien. [*giving it.*] Here is your walking ftaffe.

George. Ile proue it good vpon your carcafes,
A wifer wifard neuer met you yet,
Nor one that better could foredoome your fall :
Now I haue fingled you here alone,
I care not though you be three to one.

Kend. Villaine, haft thou betraid vs ?[2]

Georg. Momford, thou lieft, neuer was I traitor
Onely deuif'd this guile to draw you on;   [yet ; 750
For to be combatants.
Now conquere me, and then march on to London:
But / fhall goe hard but I will hold you tafke.

Gilb. Come, my Lord, cheerely, Ile kill him
        hand to hand.

Kend. A thoufand pound to him that ftrikes that
        ftroke.

---

[1] Dyce queries, 'honour'd' ; but inadmissible.
[2] Dyce queries properly, 'Thou haft'? but the forms were inter⁻
changed as meaning the same thing.

Georg. Then giue it me, for I will haue the firſt.

Here they fight: George kills Sir Gilbert [Arm-
ſtrong], and takes the other two priſoners.

Bonfield. Stay, George, we doe appeale.

George. To whom? 760

Bon. Why, to the king :
For rather had we bide what he appoynts,
Then here be murthered by a ſeruile groome.

Kend. What wilt thou doe with vs?

Georg. Euen as Lord Bonfild wiſt ;
You ſhall vnto the king ; and, for that purpoſe,
See where the Iuſtice is placed.

Enter Iuſtice.

Iuſt. Now, my Lord of Kendal, where be al
your threats?
Euen as the cauſe, ſo is the combat fallen, 770
Elſe one could neuer haue conquerd three.

Kend. I pray thee, Woodroffe, do not twit me ;
If I haue faulted, I muſt make amends.

Geor. Maſter Woodroffe, here is not a place for
many words ;
I beſeech ye, ſir, diſcharge all his ſouldiers,
That euery man may goe home vnto his owne
houſe.

Iuſtice. It ſhall be ſo. What wilt thou doc,
George?

Geor. Mafter Woodroffe, looke to your charge ;
Leaue me to my felfe.

Iuft. / Come, my Lords.   780

[*Exeunt all but George.*[1]

Geor. Here fit thou, George, wearing a willow
    wreath,
As one defpairing of thy beautious loue.
Fie, George, no more ;
Pine not away for that which cannot be.
I cannot ioy in any earthly bliffe,
So long as I doe want my Bettris.[2]

Enter Ienkin.

Ien. Who fee a mafter of mine?
George. How now firrha, whither away ?   790
Ien. Whither away ? why, who doe you take me
to bee ?
Georg. Why, Ienkin, my man.
Ien. I was fo once in deede, but now the cafe is
altered.
Georg. I pray thee, as how ?
Ien. Were not you a fortune teller to-day ?
Georg. Well, what of that ?
Ien. So fure am I become a iugler. What will
you fay if I iuggle your fweete heart ?   800

---

[1] Original 'Exit.' Dyce annotates, "Here a change of scene is
supposed."
[2] Dyce notes, "A trisyllable here—*Betteris* = *Beatrice.*"

George. Peace, prating lofell, her ielous father
Doth wait ouer her with fuch fufpitious eyes,
That, if a man but dally by her feete,
He thinks it ftraight a witch[1] to charme his daughter.

Ien. Well, what will you giue me, if I bring her
hither?

George. A fute of greene, and twentie crownes
befides.

Ien. Well, by your leaue, giue me roome. You
muft giue me fomething that you haue lately worne.

George. Here is a gowne, will that ferue you? 810
                                [*Gives gown.*

Ienkin. I, this will ferue me : keep out of my
    circle,
Leaft / you be torne in peeces with fhee deuils.—
Miftres Bettris, once, twice, thrice.

   He throwes the gown[2] *in, and fhe comes out.*

Oh is this no cunning[3]?

George. Is this my loue, or is it but her fhadow?

Ienkin. I, this is the fhadow, but heere is the
fubftance.

---

[1] ;'*i.e.* a sorcerer, as is remarked by Walker (*Crit. Exam. of the Text
of Shakespeare*, etc., ii. 89), who arranges the passage thus—
      ' Her iealous father doth wait over her
        With fuch fufpicious eyes, that, if a man
        But dally by her feet, he thinks it ftraight
        A witch to charm his daughter.' "—*Dyce.*
[2] Original misprinted ' ground.'
[3] Dyce queries '*this is* no cunning !'?

George. Tell mee fweete loue, what good fortune
    brought thee hither :   820
For one it was that fauoured George a Greene.[1]
 Bettris. Both loue & fortune brought me to my
    George,
In whofe fweete fight is all my hearts content.
 Geor. Tell mee fweete loue, how camft thou from
    thy fathers ?
 Bettris. A willing minde hath many flips in loue.
It was not I, but Wily, thy fweete boy.
 Geor. And where is Wily now ?
 Bettris. In my apparell in my chamber ftill.
 Geor. Ienkin, come hither : goe to Bradford,
And liften out your fellow Wily.—   830
Come, Bettris, let vs in,
And in my cottage we will fit and talke.
        [*Exeunt omnes*

  Enter King Edward, the King of Scots, Lord
   Warwicke, yong Cuddy, and their traine.

 Edward. Brother of Scotland, I doe hold it hard,
Seeing a league of truce was late confirmde
Twixt you and me, without difpleafure offered
You fhould make fuch inuafion in my land.
The / vowes of kings fhould be as oracles, 840

---

[1] Dyce very needlessly notes, " It is plain from Bettris's answer that
something has dropped out here."

Not blemisht with the staine of any breach ;
Chiefly where fealtie and homage willeth[1] it.
    Iames. Brother of England, rub not the sore
        afresh ;
My conscience grieues me for my deepe misdeede :
I haue the worst ; of thirtie thousand men,
There scapt not full fiue thousand from the field.
    Edward. Gramercie, Musgroue, else it had gone
        hard :
Cuddie, Ile quite thee well ere we two part.
    Iames. But had not his olde Father William
        Musgroue,
Plaid twice the man, I had not now bene here.   850
A stronger man I seldome felt before ;
But one[2] of more resolute valiance
Treads not, I thinke vpon the English ground.
    Edward. I wot wel, Musgroue shall not lose his
        hier.
    Cuddie. And it please your grace, my father was
Fiue score and three at Midsommer last past ;
Yet had king Iamie bene as good as George a
        Greene,
Yet Billy Musgroue would haue fought with him.
    Edward. As George a Greene ?
I pray thee, Cuddie, let me question thee.   860

---

[1] Dyce finically changes to ' will.'
[2] Dyce queries, ' *And* one of *valiance more resolute*
      Treads not,' etc.

Much haue I heard fince I came to my crowne,
Many in manner of a prouerbe fay,
Were he as good as G[eorge] a Green, I would
    ftrike him fure.
I pray thee tell me, Cuddie, canft thou informe me,
What is that George a Greene ?
    Cuddie. Know, my Lord, I neuer faw the man,
But mickle talke is of him in the Country ;
They / fay he is the Pinner of Wakefield towne,
But for his other qualities, I let alone.
    War. May it pleafe your grace, I know the mã
        too wel.   870
    Edward. Too well? Why fo, Warwicke ?
    War. For once he fwingde me till my bones did
        ake.
    Edward. Why, dares he ftrike an Earle?
    Warw. An Earle, my Lord ? nay he wil ftrike
        a king,
Be it not king Edward. For ftature he is framde
Like to the picture of ftoute Hercules,
And for his carriage paffeth Robin Hood.
The boldeft Earle or Baron of your land,
That offereth fcath vnto the towne of Wakefield,
George will arreft his pledge vnto the pound ;   880
And whofo refifteth beares away the blowes,
For he himfelfe is good inough for three.
    Edward. Why, this is wondrous. My L[ord]
        of Warwicke,

Sore do I long to fee this George a Greene.
But leauing him, what fhall we do, my Lord,
For to fubdue the rebels in the North?
They[1] are now marching vp to Doncafter.—
Soft, who haue we there?

Enter one with the Earle of Kendal prifoner.[2]

Cuddie. Here is a traitour, the Earle of Kendal. 890
Edward. Afpiring traitour, how darft thou
Once caft thine eyes vpon thy Soueraigne
That honour'd thee with kindenes and with fauour?
But I will make thee buy[3] this treafon deare.
Kend. / Good my Lord,—
Edward. Reply not, traitour.—
Tell me, Cuddy, whofe deede of honour
Wonne the victorie againft this rebell?   [field.
Cuddy. George a Greene, the Pinner of Wake-
Edward. George a Greene : now fhall I heare 900
Certaine what this Pinner is :   [newes
Difcourfe it briefly, Cuddy, how it befell.
Cud. Kendall and Bonfild, with Sir Gilbert
          Armftrong,
Came to Wakefield Towne difguifd,
And there fpoke ill of your grace ;
Which George but hearing, feld them at his feete,

---

[1] Dyce again finically queries 'That'?
[2] Original places this stage-direction before 'Soft, etc.'
[3] Dyce alters silently to 'by,' and explains " *i.e.* aby." But it is 'buy,' not 'by.'

And, had not refcue come into[1] the place,
George had flain them[3] in his clofe of wheate.
    Eaward. But, Cuddy,
Canft thou not tell where I might giue and grant   910
Some thing that might pleafe
And highly gratifie the pinners thoughts?
    Cuddie. This at their parting George did fay to
If the king vouchfafe of this my feruice,   [me[3];
Then, gentle Cuddie, kneele vpon thy knee,
And humbly craue a boone of him for me.
    Eaward. Cuddie, what is it?   [them,
    Cuddie. It is his will your grace would pardon
And let them liue, although they haue offended.
    Edward. I thinke the man ftriueth to be glorious. 920
Well, George hath crau'd it, and it fhall be graunted,
Which none but he in England fhould haue got-
        ten.—
Liue, Kendall, but as prifoner,
So fhalt thou end thy dayes within the tower.
    Kend. / Gracious is Edward to offending fubiects.
    Iames. My Lord of Kend[al], you are welcome
        to the court.
    Edward. Nay, but ill-come as it fals out now ;
I, . . .
Ill come in deede, were it not for George a Greene.

---

[1] = unto.   [2] Original ' him.'
[2] Dyce notes here, " Yet Cuddy a little before has told the king he
never saw George-a-Greene." Such slips frequent.

But gentle king, for fo you would auerre,   930
And Edwards betters, I falute you both,
And here I vowe by good Saint George,
You wil gaine but litle when your fummes are
    counted.
I fore doe long to fee this George a Greene :
And for becaufe I neuer faw the North,
I will forthwith goe fee it :
And for that to none I will be knowen, we will
Difguife ourfelues and fteale downe fecretly,
Thou and I, king Iames, Cuddie, and two or three,
And make a merrie iourney for a moneth.—   940
Away then, conduct him to the tower.—
Come on king Iames, my heart muft needes be
    merrie,
If fortune make fuch hauocke of our foes.
                                    [*Ex. omnes.*

*Enter Robin Hood, Mayd Marian, Scarlet, and
        Much, the Millers fonne.*

Robin. Why is not louely Marian blithe of
        cheere ?
What ayles my Lemman, that fhe gins to lowre?
Say, good Marian, why art thou fo fad?
    Marian. Nothing, my Robin, grieues me to the 950
        heart,
But whenfoeuer I doe walke abroad,

I heare no fongs but all of George a Greene ;
Bettris, his faire Lemman, paffeth me ;
And this, my Robin, gaules my very foule.

    Robin. / Content [thee] :   [ftoute,
What wreakes it vs, though George a Greene be
So long as he doth proffer vs no fcath ?
Enuie doth feldome hurt but to it felfe ;
And therefore, Marian, fmile vpon thy Robin.

    Mar. Neuer will Marian fmile vpon her Robin, 960
Nor lie with him vnder the greenwood fhade,
Till that thou go to Wakefield on a greene,
And beate the Pinner for the loue of me.

    Robin. Content thee, Marian, I will eafe thy
My merrie men and I will thither ftray ; [griefe,
And heere I vow that, for the loue of thee,
I will beate George a Greene, or he fhall beate me.

    Scarlet. As I am Scarlet, next to little Iohn,
One of the boldeft yeomen of the crew,
So will I wend with Robin all along,   970
And try this Pinner what he dares[1] do.

    Much. As I am Much, the Millers fonne,
That left my Mill to goe with thee,
And nill repent that I haue done,
This pleafant life contenteth me ;
In ought I may, to doe thee good,
Ile liue and die with Robin Hood.

---

[1] Dyce notes, " Here ' dares ' is a dissyllable : see Walker's *Shakespeare's Versification,* etc., p. 146."

Marian. And Robin, Marian fhe will goe with
To fee faire Bettris how bright fhe is of blee.[1] [thee,
 Robin. Marian, thou fhalt goe with thy Robin.— 980
Bend vp your bowes, and fee your ftrings be tight,
The arrowes keene, and euery thing be ready,
And / each of you a good bat on his necke,
Able to lay a good man on the ground.
 Scarlet. I will haue Frier Tuckes.
 Much. I will haue little Iohns.
 Robin. I will haue one made of an afhen plunke[2]
Able to beare a bout or two.—
Then come on, Marian, let vs goe ;
For before the Sunne doth fhew the morning, day,[3] 990
I will be at Wakefield to fee this Pinner, George
 a Greene.   [*Exeunt omnes.*

*Enters a Shoomaker, fitting vpon the ftage at worke ;
Ienkin to him.*

 Ienkin. My mafters, he that hath neither meate
nor money, and hath loft his credite with the Ale-
wife, for anything I know, may go fupperleffe to
bed.—But, foft, who is heere ? here is a Shoomaker : he knowes where is the beft Ale.—
Shoomaker, I pray thee tell me, where is the beft 1000
Ale in the towne ?

---

[1] " ' Bright of blee ' is an expression frequent in old ballads : ' blee '
is colour, complexion (Sax. *bleo*)."—*Dyce.*
[2] Dialectal spelling of ' plank.'
[3] Dyce ineptly queries ' *his* morning *ray.*'

Shoomaker. Afore, afore, follow thy nofe ; at the figne of the Egge fhell.

Ienkin. Come, Shoomaker, if thou wilt, and take thy part of a pot.

Shoomaker. [*coming forward.*] Sirra, downe with your ftaffe, downe with your ftaffe.   1010

Ienkin. Why, how now, is the fellow mad ? I pray thee tell me, why fhould I hold downe my ftaffe ?

Shooma[*ker.*] You wil downe with him, will you not, fir ?

Ienkin. / Why, tell me wherefore ?

Shoo. My friend, this is the towne of merry Wakefield, and here is a cuftome held, that none fhall paffe with his ftaffe on his fhoulders, but he muft haue a bout with me ; and fo fhall you, fir.

Ienkin. And fo will not I, fir.[1]

Shoo. That wil I try. Barking dogs bite not the foreft.   1020

Ienkin. [*afide.*] I would to God I were once well rid of him.

Shoomaker. Now, what, will you downe with your ftaffe ?

Ienkin. Why, you are not in earneft, are you?

Shoomaker. If I am not, take that. [*Strikes him.*

Ienkin. You whoorfen cowardly fcabbe, it is but the part of a clapperdudgeon to ftrike a man in the

---

[1] " *i.e.* will not I down with my staff."—*Dyce.*

ftreete. But dareft thou walke to the townes end
with me? 1030

Shoomaker. I, that I dare do : but ftay till I
lay in my tooles, and I will goe with thee to the
townes end prefently.

Ienkin. [*afide.*] I would I knew how to be rid
of this fellow.

Shoom. Come, fir, wil you go to the townes end
now fir ?

Ienkin. I fir, come.—Now we are at the townes
end, what fay you now ?

Shoomaker. Marry, come, let vs euen haue a 1040
bout.

Ienkin. Ha, ftay a little ; hold thy hands, I pray
thee.

Shoomaker. Why, whats the matter ?

Ienkin. Faith, I am vnder-pinner of a[1] towne, and
there is an order, which if I doe not keepe, I fhall /
be turned out of mine office.

Shoomaker. What is that, fir.

Ienkin. Whenfoeuer I goe to fight with any-
bodie, I vfe to flourifh my ftaffe thrife about my 1050
head before I ftrike, and then fhew no fauour.

Shoomaker. Well, fir, and till then I will not
ftrike thee.

Ienkin. Well, fir, here is once, twice :—here is
my hand, I will neuer doe it the third time.

---

[1] Dyce alters to 'the,' but Ienkin disguises by 'a' who he really is.

Shoomaker. Why, then, I fee we fhall not fight.

Ienkin. Faith, no : come, I will giue thee two
pots of the beft Ale, and be friends.

Shoomaker. [*afide.*] Faith, I fee it is as hard to
get water out of a flint as to get him to haue 1060
a bout with me : therefore I will enter into him
for fome good cheere.—My friend, I fee thou
art a faint hearted fellow, thou haft no ftomacke
to fight, therefore let vs go to the Alehoufe and
drinke.

Ienkin. Well, content : goe thy wayes, and fay
thy prayers, thou fcapft my hands to-day.

[*Exeunt omnes.*

Enter George a Greene and Bettris.

George. Tell me fweet loue, how is thy minde 1070
         content ?

What, canft thou brooke to liue with George a
         Greene ?

Bettris. Oh George, how little pleafing are thefe
         words ?

Came I from Bradford for the loue of thee,

And left my father for fo fweet a friend ?

Here will I liue vntill my life doe end.

George. Happy am I to haue fo fweet a loue.—

But / what are thefe come trafing here along ?

Bettris. Three men come ftriking through the
         corne, my loue.

*Enter Robin Hood, [Scarlet, Much,] and [Maid]
Marian, and his traine.*　　　1080

George. Backe againe, you foolifh trauellers,
For you are wrong, and may not wend this way.
　Robin Hood. That were great fhame. Now by
　　　my foule, proud fir,
We be three tall yeomen, and thou art but one.——
Come, we will forward in defpite of him.
　George. Leape the ditch, or I will make you fkip.
What, cannot the hieway ferue your turne
But you muft make a path ouer the corne?
　Robin. Why, art thou mad? dar'ft thou in-
　　　counter three?
We are no babes, man, look vpon our limmes.　　1090
　Geo. Sirra,
The biggeft lims haue not the ftouteft hearts.
Were ye as good as Robin Hood, and his three
　　　mery men,
Ile driue you backe the fame way that ye came.
Be ye men, ye fcorne to incounter me all at once;
But be ye cowards, fet vpon me all three,
And try the Pinner what he dares performe.
　Scarlet. Were thou as high in deedes
As thou art haughtie in wordes,
Thou well mighteft be a champion for a king:　　1100
But emptie veffels haue the loudeft foundꞩ,
And cowards prattle more than men of worth.

George. Sirra, dareſt thou trie me?

Scarlet. I, ſirra, that I dare.

    [*They fight, and George a Greene beates him.*

Much. / How now? what, art thou downe?—
Come, ſir, I am next.

    [*They fight, and George a Greene beates him.*

Robin Hood. Come, ſirra, now to me; ſpare me
                not,

For Ile not ſpare thee.   [thee. 1110

George. Make no doubt I will be as liberall to
              They fight; Robin Hood ſtayes.

Robin Hood. Stay, George, for here I doo proteſt.
Thou art the ſtouteſt champion that euer I
Layd handes vpon.

George. Soft, you ſir! by your leaue, you lye;
You neuer yet laid hands on me.

Robin Hood. George, wilt thou[1] forſake Wake-
And go with me?   [field,
Two liueries will I giue thee euerie yeere,   1120
And fortie crownes ſhall be thy fee.

George. Why, who art thou?

Robin Hood. Why, Robin Hood:
I am come hither with my Marian
And theſe my yeomen for to viſit thee.

George. Robin Hood?
Next to King Edward art thou leefe to me.
Welcome, ſweet Robin, welcome, mayd Marian;

---

[1] See the ballad at the end of this play from Dyce.

And welcome, you my friends. Will you to my
    poore houſe?
You ſhall haue wafer cakes your fill,   1130
A peece of beefe hung vp ſince Martlemas,
Mutton and veale : if this like you not,
Take that you finde, or that you bring, for me.[1]
   Robin Hood. Godamercies, good George,
Ile be thy gheſt to day.
   George. Robin, therein thou honoureſt me.
Ile leade the way.   *[Exeunt omnes.*

   Enter King Edward and King Iames [of Scots]
       diſguiſed, with two ſtaues.
   Edward. Come on, king Iames : now wee are 1140
        thus diſguiſed,
There is none (I know) will take vs to be kings :
I thinke we are now in Bradford,
Where all the merrie ſhoomakers dwell.

      Enters a Shoomaker.
   Shoomaker. [*coming forward.*] Downe with your
        ſtaues, my friends,
Downe with them.
   Edward. Downe with our ſtaues? I pray thee,
        why ſo?
   Shoomaker. My friend, I ſee thou art a ſtranger
        heere,
Elſe wouldeſt thou not haue queſtiond of the thing.
           [1] Cf. ll. 618-21.   1150

This is the towne of merrie Bradford,
And here hath beene a cuftome kept of olde,
That none may beare his ftaffe vpon his necke,
But traile it all along throughout the towne,
Vnleffe they meane to haue a bout with me.

    Edward. But heare you fir, hath the king
This cuftome ?   [granted you

    Shoomaker. King or Kaifar, none fhall paffe this
               way,
Except King Edward ;
No, not the ftouteft groome that haunts his court : 1160
There / fore downe with your ftaues.

    Edward. What were we beft to do ?

    Iames. Faith, my Lord, they are ftoute fellowes :
And becaufe we will fee fome fport,
We will traile our ftaues.

    Edward. Heer'ft thou, my friend ?
Becaufe we are men of peace and trauellers,
We are content to traile our ftaues.

    Shoomaker. The way lies before you, go along.

    Enter Robin Hood and George a Greene, difguifed. 1170

    Robin Hood. See George, two men are paffing
          through the towne,
Two luftie men, and yet they traile their ftaues.

    George. Robin,
They are fome pefants trickt in yeomans weedes.—
Hollo, you two trauellers !

Edward. Call you vs, fir ?

George. I, you. Are ye not big inough to beare
Your bats vpon your neckes, but you muſt traile
Along the ſtreetes ?   [them

Edward. Yes ſir, we are big inough ;   1180
But here is a cuſtome kept,
That none may paſſe, his ſtaffe vpon his necke,
Vnleſſe he traile it at the weapons point.
Sir, we are men of peace, and loue to ſleepe
In our whole ſkins, and therefore quietnes is beſt.

George. Baſe minded peſants, worthleſſe to be
                              men :
What, haue you bones and limmes to ſtrike a blow,
And be your hearts ſo faint you cannot fight ?
Wert not for ſhame, I would drub[1] your ſhoulders
                              well,
And / teach you manhood againſt another time.   1190

Shoom. Well preacht ſir Iacke, downe with your
                              ſtaffe.

Edward. Do you heare my friends? and you be
                              wiſe, keepe downe
Your ſtaues, for all the towne will riſe vpon you.

George. Thou ſpeakeſt like an honeſt quiet
                              fellow ;
But heare you me ; in ſpite of all the ſwaines
Of Bradford town, beare me your ſtaues vpon your
                              necks,

[1] Original ' ſhrub.'

Or to begin withall, Ile bafte you both fo well,
You were neuer better bafted in your liues.

Edward. We will hold vp our ftaues.

    George a Greene fights with the Shoomakers, and   1200
        beates them all downe.

George. What, haue you any more ?
Call all your towne forth, cut, and longtaile.[1]

    The Shoomakers fpy George a Greene.

Shoomaker. What, George a Greene, is it you ?
               A plague found[2] you !
I thinke you long'd to fwinge me well :
Come George, we will crufh a pot before we part.

    George. A pot, you flaue, we will haue an
        hundred.—

---

[1] See Glossarial Index, *s.v.*, for a full note. " This expression, it would
seem, was originally applied to dogs : ' Yea, euen their verie *dogs*, Rug,
Rig, and Rifbie, yea, *cut and long-taile,* they fhall be welcome.'—Ulpian
Fulwell's ' Art of Flattery,' 1576, sig. G 3. In his note on ' call me cut,'
Twelfth Night, Act II., sc. iii. (Shakespeare ii. 671, ed. 1858,) Mr. Collier
writes : ' " Cut " (as Steevens suggests) was probably abbreviated from
curtal, a horse whose tail has been docked ; and hence the frequent
opposition, in old comic writers, of *cut* and *long-tail.* The Rev. Mr.
Dyce, in a note on " Wit at Several Weapons " (B. & F. iv. 39) says that
cut and longtail means " dogs of all kinds." What marks of admiration
would he not have placed after it, if any other editor had committed
such a mistake ! ' But Mr. Collier's memory must be sadly impaired ;
for his note on ' come cut and long-tail,' *Merry Wives of Windsor,*
Act III., sc. iv. (Shakespeare i. 222, ed. 1858), runs thus : ' A phrase
expressive of dogs of every kind ; which Slender applies to persons pre-
cisely in the same way as by [*sic*] Pompey in Beaumont and Fletcher
" Wit at Several Weapons " (edit. Dyce, iv. p. 39),' etc."

[2] = confound.

Heere, Will Perkins, take my purfe, fetch me
A ftand of Ale, and fet [it] in the Market place,   1210
That all may drinke that are athirft this day ;
For this is for a fee to welcome Robin Hood
To Bradford towne.

They bring out the ftande of ale, and they fall a
drinking.

Here, Robin, fit thou here ;
For thou art the beft man at / the boord this day.
You that are ftrangers, place yourfelues where you
Robin,   [will.
Heer's a caroufe to good King Edwards felf ;   1220
And they that loue him not, I would we had
The bafting of them a litle.

Enter the Earle of Warwicke with other noblemen,
bringing out the Kings garments : then George
a Greene and the reft kneele downe to the King.

Edward. Come, mafters, all fellowes.—Nay,
Robin,
You are the beft man at the boord to-day.—
Rife vp, George.   [were, then :
George. Nay, good my Liege, ill nurtur'd we
Though we Yorkefhire men be blunt of fpeech,   1230
And litle fkill'd in court, or fuch quaint fafhions,
Yet nature teacheth vs duetie to our king.
Therefore I
Humbly befeech you pardon George a Green[e].

Robin. And, good my Lord, a pardon for poore
    Robin,
And for vs all a pardon, good King Edward.
    Shoomaker. I pray you, a pardon for the Shoo-
    makers.
    Edward. I frankely grant a pardon to you all :
                            [*They rife.*
And, George a Greene,[1] giue me thy hand ;
There is none in England that fhall do thee wrong. 1240
Euen from my court I came to fee thy felfe ;
And now I fee that fame fpeakes nought but trueth.
    George. I humbly thanke your royall Maieftie.
That which I did againft the Earle of Kendal,
Twas [2] but a fubiects duetie to his Soueraigne,
And / therefore little merit[s] fuch good words.
    Edward. But ere I go, Ile grace thee with good
Say what King Edward may performe,   [deeds :
And thou fhalt haue it, being in Englands bounds.
    George. I haue a louely Lemman,
As bright of blee as is the filuer moone,   1250
And olde Grimes her father, will not let her match

---

[1] "Mr. Collier (*Hist. of Engl. Dram. Poet.* iii. 167) cites this passage
with the following regulation :—
        'And George-a-Greene, give me thy hand : there is
        None in England that fhall do thee wrong,'—
observing that 'the word "England" is to be pronounced as a trisyllable.' But though our early poets occasionally use 'England' as a
trisyllable, they certainly never intended it to be accented 'Engéland.' "
—*Dyce.*
    [2] Original, "It was.'

With me, becaufe I am a Pinner,
Although I loue her, and fhe me, dearely.

   Edward. Where is fhe?

   George. At home at my poore houfe,
And vowes neuer to marrie vnleffe her father
Giue confent ; which is my great griefe, my Lord.

   Edward. If this be all, I will difpatch it ftraight ;
Ile fend for Grime, and force him giue his grant :   1260
He will not denie king Edward fuch a fute.

Enter Ienkin, and fpeakes.

   [*Ienkin.*] Ho, who faw a mafter of mine ? Oh
he is gotten into company, an a bodie fhould rake
hell for companie.

   George. Peace, ye flaue : fee where King Edward
is.

   Edward. George, what is he ?

   George. I befeech your grace pardon him, he is
my man.

   Shoomaker. Sirra, the king hath bene drinking 1270
with vs, and did pledge vs too.

   Ienkin. Hath he fo? kneele ; I dub you gentlemen.

   Shoomaker. Beg it of the King, Ienkin.

   Ienkin. I wil.—I befeech your worfhip grant
me one thing.

   Edward. / What is that ?

Ienkin. Hearke in your eare.

> *He whifpers the king in the eare.*

Edward. Goe your wayes, and do it.   1280

Ienkin. Come, downe on your knees, I haue got it.

Shoomaker. Let vs heare what it is firſt.

Ienkin. Mary, becauſe you haue drunke with the king, and the king hath ſo gracioufly pledgd you, you ſhall be no more called Shoomakers; but you and yours, to the worlds ende, ſhall be called the trade of the gentle craft.

Shoomaker. I befeech your maieſtie reforme this which he hath ſpoken.   1290

Ienkin. I befeech your worſhip confume this which he hath ſpoken.

Edward. Confirme it, you would ſay.—
Well, he hath done it for you, it is ſufficient.—
Come, George, we will goe to Grime, and haue thy loue.

Ienkin. I am ſure your worſhip will abide; for yonder is comming olde Mufgroue and mad Cuddie his ſonne.—Maſter, my fellow Wilie comes dreſt like a woman, and Maſter Grime will marrie Wilie. Heere they come.   300

> *Enter Mufgroue and Cuddie, and maſter Grime Wilie, Mayd Marian and Bettris.*

Edward. Which is thy old father, Cuddie?

Cuddie. / This, if it pleafe your maieftie.

> [Mufgroue *kneels.*

Edward. Ah old Mufgroue, ftand[1] vp ;
It fits not fuch gray haires to kneele.

Mufgroue. [*rifing.*] Long liue
My Soueraigne, long and happie be his dayes :
Vouchfafe, my gracious Lord, a fimple gift,   1310
At Billy Mufgroues hands :
King Iames at Meddellom caftle[2] gaue me this ;
This wonne the honour, and this giue I thee.

> [*Gives fword to K. Edward.*

Edward. Godamercie, Mufgroue, for this friendly
> gift,
And for thou feldft a king with this fame weapon,
This blade fhall here dub valiant Mufgroue knight.

Mufgr. Alas what hath your highnes done ? I
> am poore.   [caftle,

Edw. To mend thy liuing take thou Meddellom-
The hold of both[3] ; and if thou want liuing, com- 1320
> plaine,
Thou fhalt haue more to maintaine thine eftate.
George, which is thy loue ?

---

[1] Original 'kneele.'

[2] " = Middleham-castle : Grose, in his *Antiq. of England and Wales*, vol. iv., gives two views of this castle, and is at the trouble to inquire what foundation the present play has on history : well might Ritson (*Robin Hood*, vol. i., p. xxix) sneer at 'his very gravely sitting down and debating his opinion in form.' "—*Dyce.*

[3] " 'The hold of both,' etc.: corrupted."—*Dyce.* Query 'Take hold of both,' *i.e.* the sword and the castle ?

George. This, if pleafe your maieftie.

Edward. Art thou her aged father?

Grime. I am, and it like your maieftie.

Edward. And wilt not giue thy daughter vnto
   George?

Grime. Yes, my lord, if he will let me marrie
With this louely laffe.

Edward. What fayft thou, George? [confent.

George. With all my heart, my Lord, I giue 1330

Grime. Then do I giue my daughter vnto
   George.   [end.

Wilie. Then fhall the marriage foone be at an
Witneffe my Lord, if that I be a woman:

     [Throws off his difguife.

For I am Wilie, boy to George a Greene,
Who for my mafter wrought this fubtill fhift.

Edward. What, is it a boy? what fayft thou to
   this, Grime?

Grime. Mary, my Lord, I thinke, this boy hath
More knauerie than all the world befides.
Yet am I content that George fhall both haue 1340
My daughter and my lands.   [worth:

Edward. Now George, it refts I gratifie thy
And therefore here I doe bequeath to thee,
In full poffeffion, halfe that Kendal hath;
And what as Bradford holds of me in chiefe,
I giue it frankely vnto thee for euer.
Kneele downe George.

George. What will your maieſtie do ?

Edward. Dub thee a knight, George.

George. I beſeech your grace, grant me one 1350
    thing.

Edward. What is that?

George. Then let me liue and die a yeoman ſtill :

So was my father, ſo muſt liue his ſonne.

For tis more credite to men of baſe degree,

To do great deeds, than men of dignitie.

Edward. Well, be it ſo George.

Iames. I beſeech your grace deſpatch with me,

And ſet downe my ranſome.

    Edward. George a Greene, ſet downe the king
        of Scots

His ranſome. 1360

George. I beſeech your grace pardon me,

It paſſeth my ſkill.

Edward. Do it, the honor's thine.

George. Then let king Iames make good

Thoſe townes which he hath burnt vpon the
    borders ;

Giue a ſmall penſion to the fatherleſſe,

Whoſe fathers he cauſ'd murthered in thoſe warres;

Put in pledge for theſe things to your grace,

And ſo returne.

    [*Edward.*] King Iames, are you content? 1370

Iamie. I am content, and like your maieſtie,

And will leaue good caſtles in ſecuritie.

Edward. I craue no more.—Now George a
        Greene,
Ile to thy houfe ; and when I haue fupt,
Ile go to Afke,
And fee if Iane a Barley be fo faire
As good King Iames reports her for to be.
And for the ancient cuftome of *Vaile ftaffe*,
Keepe it ftill, clayme priuiledge from me :
If any afke a reafon why ? or how ?   1380
Say, Englifh Edward vaild his ftaffe to you.

FINIS. /

APPENDIX (*from Dyce*).

" Specimen of *The Hiſtory of George-a-Greene*, on which the preceding play is founded.

" ' Richard having ſettled his affairs, he prepar'd for a voyage to the Holy Land, in coniunction with Philip the Second, then king of France. During his abſence he conſtituted the biſhop of Ely, then chancellor of England, vicegerent of the kingdom. This biſhop being on the one ſide covetous, and by many uniuſt impoſitions oppreſſing the nation, and the kings brother ambitious on the other, as preſuming much upon his royal birth and his great poſſeſſions, ſome perſons fomented great factions and com-binations againſt the tyranizing prelate ; ſo that all things grew out of frame and order ; and great diſtractions enſued ; nay, a third ulcer, worſe than the former, broke into open rebellion—namely, an inſurrection was raiſed by the Earl of Kendal, with divers of his adherents, as, the Lord Bouteil, Sir Gilbert Armeſtrong, and others. Theſe having gather'd an army of ſome twenty thouſand malecontents, made publick proclamation, that they came into the field for no other cauſe, but to purchaſe their country-men's liberty, and to free them from the great and inſufferable oppreſſion which they then liv'd under by the prince and prelate. This drew to the earl many followers for the preſent, ſo that he ſeemed to have got together a very potent army. But the main reaſon of this rebellion was, that when the earl was but a child, a wizard had prophefy'd of him, That Richard and he ſhould meet in London, and the king ſhould

there vail his bonnet unto him : and this prediction of the
footh-fayer prov'd afterwards to be true, but not as he vainly
had expounded it.   The earl having led his army into the
north, ftruck a great terror into all thofe honeft fubiects,
that tender'd their allegiance to their abfent king and
fovereign, and wifh'd well to the good of the commonwealth
and the fafety of the kingdom ; yet many were forced
through fear to fupply his men with neceffary provifions,
left otherwife they fhould have made fpoil and havock of
all they had.   Now, the earl being for fome time deftitute
of many things that are ufeful and commodious for an army,
and encamping fome five miles from the town of Wakefield,
the three confederates drew a commiffion, and, having
fign'd it with their own feals, fent it by one Mannering,
a fervant of the earl's, to the bailiff and towns-men of
Wakefield, requiring feemingly, by way of intreaty, to fend
unto his hoft fuch a quantity of provifion, of corn and
cattle, with other neceffaries (of which he was then in great
want), and withal, fuch a fum of money as he demanded for
the payment of fo many foldiers ; to which this Mannering
was to perfwade them by all fair means poffible ; but, if
they fhould deny his requeft, he was to threaten them with
fire and fword, with all the violence that could be fuggefted
to them.   The news of this commiffion coming to their
knowledge, the bailiff fent abroad to the neighbouring
iuftices, as to Mr. Grymes and others ; fo that he and his
brethren appointed to give them a meeting in the town-
houfe, where many of the commons were to be prefent, and,
amongft others, George A Green propofed to be there, to
hear what would become of the bufinefs.   The fummons
being made, the affembly met, and the meffenger appear'd,
fhow'd his warrant, and, according to his orders, told
them what great conveniences would grow in fupplying the

army, and withal entreated from the lords their love and
favour. The bailiff and the iuftices were loth, it being
contrary to their allegiance to grant their requeft : yet they
were fearful withal peremptorily to deny it, and ftood
wavering long and debating amongft themfelves what they
had beft do for their own fafeties ; which Mannering feeing
without doing any reverence at all unto the bench, he began
to alter his phrafes, and changed the copy of his countenance, firft taunting and deriding their faint-hearted coward-
ize, and afterward threatening them, that if they gave not
prefent fatisfaction to his demand, the army would inftantly
remove, make havock and fpoil of their goods and chattels,
ravifh their daughters, and deflower their wives before their
faces, and make a bonfire of the town, to the terrifying of
others, whofe infolence durft oppofe the earl his mafter's
commiffion. At this [thefe] haughty and infufferable men-
aces, whilft the bench fate quaking, George preffeth forward
in the face of the court, and defireth, by the favour of
the bench, to have the liberty, according to his plain and
weak underftanding, to give the meffenger an anfwer ;
which being granted him, he boldly ftept up to him, and
demanded his name ; who made him anfwer, that his name
was Mannering. Mannering (faith he) ; that name was ill
beftow'd on one who can fo forget all manners, as to
ftand cover'd before a bench upon which the maiefty of his
fovereign was reprefented : which manners (faith he) fince
thou wanteft, I will teach thee ; and withal, firft fnatching his
bonnet from his head, trod upon it, then fpurn'd it before
him. At which the other being inraged, afk'd him, How
he durft to offer that violence to one who brought fo ftrong
a commiffion ? Your commiffion (faith George), I cry your
[you] mercy, fir ; and withal, defired the favour of the
bench, that he might have the liberty to perufe it ; which

being granted, I, marry, (faith he, having read it,) I cannot
chufe but fubmit myfelf to this authority; and making an
offer as if he meant to kifs it, tore it in pieces. Mannering
feeing this, began to ftamp, ftare, and fwear; but George
taking him faft by the collar, fo fhook him as if he had
purpofed to have made all his bones loofe in his fkin, and
drawing his dagger, and pointing it to his bofom, told him,
He had devifed phyfick to purge his cholerick blood; and
gathering up the three feals, told him, It was thefe three
pills, which he muft inftantly take and fwallow, and [or]
never more expect to return to his mafter; nor did he leave
him, or take the dagger from his breaft, till he had feen it
down, and afterwards, when he had perceiv'd that they had
almoft choak'd him, he call'd for a bottle of ale, and faid
thefe words: It fhall never be faid, that a meffenger fhall be
fent by fuch great perfons to the town of Wakefield, and
that none would be fo kind as to make him drink; therefore here (faith he), Mannering, is a health to the confufion
of the traitor thy mafter, and all his rebellious army; and
pledge it me without evafion or delay, or I vow, by the
allegiance which I owe to my prince and fovereign, that
thou haft drunk thy laft already. Mannering, feeing there
was no remedy, and feeling the wax ftill fticking in his
throat, drank it off fupernaculum; which the other feeing,
Now (faith he) commend me to thy mafter and the reft, and
tell them, one George A Green, no better man than the
Pindar of the town of Wakefield, who tho' I have torn their
commiffion, yet I have fent them their feals fafe back again
by their fervant. Whatfoever Mannering thought, little
was he heard to fpeak, but went away muttering the devil's
Pater Nofter, and fo left them. Every body commended
the refolution of George, and, by his fole encouragement,
purpofed henceforward to oppofe themfelves againft the

infurrection of the rebels.'—Thoms's *Early Romances,* vol. ii., p. 174, ed. 1858."

" BALLAD—' *The Iolly Pinder of Wakefield, with Robin Hood, Scarlet, and Iohn.*

" From an old black letter copy in A. à Wood's collection, compared with two other copies in the British Museum, one in black letter. It should be sung ' To an excellent tune,' which has not been recovered.

"Several lines of this ballad are quoted in the two old plays of the *Downfall* and *Death of Robert earle of Huntington,* 1601, 4to, b. 1, but acted many years before. It is also alluded to in Shakespeare's *Merry Wiues of Windfor,* Act I., Sc. 1, and again in his Second Part of *King Henry IV.,* Act V., Sc. 3;

' In Wakefield there lives a iolly pindèr,
   In Wakefield all on a green,
   In Wakefield all on a green :
There is neither knight nor fquire, faid the pindèr,
   Nor baron that is fo bold,
   Nor baron that is fo bold,
Dare make a trefpàfs to the town of Wakefield,
   But his pledge goes to the pinfold, etc.

All this be heard three witty young men,
   'Twas Robin Hood, Scarlet, and Iohn ;
With that they efpy'd the iolly pindèr,
   As he fat under a thorn.

Now turn again, turn again, faid the pindèr,
   For a wrong way you have gone ;
For you have forfaken the kings highway,
   And made a path over the corn.

O that were a fhame, faid iolly Robin,
   We being three, and thou but one.
The pinder leapt back then thirty good foot,
   'Twas thirty good foot and one.

He leaned his back faſt unto a thorn,
  And his foot againſt a ſtone,
And there he fought a long ſummers day,
  A ſummers day ſo long,
Till that their ſwords on their broad bucklèrs
  Were broke faſt into their hands.

Hold thy hand, hold thy hand, ſaid bold Robin Hood,
  And my merry men every one ;
For this is one of the beſt pindèrs,
  That ever I tryed with ſword.

And wilt thou forſake thy pinders craft,
  And live in the green-wood with me ?
At Michaelmas next my cov'nant comes out,
  When every man gathers his fee ;

Then I'le take my blew blade all in my hand,
  And plod to the green-wood with thee.
Haft thou either meat or drink, ſaid Robin Hood,
  For my merry men and me ?

I have both bread and· beef, ſaid the pindèr,
  And good ale of the beſt.
And that is meat good enough, ſaid Robin Hood,
  For ſuch unbidden gueſts.[1]

O wilt thou forſake the pinder his craft,
  And go to the green-wood with me ?
Thou ſhalt have a liuery twice in the year,
  The one green, the other brown.

If Michaelmas day was come and gone,
  And my maſter had paid me my fee,
Then would I ſet as little by him
  As my maſter doth by me.'
                Ritson's *Robin Hood*, vol. ii., p. 16."

  [1] " Qy., rather, ' gueſt ' [a plural] ? "—*Dyce.*

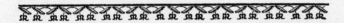

VII.

SELIMUS.

1594.

NOTE.

For the exemplar of 'Selimus' (1594) I have once more to thank his Grace the Duke of Devonshire. Opposite is the title-page. For our reasons for including 'Selimus' among the productions of Greene, see Storojenko's annotated Biography (in Vol. I.).   G.

THE
First part of the Tra-

gicall raigne of Selimus, fometime Emperour of the Turkes, and grandfather to him
that now raigneth.

Wherein is fhowne how hee moft vnnaturally
raifed warres againft his owne father *Baiazet*, and pre-
uailing therein, in the end caufed him to
be poyfoned.

Alfo with the murthering of his two brethren,
Corcut, and *Acomat*.

As it was playd by the Queenes Maiefties
Players.

LONDON
Printed by Thomas Creede, dwelling in Thames
ftreete at the figne of the Kathren wheele,
neare the olde Swanne.
1594.

Prologue.

No fained toy nor forged Tragedie,
Gentles we here prefent vnto your view,
But a moft lamentable hiftorie
Which this laft age acknowledgeth for true.
Here fhall you fee the wicked fonne purfue
His wretched father with remorflefle fpight :
And danted once, his force againe renue,
Poyfon his father, kill his friends in fight.
You fhall behold him character in bloud,   10
The image of an vnplacable King,
And like a fea or high refurging floud,
All obftant lets, downe with his fury fling.
Which if with patience of you fhalbe heard,
VVe haue the greateft part of our reward.
                             Exit   16

[Dramatis Personæ.[1]

Baiazet, *Emperour of Turkie.*

Selimus (or Selim), *Emperour of the Turkes (youngeſt ſon of Baiazet).*

Acomat, } *ſons of Baiazet.*
Corcut, }

Mustaffa, *high official of Baiazet.*

Aga.

Cherseoli.

Sinam Bassa.

Cali Bassa.

Hali Bassa.

Prince Mahomet, *ſon of Baiazet's eldeſt ſon, deceaſed.*

Ottrante.

Occhiali.

Regan.

Tonombey, *a great warrior.*

Visir.

Belierbey of Natolia.

Aladin, } *ſons of Acomat.*
Amurath, }

Bullithrumble, *a ſhepheard.*

Abraham, *the Iew.*

Ianiſſaries, Souldiers, Meſſengers, Page.

Zonara, *ſiſter to Mahomet.*

Solyma, *ſiſter to Selimus, wife to Muſtaffa.*

Queene Amasia, *wife of Acomat.*]

[1] No list of 'characters' in the original : above made out from the Play itself.   G.

THE FIRST PART OF THE

moſt tyrannicall Tragedie and raigne of
Selimus, Emperour of the Turkes, and
grandfather to him that now raigneth.

Enter Baiazet *Emperour of Turkie*, Muſtaffa,
Cherſeoly, *and the* Ianniſaries.

Baiazet.

Eaue me my Lords vntill I call you
    foorth,
For I am heauie and diſconſolate.
       Exeunt all but *Baiazet.* 10
So *Baiazet,* now thou remainſt
    alone,
Vnrip the thoughts that harbour in thy breſt
And eate thee vp; for arbiter heres none,
That may diſcrie the cauſe of thy vnreſt,
Vnleſſe theſe walles thy ſecret thoughts declare:

And Princes walles they fay, vnfaithful are.
Why, thats the profit of great regiment,
That all of vs are fubiect vnto feares,
And this vaine fhew and glorious intent,
Priuie fufpition on each fcruple reares.   20
I, though on all the world we make extent,
From the South-pole vnto the Northren beares,
And ftretch our raign from Eaft to Weftern fhore,
Yet doubt and care are with vs euermore.
Look how the earth clad in her fommers pride,
Embroyder[e]th her mantle gorgioufly
With fragrant hearbes, and flowers gaily dide,
Spreading / abroade her fpangled Tapiftrie :
Yet vnder all a loathfome fnake doth hide.
Such is our life, vnder Crownes, cares do lie,   30
And feare, the fcepter ftill attends vpon.
Oh who can take delight in kingly throne?
Publike diforders ioyn'd with priuate carke,
Care of our friends, and of our children deare,
Do toffe our liues, as waues a filly barke.
Though we be fearelefle, 'tis not without feare,
For hidden mifchiefe lurketh in the darke:
And ftormes may fall, be the day nere fo cleare.
He knowes not what it is to be a King,
That thinks a fcepter is a pleafant thing.   40
Twice fifteene times hath faire *Latonaes* fonne
Walked about the world with his great light
Since I began,—would I had nere begunne—

To fway this fcepter.   Many a carefull night
When *Cynthia* in haft to bed did runne,
Haue I with watching vext my aged fpright !
Since when, what dangers I haue ouer paft,
Would make a heart of adamant agaft.
The Perfian *Sophi*, mightie *Ifmaell*
Tooke the *Leuante* cleane away from mee;   50
And *Caraguis Baffa*, fent his force to quell,
Was kild himfelfe, the while his men did flee.
Poore *Hali Baffa* hauing once fped well
And gaind of him a bloodie victorie,
Was at the laft flaine fighting in the field ;
Charactering honor in his batt'red fhield.
Ramirchan[1] the Tartarian Emperour,
Gathering to him a number numberleffe,
Of bigbond Tartars, in a hapleffe houre
Encountred me ; and there my chiefeft bleffe   60
Good *Alemfhae*, (ah this remembrance foure)
Was flaine, the more t'augment my fad diftreffe.
In leefing *Alemfhae*,[2] poore I loft more
Then / euer I had gained theretofore.
Well may thy foule reft in her lateft graue,
Sweete *Alemfhae*, the comfort of my dayes ;
That thou might'ft liue, how often did I craue !
How often did I bootleffe praiers raife
To that high power that life firft to thee gaue !

[1] = Ramir Chan Kan. See l. 513.
[2] I place comma here, not after ‘poore’ as in original.

Truſtie waſt thou to me at all aſſaies ;　　　　70
And deereſt child, thy father oft hath cride
That thou hadſt liu'd, ſo he himſelfe had dide.
The Chriſtian Armies, oftentimes defeated
By my victorious fathers valiance,
Haue all my Captaines famouſly confronted,
And crackt in two our vncontrolled lance.
My ſtrongeſt garriſons they haue ſupplanted,
And ouerwhelmed me in ſad miſchance ;
And my decreaſe ſo long wrought their increaſe,
Till I was forc'd conclude a friendly peace.　　80
Now all theſe are but forraine dammages
Taken in warre, whoſe die vncertaine is ;
But I ſhall haue more home-borne outrages,
Vnleſſe my diuination aimes amiſſe.
I haue three ſonnes all of vnequall ages,
And all in diuerſe ſtudies ſet their bliſſe.
Corcut my eldeſt, a Philoſopher,
Acomat pompous, *Selim*[1] a warriour.
Corcut in faire *Magneſia* leades his life
In learning Arts, and *Mahounds* dreaded lawes :　90
Acomat loues to court it with his wife,
And in a pleaſant quiet ioyes[2] to pauſe ;
But *Selim* followes warres in diſmall ſtrife,
And ſnatcheth at my Crowne with greedy clawes ;
But he ſhall miſſe of that he aimeth at,

---

[1] Misprinted 'Selmi.'
[2] = enjoys or makes it his joy.

For I referue it for my *Acomat*.
For *Acomat*?   Alaffe it cannot be !
Stearne *Selimus* hath wonne my peoples hart ;
The Ianiffaries loue him more then me.
And / fee, here comes a luck[l]effe meffenger,   100
To prooue that true, which my mind did foretell.
Does *Selim* make fo fmall account of vs,
That he dare marry[1] without our confent,
And to that diuell too of *Tartaris*?
And could he then vnkind, fo foone forget
The iniuries that *Ramir* did to me,
Thus to confort himfelfe with him gainft me ?

    Cher[f]e[oli]. Your maieftie mifconfters *Selimus* ;
It cannot be, that he in whofe high thoughts
A map of many valures is enfhrin'd,   110
Should feeke his fathers ruine and decay.
Selimus is a Prince of forward hope,
Whofe only name affrights your enemies ;
It cannot be he fhould prooue falfe to you.

    Baia. Can it not be ?   Oh yes *Cherfeoli* ;
For *Selimus* hands do itch to haue the Crowne ;
And he wil haue it, or elfe pull me downe.
Is he a Prince? ah no he is a fea,
Into which runne nought but ambitious reaches,
Seditious complots, murther, fraud and hate.   120
Could he not let his father know his mind,
But match himfelfe where[2] I leaft thought on it ?

---

[1] Mifprinted 'matry.'   [2] Mifprinted 'when.'

Muſt. Perhaps my Lord *Selimus* lou'd the dame,
And feard to certifie you of his loue,
Becauſe her father was your enemie.

 Baia. In loue *Muſtaffa*? *Selimus* in loue?
If he be, Lording, tis not Ladies loue
But loue of rule, and kingly ſoueraigntie.
For wherefore ſhould he feare t'aſke my conſent?
Truſtie *Muſtaffa*, if he had fear'd me,   130
He neuer would haue lou'd mine enemie.
But this his marriage with the Tartars daughter,
Is but the prologue to his crueltie,
And quickly ſhall we haue the Tragedie.
Which though he act with meditated brauerie,
The / world will neuer giue him plauditie.
What, yet more newes?

     Sound within.   Enters another Meſſenger.

 Meſſ. Dread Emperour, *Selimus* is at hand;
Two hundreth thouſand ſtrong Tartarians   140
Armed at all points dooes he lead with him,
Beſides his followers from *Trebiſond*.

 Baia. I thought ſo much of wicked *Selimus*:
Oh forlorne hopes and hapleſſe *Baiazet*.
Is dutie then exiled from his breſt,
Which nature hath inſcrib'd with golden pen,
Deepe in the hearts of honourable men?
Ah *Selim*, *Selim*, wert thou not my ſonne,
But ſome ſtrange vnacquainted forreiner,
Whom I ſhould honour as I honour'd thee;   150

Yet would it greeue me euen vnto the death,
If he fhould deale as thou haft dealt with me.
And thou my fonne to whom I freely gaue
The mightie Empire of great *Trebifond*,
Art too vnnaturall to requite me thus.
Good *Alemfhae*, hadft thou liud till this day,
Thou wouldft haue blufhed at thy brothers mind.
Come fweete *Muftaffa*, come *Cherfeoli*,
And with fome good aduice recomfort me.

                                    Exeunt All. 160

   Enter *Selimus, Sinam Baffa, Otrante, Occhialie*,
                and the fouldiers.

   Seli. Now *Selimus*, confider who thou art ;
Long haft thou marched in difguif'd attire,
But now vnmafke thy felfe, and play thy part,
And manifeft the heate of thy defire ;
Nourifh the coales of thine ambitious fire.
And thinke that then thy Empire is moft fure,
When men for feare thy tyrannie endure.
Thinke that to thee there is no vvorfe reproach,   170
Then / filiall dutie in fo high a place.
Thou oughtft to fet barrels of blood abroach,
And feeke with fwoord whole kingdomes to dis-
        place :
Let *Mahounds* lawes be lockt vp in their cafe,
And meaner men and of a bafer fpirit,
In vertuous actions feeke for glorious merit.

I count it facriledge, for to be holy,
Or reuerence this thred-bare name of good ;
Leaue to old men and babes that kind of follie,
Count it of equall value with the mud :   180
Make thou a paffage for thy gufhing floud,
By flaughter, treafon, or what elfe thou can,
And fcorne religion ; it difgraces man.
My father *Baiazet* is weake and old,
And hath not much aboue two yeares to liue ;
The Turkifh Crowne of Pearle and *Ophir* gold,
He meanes to his deare *Acomat* to giue.
But ere his fhip can to her hauen driue,
Ile fend abroad my tempefts in fuch fort,
That fhe fhall finke before fhe get the port.   190
Alaffe, alaffe, his highneffe aged head
Is not fufficient to fupport a Crowne ;
Then *Selimus*, take thou it in his fteed ;
And if at this thy boldneffe he dare frowne,
Or but refift thy will, then pull him downe :
For fince he hath fo fhort a time t'enioy it,
Ile make it fhorter, or I will deftroy it.[1]
Nor paffe I what our holy votaries
Shall here obiect againft my forward minde,
I wreake[2] not of their foolifh ceremonies,   200
But meane to take my fortune as I finde :
Wifedome commands to follow tide and winde,
And catch the front of fwift occafion

---

[1] Misprinted 'him.'   [2] = reck = reckon.

Before fhe be too quickly ouergone :
Some man will fay I am too impious,
Thus to laie fiege againft my fathers life,
And / that I ought to follow vertuous
And godly fonnes ; that vertue is a glaffe
Wherein I may my errant life behold,
And frame my felfe by it in auncient mould.   210
Good fir, your wifedomes ouerflowing wit,
Digs deepe with learnings wonder-working fpade :
Perhaps you thinke that now forfooth you fit
With fome graue wifard[1] in a pratling fhade.
Auant fuch glaffes ; let them view in me,
The perfect picture of right tyrannie.
I like[2] a Lions looke not worth a leeke,
When euery dog depriues him of his pray :
Thefe honeft termes are farre inough to feeke.
When angry Fortune menaceth decay,
My refolution treads a nearer way.   220
Giue me the heart confpiring with the hand,
In fuch a caufe my father to withftand.
Is he my father? why, I am his fonne ;
I owe no more to him then he to me.
If he proceed as he hath now begunne,
And paffe from me the Turkifh Seigniorie,
To *Acomat*, then *Selimus* is free :
And if he iniure me that am his fonne,
Faith all the loue twixt him and me is done.   230

---

[1] = wise man, not a witch.   [2] Query—take = I like . . . [to be].

But for I fee the fchoolemen are prepard,
To plant gainft me their bookifh ordinance,
I meane to ftand on a fentencious gard ;
And without any far fetcht circumftance,
Quickly vnfold mine owne opinion,
To arme my heart with irreligion.
When firft this circled round, this building faire,
Some God tooke out of the confufed maffe,
(What God I do not know, nor greatly care)
Then euery man of his owne dition[1] was,   240
And euery one his life in peace did paffe.
Warre was not then, and riches were not knowne,
And / no man faid, this, or this, is mine owne.
The plough-man with a furrow did not marke
How farre his great poffeffions did reach ;
The earth knew not the fhare, nor feas the barke.
The fouldiers entred not the battred breach,
Nor Trumpets the tantara loud did teach.
There needed them no iudge, nor yet no law,
Nor any King of whom to ftand in awe.   250
But after *Ninus*, warlike *Belus* fonne,
The earth with vnknowne armour did array,[2]
Then firft the facred name of King begunne,
And things that were as common as the day,
Did then to fet poffeffours firft obey.
Then they eftablifht lawes and holy rites,
To maintaine peace, and gouerne bloodie fights.

[1] *Sic.*   [2] Misprinted 'warray' : but qy. worrie?

Then fome fage man, aboue the vulgar wife,
Knowing that lawes could not in quiet dwell,
Vnleffe they were obferued ; did firft deuife 260
The names of Gods, religion, heauen, and hell,
And gan of paines, and faind rewards, to tell.
Paines for thofe men which did neglect the law,
Rewards, for thofe that liu'd in quiet awe.
Whereas indeed they were meere fictions,
And if they were not, *Selim* thinkes they were ;
And thefe religious obferuations,
Onely bug-beares to keepe the world in feare,
And make men quietly a yoake to beare.
So that religion of it felfe a bable, 270
Was onely found to make vs peaceable.
Hence in efpeciall come the foolifh names,
Of father, mother, brother, and fuch like :
For who fo well his cogitation frames,
Shall finde they ferue but onely for to ftrike
Into our minds a certaine kind of loue.
For thefe names too are but a policie,
To keepe the quiet of focietie.
Indeed / I muft confeffe they are not bad,
Becaufe they keepe the bafer fort in feare ; 280
But we, whofe minde in heauenly thoughts is clad,
Whofe bodie doth a glorious fpirit beare,
That hath no bounds, but flieth euery where ;
Why fhould we feeke to make that foule a flaue,
To which dame Nature fo large freedome gaue?

Amongſt vs men, there is ſome difference,
Of actions, tearmd by vs good or ill :
As he that doth his father recompence,
Differs from him that doth his father kill.
And yet I thinke, thinke other what they will,   290
That Parricides, when death hath giuen them
Shall haue as good a part as [have] the beſt ;   [reſt,
And thats iuſt nothing : for as I ſuppoſe
In deaths voyd kingdome raignes eternall night ;
Secure of euill, and ſecure of foes,
Where nothing doth the wicked man affright,
No more then him that dies in doing right.
Then ſince in death nothing ſhall to vs fall,
Here while I liue, Ile haue a ſnatch at all,
And that can neuer, neuer be attaind,   300
Vnleſſe old *Baiazet* do die the death.
For long inough the gray-beard now hath raign'd,
And liu'd at eaſe, while others liu'd vneath ;
And now its time he ſhould reſigne his breath.
T'were good for him if he were prèſſed out,
T'would bring him reſt, and rid him of his gout.
Reſolu'd to do it, caſt to compaſſe it
Without delay, or long procraſtination ;
It argueth an vnmatured wit,
When all is readie for ſo ſtrong inuaſion,   310
To draw out time ; an vnlookt for mutation
May ſoone preuent vs if we do delay ;

---

[1] Misprinted 'vnmanured.'

Quick fpeed is good, vvhere vvifedome leades the
Occhiali ?   [vvay.

   Occhi. / My Lord.

   Sel. Lo flie boy to my father *Baiazet*,
And tell him *Selim* his obedient fonne,
Defires to fpeake with him and kiffe his hands ;
Tell him I long to fee his gratious face,
And that I come with all my chiualrie,   320
To chafe the Chriftians from his Seigniorie :
In any wife fay I muft fpeake with him.

                      Exit Occhiali.

Now *Sinam* if I fpeed.

   Sinam. What then my Lord?

   Sel. What then? why *Sinam* thou are nothing
          woorth,
I will endeuour to perfuade him, man,
To giue the Empire ouer vnto me ;
Perhaps I fhall attaine it at his hands :
If I can not, this right hand is refolu'd,   330
To end the period with a fatall ftabbe.

   Sin. My gratious Lord, giue *Sinam* leaue to
          fpeake :
If you refolue to worke your fathers death,
You venture life ; thinke you the Ianiffaries
Will fuffer you to kill him in their fight,
And let you paffe free without punifhment ?

   Sel. If I refolue ? as fure as heauen is heauen,
I meane to fee him dead, or my felfe King ;

As for the *Baſſaes*, they are all my friends,
And I am ſure would pawne their deareſt blood,   340
That *Selim* might be Emperour of Turkes,

   Sin. Yet *Acomat* and *Corcut* both ſuruiue,
To be reuenged for their fathers death.

   Sel. Sinam, if they or twentie ſuch as they,
Had twentie ſeuerall Armies in the field ;
If *Selimus* were once your Emperour
Ide dart abroad the thunderbolts of warre,
And mow their hartleſſe ſquadrons to the ground.

   Sin. Oh yet my Lord after your highneſſe death,
There is a hell and a reuenging God.   350

   Sel. / Tuſh *Sinam*, theſe are ſchoole conditions,
To feare the diuell or his curſed damme :
Thinkſt thou I care for apparitions,
Of *Siſiphus* and of his backward ſtone,
And poore *Ixions* lamentable mone ?
No[1] no, I thinke the caue of damned ghoaſts,
Is but a tale to terrifie yoong babes :
Like diuels faces ſcor'd on painted poaſts,
Or fained circles in our aſtrolabes.
Why, theirs[2] no difference when we are dead ;   360
And death once come then all alike are ſped.
Or, if there were, as I can ſcarce beleeue,
A heauen of ioy, and hell of endleſſe paine ;
Yet by my ſoule it neuer ſhould mee greeue,
So I might on the Turkiſh Empire raigne,

---

    [1] Misprinted 'Now.'   [2] = there's.

To enter hell, and leaue[1] faire heauens gaine.
An Empire *Sinam*, is fo fweete a thing,
As I could be a diuell to be a King.
But go we Lords, and folace in our campe,
Till the returne of yoong *Occhiali* :   370
And if his anfwer be to thy defire,
Selim, thy minde in kingly thoughts attire.

Exeunt All.

Enter *Baiazet, Muftaffa, Cherfeoli, Occhiali,* and
the Ianifferies.

Baia. Euen as the great Ægyptian *Crocodile*
Wanting his praie, with artificiall teares,
And fained plaints, his fubtill tongue doth file,
T'entrap the filly wandring traueller,
And moue him to aduance his footing neare ;   380
That when he is in danger of his clawes,
He may deuour him with his famifhed iawes :
So plaieth craftie *Selimus* with me.
His haughtie thoughts ftill wait on Diadems,
And not a ftep but treads to maieftie.
The / Phœnix gazeth on the Suns bright beames,
The Echinæis fwimmes againft the ftreames.
Nought but the Turkifh fcepter can him pleafe,
And there I know lieth his chiefe difeafe.
He fends his meffenger to craue acceffe,   390
And faies he longs to kiffe my aged hands ;

[1] Mifprinted 'leane on.'

But howfoeuer he in fhew profeffe,
His meaning with his words but weakly ftands.
And fooner will the *Syrteis* boyling fands,
Become a quiet roade for fleeting fhippes,
Then *Selimus* heart agree with *Selims* lippes.
Too well I know the Crocodiles fained teares,
Are but [the] nettes wherein to catch his pray ;
Which who fo mou'd with foolifh pitie heares,
Will be the authour of his owne decay.   400
Then hie thee *Baiazet* from hence away :
A fawning monfter is falfe *Selimus*,
Whofe faireft words are moft pernicious.
Yoong man, would *Selim* come and fpeak with vs ?
What is his meffage to vs, canft thou tell ?

 Occhi. He craues my Lord another feigniorie,
Nearer to you and to the Chriftians,
That he may make them know, that *Selimus*
Is borne to be a fcourge vnto them all.

 Baia. Hee's born to be a fcourge to me & mine.   410
He neuer would haue come with fuch an hoaft,
Vnleffe he meant my ftate to vndermine.
What though in word he brauely feeme to boaft
The forraging of all the Chriftian coaft ?
Yet we haue caufe to feare when burning brands,
Are vainly giuen into a mad mans hands.
Well, I muft feeme to winke at his defire,
Although I fee it plainer then the light,
My lenitie addes fuell to his fire ;

Which now begins to breake in flaſhing bright.   420
Then *Baiazet* chaſtiſe his ſtubborne ſpright,
Leaſt / theſe ſmall ſparkles grow to ſuch a flame,
As ſhall conſume thee and thy houſes name.
Alaſſe, I ſpare when all my ſtore is gone,
And thruſt my ſickle where the corne is reapt.
In vaine I ſend for the phiſition,
When on the patient is his graue duſt heapt.
In vaine,—now all his veines in venome ſteept[1]
Break out in bliſters that will poyſon vs,—
VVe ſeeke to giue him an Antidotus.   430
He that will ſtop the brooke, muſt then begin
VVhen ſommers heate hath dried vp his ſpring,
And when his pittering ſtreames are low & thin ;
For let the winter aide vnto him bring,
He growes to be of watry flouds the King.
And though you dam him vp with loftie rankes,
Yet will he quickly ouerflow his bankes.
Meſſenger, go and tell yoong *Selimus*,
We giue to him all great *Samandria*,
Bordring on *Bulgrade* of *Hungaria*,   440
Where he may plague thoſe Chriſtian runnag[at]es,
And ſalue the wounds that they haue giuen our
    ſtates.
Cherſeo[*li*], go and prouide a gift,
A royall preſent for my *Selimus* ;
And tell him, meſſenger, another time

       [1] Miſprinted 'ſleept.'

He fhall haue talke inough with *Baiazet*.

> *Exeunt Cherfeoli* and *Occhiali*.

And now what counfell giues *Muftaffa* to vs?
I feare this haftie reckoning will vndo vs.

Muft. Make hafte my Lord from *Andri*[a]*nople* 450
And let vs flie to faire *Bizantium* ;   [walles,
Leaft if your fonne before you take the towne,
He may with little labour winne the crowne.

Baia. Then do fo good *Muftaffa* ; call our gard,
And gather all our warlike Ianiffaries ;
Our chiefeft aid is fwift celeritie :
Then let our winged courfers tread the winde,
And / leaue rebellious *Selimus* behinde.

> *Exeunt All*.

> *Enter Selimus, Sinam, Occhiali, Ottrante*   460
> and their fouldiers.

Selim. And is his anfwere fo *Occhiali* ?
Is *Selim* fuch a corfiue to his heart,
That he cannot endure the fight of him?
Forfooth he giues thee all *Samandria*,
From whence our mightie Emperour *Mahomet*,
Was driuen to his country backe with fhame.
No doubt thy father loues thee *Selimus*,
To make thee Regent of fo great a land ;
Which is not yet his owne, or if it were,   47(
What dangers wayt on him that fhould it ftere !

Here the *Polonian* he comes hurtling in
Vnder the conduct of some forraine prince,
To fight in honour of his crucifix !
Here the *Hungarian* with his bloodie croffe,
Deales blowes about to win *Belgrade* againe.
And after all, forfooth *Bafilius*
The mightie Emperour of *Ruffia*,
Sends in his troups of flaue-borne *Mufcouites* ;
And he will fhare with vs, or elfe take all.   480
In giuing fuch a land fo full of ftrife,
His meaning is to rid me of my life.
Now by the dreaded name of *Termagant*,
And by the blackeft brooke in loathfome hell,
Since he is fo vnnatural to me,
I will prooue as vnnatural as he.
Thinks he to ftop my mouth with gold or pearle ?
Or ruftie iades fet from *Barbaria* ?
No let his minion, his philofopher,
Corcut and *Acomat*, be enrich'd with them.   490
I will not take my reft, till this right hand
Hath puld the Crowne from off his cowards head,
And / on the ground his baftards gore-blood fhead ;
Nor fhall his flight to old *Bizantium*
Difmay my thoughts, which neuer learnd to ftoup.
March *Sinam* march in order after him :
Were his light fteeds as fwift as *Pegafus*,
And trode the ayrie pauement with their heeles,
Yet *Selimus* would ouertake them foone.

And though the heauens do nere so crosly frowne, 500
In spight of heauen, shall *Selim* weare the crowne.

Exeunt.

Alarum within. Enter *Baiazet, Muftaffa, Cherfeoli* and the Ianiffaries, at one doore. *Selimus,
   Sinam, Ottrante, Occhiali,* and their fouldiers
   at another.

   Baia. Is this thy dutie fonne vnto thy father
So impioufly to leuell at his life ?
Can thy foule wallowing in ambitious mire,
Seeke for to reaue that breft with bloudie knife,   510
From whence thou hadft thy being *Selimus* ?
Was this the end for which thou ioyndft thy felfe,
With that mifchieuous traytor *Ramirchan* ? [1]
Was this thy drift to fpeake with *Baiazet* ?
Well hoped I (but hope I fee is vaine)
Thou wouldft haue bene a comfort to mine age,
A fcourge and terrour to mine enemies ;
That this thy comming with fo great an hoaft,
Was for no other purpofe and intent,
Then for to chaftife thofe bafe Chriftians   520
Which fpoile my fubiects welth with fire & fword :
Well hoped I the rule of *Trebifond,*
Would haue increafde the valour of thy minde,
To turne thy ftrength vpon the [2] Perfians.
But thou, like to a craftie *Polipus,*

---

[1] See l. 57.   [2] Misprinted 'thy.'

Doeſt turne thy hungry iawes vpon thy ſelfe ;
For what am I *Selimus* but thy ſelfe ?
VVhen / courage firſt crept in thy manly breſt
And thou beganſt to rule the martiall ſword,
How oft ſaid thou the ſun ſhuld change his courſe, 530
VVater ſhould turne to earth, & earth to heauen ;
Ere thou wouldſt prooue diſloyall to thy father.
O *Titan* turne thy breathleſſe courſers backe,
And enterpriſe thy iourny from the Eaſt.
Bluſh *Selim,* that the world ſhould ſay of thee
That by my death thou gaindſt the Emperie.

    Seli. Now let my cauſe be pleaded *Baiazet*,
For father I diſdaine to call thee now ;
I tooke not Armes to ſeaze vpon thy crowne,
For that if once thou hadſt bene layd in graue,   540
Should ſit vpon the head of *Selimus*
In ſpight of *Corcut* and [of] *Acomat.*
I tooke not Armes to take away thy life ;
The remnant of thy dayes is but a ſpan ;
And fooliſh had I bene to enterprize
That which the gout and death would do for me.
I tooke not armes to ſhed my brothers blood,
Becauſe they ſtop my paſſage to the crowne ;
For whilſt thou liu’ſt *Selimus* is content
That they ſhould liue ; but when thou once art 550
    dead,
VVhich of them both, dares *Selimus* withſtand ?
I ſoone ſhould hew their bodies in peecemeale,

As eafie as a man would kill a gnat.
But I tooke armes, vnkind, to honour thee,
And win againe the fame that thou haft loft.
And thou thoughtft fcorne *Selim* fhould fpeake
    wit[h thee] ;
But had it bene your darling *Acomat*
You would haue met him half the way your felfe.
I am a Prince, and though your yoonger fonne,
Yet are my merits better then both theirs ;   560
But you do feeke to difinherit me,
And meane t'inueft *Acomat* with your crowne.
So he fhall haue a princes due reward,
That / cannot fhew a fcarre receiu'd in field.
VVe that haue fought with mighty *Prefter Iohn*,
And ftript th' Ægyptian foldan of his camp,
Venturing life and liuing to honour thee;
For that fame caufe fhall now difhonour'd be.
Art thou a father?   Nay falfe *Baiazet*
Difclaime the title which thou doeft not merit.   570
A father would not thus flee from his fonne,
As thou doeft flie from loyall *Selimus*.
Then *Baiazet* prepare thee to the fight ;
Selimus once thy fonne, but now thy foe,
VVill make his fortunes by the fword [and fhield] ;
And fince thou fear'ft as long as I do liue,
Ile alfo feare, as long as thou doeft liue.
                  Exit Selim and his company.
   Ba. My heart is ouerwhelm'd with fear & grief ;

VVhat difmall Comet blazed at my birth,   580
VVhofe influence makes my ftrong vnbrideled
In fteed of loue to render hate to me ?   [fonne [1]
Ah Baffaies if that euer heretofore
Your Emperour ought[2] his fafetie vnto you,
Defend me now gainft my vnnaturall fonne :
Non timeo mortem: mortis mihi difplicet author.

               Exit *Baiazet* and his company.

Alarum, *Muftaffa* beates *Selimus* in, then *Ottrante*
    and *Cherfeoli* enter at diuerfe doores.

Cherfe. Yield thee *Tartarian*, or thou fhalt die; 590
Vpon my fwords fharpe point ftandeth pale death
Readie to riue in two thy caitiue breft.
   Ott. Art thou that knight that like a lion fierce,
Tiring his ftomacke on a flocke of lambes,
Haft broke our rankes & put them cleane to flight?
   Cherfe. / I, and vnleffe thou looke vnto thy felfe,
This fword here,[3] drunke in the *Tartarian* blood,
Shall make thy carkaffe as the outcaft dung.
   Ottran. Nay, I haue matcht a brauer knight
          then you,
Strong *Alemfhae*, thy maifters eldeft fonne ;   600
Leauing his bodie naked on the plaines :
And *Turke*, the felfe fame end for thee remaines.
   They fight. He killeth *Cherfeoli*, and flieth.

---

[1] Misprinted 'fonnes.'   [2] = owed.   [3] Misprinted 'nere.'

Alarum.   Enter *Selimus.*

Selim. Shall *Selims* hope be buried in the duſt?
And *Baiazet* triumph ouer his fall?
Then oh thou blindfull miſtreſſe of miſhap,
Chiefe patroneſſe of *Rhamus* golden gates,
I will aduance my ſtrong reuenging hand,
And plucke thee from thy euer turning wheele.   610
Mars, or *Minerua*, *Mahound*, *Termagaunt*,
Or who ſo ere you are that fight gainſt me,
Come and but ſhew your ſelues before my face,
And I will rend you all like trembling reedes.
Well, *Baiazet*, though Fortune ſmile on thee,
And deck thy camp with glorious victorie,
Though *Selimus* now conquered by thee,
Is faine to put his ſafetie in ſwift flight;
Yet ſo he flies, that like an angry ramme,
Heele turne more fiercely then before he came.   620

                         Exit Selimus.

Enter *Baiazet*, *Muſtaffa*, the ſouldier with the bodie
       of *Cherſeoli*, and *Ottrante* priſoner.

Baia. Thus haue we gain'd a bloodie victorie,
And though we are the maiſters of the field,
Yet haue we loſt more then our enemies:
Ah luckleſſe fault of my *Cherſeoli*!
As dear and dearer wert thou vnto me,
Then any of my ſonnes, then mine owne ſelfe.

When I was glad, thy heart was full of ioy ;   630
And / brauely haft thou died for *Baiazet.*
And though thy bloudleffe bodie here do lie,
Yet thy fweet foule in heauen for euer bleft,
Among the ftarres enioyes eternall reft.
What art thou, warlike man of *Tartarie,*
Whofe hap it is to be our prifoner ?

  Ottran. I am a Prince, *Ottrante* is my name;
Chiefe captaine of the *Tartars* mightie hoaft.

  Ba. Ottrante ? Waft not thou that flue my fon ?

  Ottran. I, and if fortune had but fauour'd me, 640
Had fent the fire to keepe him company.

  Baia. Off with his head and fpoyle him of his
And leaue his bodie for the ayrie birds. [Armes ;
                     Exit one with *Ottrante.*
The vnreuenged ghoaft of *Alemfhae,*
Shall now no more wander on *Stygian* bankes,
But reft in quiet in th'*Elyfian* fields.
Muftaffa, and you worthie men at Armes,
That left not *Baiazet* in greateft need,
When we arriue at *Conftantines* great Tour,[1] 650
You fhalbe honour'd of your Emperour.
                     Exeunt All.

  Enter *Acomat, Vifir, Regan* and a band of
          fouldiers.

  Aco. Perhaps you wonder why prince *Acomat,*

        [1] Qy.—towne?

Delighting heretofore in foolifh loue,
Hath chang'd his quiet to a fouldiers ftate ;
And turnd the dulcet tunes of *Himens* fong,
Into *Bellonas* horrible outcries ;
You thinke it ftrange, that whereas I haue liu'd,   660
Almoft a votarie to wantonneffe ;
To fee me now[1] laie off effeminate robes,
And arme my bodie in an iron wall.
I haue enioyed quiet long inough,
And furfeted with pleafures fu[r]quidrie ;
A field of dainties I haue paffed through,
And / bene a champion to faire *Cytheree*.
Now, fince this idle peace hath weeried me,
Ile follow *Mars*, and warre another while,
And die my fhield in dolorous vermeil.   670
My brother *Selim* through his manly deeds,
Hath lifted vp his fame vnto the fkies,
While we like earth wormes lurking in the weeds,
Do liue inglorious in all mens eyes.
What lets me then from this vaine flumber rife,
And by ftrong hand atchieue eternall glorie,
That may be talkt of in all memorie ?
And fee how fortune fauours mine intent :
Heard you not Lordings, how prince *Selimus*
Againft our royall father armed went ?   680
And how the Ianiffaries made him flee
To *Ramir* Emperour of *Tartarie* ?

---

[1] Misprinted 'low.'

This his rebellion greatly profits me ;
For I fhall fooner winne my fathers minde,
To yeeld me vp the Turkifh Empir[i]e ;
Which if I haue, I am fure I fhall finde
Strong enemies to pull me downe againe,
That faine would haue prince *Selimus* to raigne.
Then ciuill difcord, and contentious warre,
Will follow *Acomats* coronation.   690
Selim no doubt will broach feditious iarre,
And *Corcut* too will feeke for alteration.
Now to preuent all fuddaine perturbation,
We thought it good to mufter vp our power,
That danger may not take it vnprouided.

   Vifir. I like your highneffe refolution well ;
For thefe fhould be the chiefe arts of a king,
To punifh thofe that furioufly rebell,
And honour thofe that facred counfell bring ;
To make good lawes, ill cuftomes to expell,   700
To nourifh peace, from whence your riches fpring,
And when good quarrels call you to the field
T'excell / your men in handling fpeare & fhield.
Thus fhall the glory of your matchleffe name,
Be regiftred vp in immortall lines :
Whereas that prince that followes luftfull game,
And to fond toyes his captiue minde enclines,
Shall neuer paffe the temple of true fame ;
Whofe worth is greater then the *Indian* mines.
But is your grace affured certainly   710

That *Baiazet* doth fauour your requeſt?
Perhaps you may make him your enemie ;
You know how much your father doth deteſt,
Stout [dis]obedience and obſtinacie.
I ſpeake not this as if I thought it beſt,
Your highneſſe ſhould your right in it neglect,
But that you might be cloſe and circumſpect.

   Aco. We thank thee *Viſir* for thy louing care ;
As for my father *Baiazets* affection,
Vnleſſe his holy vowes forgotten are,   720
I ſhall be ſure of it by his election.
But[1] after *Acomats* erection
We muſt forecaſt what things be neceſſary,
Leaſt that our kingdome be too momentary.

   Reg. Firſt, let my Lord be ſeated in his throne,
Enſtalled by great *Baiazets* conſent ;
As yet your harueſt is not fully growne,
But in the greene and vnripe blade is pent ;
But when you once haue got the regiment,
Then may your Lords more eaſily prouide   730
Againſt all accidents that may betide.

   Acomat. Then ſet we forward to *Bizantium*,
That we may know what *Baiazet* intends.
Aduiſe thee *Acomat*, whats beſt to do ;
The Ianiſſaries fauour *Selimus*,
And they are ſtrong vndanted enemies,
Which will in Armes gainſt thy election riſe.

           [1] Misprinted 'By.'

Then will[1] them to thy wil with precious gifts,
And / ſtore of gold ; timely largition
The ſtedfaſt perſons from their purpoſe lifts : 740
But then beware leaſt *Baiazets* affection
Change into hatred by ſuch premunition.
For then he'[ll] thinke that I am factious,
And imitate my brother *Selimus.*
Beſides, a prince his honour doth debaſe,
That begs the common ſouldiers ſuffrages ;
And if the Baſſaes knew I ſought their grace,
It would the more increaſe their inſolentneſſe.
To reſiſt them were ouerhardineſſe,
And worſe it were to leaue my enterprize. 750
Well how ſo ere, reſolue to venture it,
Fortune doth fauour euery bold aſſay ;
And t'were a trick of an vnſetled wit
Becauſe the bees haue ſtings with them alway,
To f[e]are our mouthes in honie to embay.
Then reſolution for me leades the dance,
And thus reſolu'd, I meane to trie my chance.

Exeunt all.

Enter *Baiazet, Muſtaffa, Calibaſſa, Halibaſſa,*
and the Ianiſſaries. 760

Baia. What prince ſo ere, truſts to his mightie
Ruling the reines of many nations, [pow'r,
And feareth not leaſt fickle fortune loure,

[1] = wile, entice.

Or[1] thinkes his kingdome free from alterations;
If he were in the place of *Baiazet*,
He would but litle by his fcepter fet.
For what hath rule that makes it acceptable ?
Rather what hath it not worthie of hate?
Firft of all is our ftate ftill mutable,
And our continuance at the peoples rate ;   77°
So that it is a flender thred, whereon
Depends the honour of a princes throne.
Then do we feare, more then the child new borne,
Our / friends, our Lords, our fubiects, & our fonne.[2]
Thus is our minde in fundry pieces torne
By care, by feare, fufpition, and diftruft ;
In wine, in meate we feare pernicious poyfon ;
At home, abroad, we feare feditious treafon.
Too true that tyrant *Dionyfius*
Did picture out the image of a King,   780
When *Damocles*[3] was placed in his throne,
And ore his head a threatning fword did hang,
Faftned vp onely by a horfes haire.
Our chiefeft truft is fecretly, diftruft ;
For whom haue we whom we may fafely truft,
If our owne fonnes, neglecting awfull dutie,
Rife vp in Armes againft their louing father?[4]
Their heart is all of hardeft marble wrought,
That can laie wayt to take away their breath,

[1] Mifprinted ' Ar.'   [2] Mifprinted 'fonnes.'
[3] Mifprinted 'Daniocles.'   [4] Mifprinted 'fathers.'

From whom they firſt fucked this vitall ayre : 790
My heart is heauie, and I needs muſt ſleepe.
Baſſaes, withdraw your ſelues from me awhile,
That I may reſt my ouerburdned ſoule.
    They ſtand aſide while the curtins are drawne.
Eunuchs, plaie me ſome muſicke while I ſleepe.

        Muſicke within.

  Muſt. Good *Baiazet*, who would not pitie thee,
Whom thine owne ſonne ſo vildly perſecutes ?
More mildly do th'vnreaſonables[t] beaſts
Deale with their dammes, then *Selimus* with thee. 800
  Halibas. Muſtaffa, we are princes of the land,
And loue our Emperour as well as thou ;
Yet will we not for pitying his eſtate,
Suffer our foes our wealth to ruinate.
If *Selim* haue playd falſe with *Baiazet*
And ouerſlipt the dutie of a ſonne,
Why, he was mou'd by iuſt occaſion.
Did he not humbly ſend his meſſenger
To craue acceſſe vnto his maieſtie ?
And / yet he could not get permiſſion 810
To kiſſe his hands, and ſpeake his mind to him.
Perhaps he thought his aged fathers loue
Was cleane eſtrang'd from him, and *Acomat*
Should reape the fruite that he had laboured for.
Tis lawfull for the father to take Armes,
I and by death chaſtize his rebell ſonne.

G. XIV   15

Why fhould it be vnlawfull for the fonne,
To leauie Armes gainft his iniurious fire?
   Muft. You reafon *Hali* like a fophifter;
As if t'were lawfull for a fubiect prince   820
To rife in Armes [a]gainft his foueraigne,
Becaufe he will not let him haue his will:
Much leffe ift lawfull for a mans owne fonne.
If *Baiazet* had iniur'd *Selimus*,
Or fought his death, or done him fome abufe,
Then *Selimus* caufe had bene more tollerable.
But *Baiazet* did neuer iniure him,
Nor fought his death, nor once abufed him;
Vnleffe becaufe he giues him not the crowne,
Being the yoongeft of his highneffe fonnes.   830
Gaue he not him an Empire for his part,
The mightie Empire of great *Trebifond*?
So that if all things rightly be obferu'd,
Selim had more then euer he deferu'd:
I fpeake not this becaufe I hate the prince,
For by the heauens I loue yoong *Selimus*,
Better then either of his brethren.
But for I owe alleagiance to my king,
And loue him much that fauours me fo much.
Muftaffa, while old *Baiazet* doth liue,
Will be as true to him as to himfelfe.   840
   Cali. Why braue *Muftaffa*, *Hali* and my felfe
Were neuer falfe vnto his maieftie.
Our father *Hali* died in the field,

Againſt the *Sophi*, in his highneſſe warres.
And / we will neuer be degenerate.
Nor do we take part with prince *Selimus*,
Becauſe we would depoſe old *Baiazet*,
But for becauſe we would not *Acomat*
That leads his life ſtill in laſciuious pompe,   850
Nor *Corcut*, though he be a man of woorth,
Should be commander of our Empir[i]e.
For he that neuer ſaw his foe mans face,
But alwaies ſlept vpon a Ladies lap,
Will ſcant endure to lead a ſouldiers life.
And he that neuer handled but his penne,
Will be vnſkilfull at the warlike lance.
Indeed his wiſedome well may guide the crowne,
And keepe that ſafe his predeceſſors got :
But being giuen to peace as *Corcut* is,   860
He neuer will enlarge the Empir[i]e :
So that the rule and power ouer vs,
Is onely fit for valiant *Selimus*.
    Muſt. Princes, you know how mightie *Baiazet*
Hath honoured *Muſtaffa* with his loue.
He gaue his daughter beautious *Solima*,
To be the ſoueraigne miſtreſſe of my thoughts.
He made me captaine of the Ianiſſaries,
And too vnnaturall ſhould *Muſtaffa* be,
To riſe againſt him in his dying age.
Yet know, you warlike peere[s], *Muſtaffa* is   870
A loyall friend vnto prince *Selimus* ;

And ere his other brethren get the crowne,
For his fake, I my felfe will pull them downe.
I loue, I loue them dearly, but the loue
Which I do beare vnto my countries good,
Makes me a friend to noble *Selimus* ;
Onely let *Baiazet* while he doth liue
Enioy in peace the Turkifh Diademe.
When he is dead, and layd in quiet graue,   880
Then none but *Selimus* our helpe fhall haue.

Sound / within.   A Meffenger enters, *Baiazet*
awaketh.

Baia. How now, *Muftaffa*, what newes haue we
there ?
Is *Selim* vp in Armes gainft me againe ?
Or is the *Sophi* entred our confines ?
Hath the Ægyptian fnatch'd his crowne againe ?
Or haue the vncontrolled Chriftians
Vnfheath'd their fwords to make more war on vs ?
Such newes, or none will come to *Baiazet*.   890
Muft. My gratious Lord, heres an Embaffador
Come from your fonne the Soldan *Acomat*.
Baia. From *Acomat* ? oh let him enter in.

Enter Regan.

Embaffadour, how fares our louing fonne ?
Reg. Mightie commander of the warlike Turks,
Acomat Souldane of *Amafia*,

Greeteth your grace by me his meſſenger.

He giues him a Letter.

And gratulates your highneſſe good ſucceſſe,   900
Wiſhing good fortune may befall you ſtill.

   Baia. Muſtaffa read.

    He giues the letter to *Muſtaffa*, and ſpeakes
           the reſt to himſelfe.

Acomat craues thy promiſe *Baiazet*,
To giue the Empire vp into his hands,
And make it ſure to him in thy life time.
And thou ſhalt haue it louely *Acomat*,
For I haue bene encombred long inough,
And vexed with the cares of kingly rule ;   910
Now let the trouble of the Empirie
Be buried in the boſome of thy ſonne.
Ah *Acomat*, if thou haue ſuch a raigne
So full of ſorrow as thy fathers was,
Thou wilt accurſe the time, the day and houre,
In which thou was eſtabliſh'd Emperour.

     Sound.   A Meſſenger from *Corcut.*

Yet / more newes ?

   Meſſ. Long liue the mightie Emperor *Baiazet* ;
Corcut the Soldan of *Magneſia*,   920
Hearing of *Selims* worthie ouerthrow,
And of the comming of yoong *Acomat* ;
Doth certifie your maieſtie by me,
How ioyfull he is of your victorie.

And therewithall he humbly doth require
Your grace would do him iuſtice in his cauſe.
His brethren both, vnworthie ſuch a father,
Do ſeeke the Empire while your grace doth liue,
And that by vndirect ſiniſter meanes.
But *Corcuts* mind free from ambitious thoughts,   930
And truſting to the goodneſſe of his cauſe,
Ioyned vnto your highneſſe tender loue,
Onely deſires your grace ſhould not inueſt
Selim nor *Acomat*, in the Diademe,
Which appertaineth vnto him by right;
But keepe it to your ſelfe the while you liue :
And when it ſhall the great creator pleaſe,
Who hath the ſpirits of all men in his hands,
Shall call your highneſſe to your lateſt home,
Then will he alſo ſue to haue his right.   940
      Baia. Like to a ſhip ſayling without ſtarres
            [ſight]
Whom waues do toſſe one way and winds another,
Both without ceaſing ; euen[1] ſo my poore heart
Endures a combat between loue and right.
The loue I beare to my deare *Acomat*,
Commands me giue my ſuffrage vnto him,
But *Corcuts* title, being my eldeſt ſonne,
Bids me recall my hand, and giue it him.
Acomat, he would haue it in my life,
But gentle *Corcut* like a louing ſonne,   950

          [1] = e'en.

Defires me liue and die an Emperour,
And at my death bequeath my crowne to him.
Ah *Corcut* thou I fee lou'ft me indeed :
Selimus / fought to thruft me downe by force,
And *Acomat* feekes the kingdome in my life ;
And both of them are grieu'd thou liu'ft fo long.
But *Corcut* numbreth not my dayes as they ;
O how much dearer loues he me then they !
Baffaes, how counfell you your Emperour ?

    Muft. My gratious Lord, my felf wil fpeak 960
        for al ;
For all I know are minded as I am.
Your highneffe knowes the Ianiffaries loue,
How firme they meane to cleaue to your beheft,
As well you might perceiue in that fad fight,
When *Selim* fet vpon you in your flight.
Then we do all defire you on our knees,
To keepe the crowne and fcepter to your felfe.
How grieuous will it be vnto your thoughts
If you fhould giue the crowne to *Acomat,*
To fee the brethren difinherited,   970
To flefh their anger one vpon another,
And rend the bowels of this mightie realme.[1]
Suppofe that *Corcut* would be well content,
Yet thinkes your grace if *Acomat* were king
That *Selim* ere long would ioine league with him ?
Nay he would breake from forth his *Trebifond,*

            [1] Mifprinted 'raigne.'

And waſte the Empire all with fire and ſword.
Ah then too weake would be poore *Acomat*,
To ſtand againſt his brothers puiſſance,
Or ſaue himſelfe from his enhanced hand.   980
While Iſmael and the cruell Perſians,
And the great Soldane of th'Egyptians,
Would ſmile to ſee our force diſmembred ſo ;
I, and perchance the neighbour Chriſtians
Would take occaſion to thruſt out their heads.
All this may be preuented by your grace,
If you will yeeld to *Corcuts* iuſt requeſt,
And keepe the kingdome to you while you liue ;
Meanetime we that your graces ſubiects are,
May / make vs ſtrong, to fortifie the man,   990
Whō at your death your grace ſhal chuſe as
    king.
    Baia. O how thou ſpeakeſt euer like thy ſelfe,
Loyall *Muſtaffa* ; well were *Baiazet*
If all his ſonnes, did beare ſuch loue to him.
Though loth I am longer to weare the crowne,
Yet for I ſee it is my ſubiects will,
Once more will *Baiazet* be Emperour.
But we muſt ſend to pacifie our ſonne,
Or he will ſtorme, as earſt did *Selimus*.
Come let vs go vnto our councell Lords,[1]   1000
And there conſider what is to be done.
                              Exeunt All.

_____

[1] Misprinted 'Lord.'

Enter *Acomat, Regan, Viſir,* and his ſouldiers.
   Acomat muſt read a letter, and then renting
   it ſay :

Aco. Thus will I rend the crowne from off thy
Falſe-hearted and iniurious[1] *Baiazet,*   [head,
To mocke thy ſonne that loued thee ſo deare.
What ? for becauſe the head-ſtrong Ianiſſaries
Would not conſent to honour *Acomat,*
And their baſe Baſſaes vow'd to *Selimus,*   1010
Thought me vnworthie of the Turkiſh crowne ;
Should he be rul'd and ouerrul'd by them.
Vnder pretence of keeping it himſelfe,
To wipe me cleane for euer being king ?
Doth he eſteeme ſo much the Baſſaes words,
And prize their fauour at ſo high a rate,
That for to gratifie their ſtubborne mindes,
He caſts away all care, and all reſpects
Of dutie, promiſe, and religious oathes ?
Now by the holy Prophet *Mahomet*   1020
Chiefe preſident and patron of the Turkes,
I meane to chalenge now my right by Armes,
And winne by ſword that glorious dignitie
Which he iniurioufly[2] detaines from me.
Haply / he thinkes becauſe that *Selimus*
Rebutted by his warlike Ianiſſaries,
Was faine to flie in haſt from whence he came ;

[1] Query—vniuſt ?   [2] Query—vniuſtly ?   See context in both cases.
Cf. l. 1291, where 'iniurioufly' occurs.

That *Acomat* by his example mou'd,
Will feare to manage Armes againſt his ſire.
Or that my life forepaſſed in pleaſures court,   1030
Promiſes weake reſiſtance in the fight ;
But he ſhall know that I can vſe my ſwoord,
And like a lyon ſeaze vpon my praie.
If euer *Selim* mou'd him heretofore,
Acomat meanes to mooue him ten times more.

  Viſir. T'were good your grace would to *Amaſia*,
And there increaſe your camp with freſh ſupply.

  Aco. Viſir I am impatient of delaie ;
And ſince my father hath incenſt me thus,
Ile quēch thoſe kindled flames with his hart blood. 1040
Not like a ſonne, but a moſt cruell foe,
Will *Acomat* be henceforth vnto him.
March to *Natolia*, there we will begin
And make a preface to our maſſacres.
My nephew *Mahomet*, ſonne to *Alemſhae*,
Departed lately from *Iconium*,
Is lodged there ; and he ſhall be the firſt
Whom I will ſacrifice vnto my wrath.

         Exeunt All.

Enter the yoong Prince *Mahomet*, the *Belierbey* of 1050
  Natolia, and one or two ſouldiers.

  Naho. Lord Gouernour, what thinke you beſt
If we receiue the Souldaine *Acomat*, [to doo ?
Who knoweth not but his blood-thirſtie ſwoord

Shall be embowell'd in our country-men.
You know he is difpleafde with *Baiazet*,
And will rebell,—as *Selim* did to fore,—
And would to God, with *Selims* ouerthrow.
You know his angrie heart hath vow'd reuenge
On all the fubiects of his fathers land.   1060

    Bel. / Yoong prince, thy vncle feekes to haue
           thy life,
Becaufe by right the Turkifh crowne is thine ;
Saue thou thy felfe by flight or otherwife,
And we will make refiftance as we can.
Like an Armenian tygre, that hath loft
Her loued whelpes, fo raueth *Acomat* :
And we muft be fubiect [vn]to his rage,
But you may liue to venge your citizens :
Then flie good prince before your vncle come.
    Maho. Nay good my Lord, neuer fhall it be faid 1070
That *Mahomet* the fonne of *Alemfhae*,
Fled from his citizens for feare of death ;
But I will ftaie, and helpe to fight for you,
And if you needs muft die, ile die with you.
And I among the reft with forward hand,
Will helpe to kill a common enemie.
                    Exeunt All.

    Enter *Acomat, Vifir, Regan,* and the fouldiers.

    Aco. Now faire *Natolia,* fhall thy ftately walles
Be ouerthrowne and beaten to the ground ;   1080

My heart within me for reuenge ftill calles.
Why *Baiazet*, thought'ft thou that *Acomat*
Would put vp fuch a monftrous iniurie ?
Then had I brought my chiualrie in vaine,
And to no purpofe drawne my conquering blade ;
VVhich now vnfheath'd, fhall not be fheath'd againe,
Till it a world of bleeding foules hath made.
Poore *Mahomet*, thou thoughtft thy felfe too fure,
In thy ftrong citie of *Iconium*,
To plant thy Forces in *Natolia*,   1090
VVeakned fo much before by *Selims* fwoord.
Summon a parley to the citizens,
That they may heare the dreadfull words I fpeak,
And die in thought before they come to blowes.

   All. A parley. *Mahomet*, *Belierbey*, and fouldiers
             on the walles.

   Maho. / What craues our vncle *Acomat* with vs ?
   Aco. That thou & all the citie yeeld themfelues ;
Or by the holie rites of *Mahomet*
His wondrous tomb, and facred *Alcoran*
You all fhall die ; and not a common death,   1100
But euen as monftrous as I can deuife.
   Maho. Vncle, if I may call you by that name,
Which cruelly hunt for your nephewes blood ;
You do vs wrong thus to befiege our towne,
That nere deferu'd fuch hatred at your hands,
Being your friends and kinfmen as we are.

Aco. In that thou wrongſt me that thou art my
    kinſman.

Maho. Why, for I am thy nephew doeſt thou
    frowne?

Aco. I, that thou art ſo neare vnto the crowne.

Maho. Why vncle I reſigne my right to thee,   1110
And all my title were it nere ſo good.

Aco. Wilt thou? then know aſſuredly from me,
Ile ſeale the reſignation with thy blood;
Though *Alemſhae* thy father lou'd me well.
Yet *Mahomet*, his [1] ſonne ſhall downe to hell.

Mah. Why vncle doth my life put you in feare?

Aco. It ſhall not nephew, ſince I haue you here.

Maho. VVhen I am dead, more[2] hindrers ſhalt
    thou finde.

Acon. VVhen ones cut off, the fewer are behinde.

Maho. Yet thinke the gods do beare an equall 1120
    eye.

Aco. Faith if they all were ſquint-ey'd, what
    care I?

Maho. Then *Acomat*[3] know we will rather die,
Then yeeld vs vp into a tyrants hand.

Aco. Beſhrew me but you be the wiſer *Mahomet*;
For if I do but catch you boy aliue,
Twere better for you runne through Phlegiton.
Sirs ſcale the walles, and pull the caitiues downe,
I giue to you the ſpoyle of all the towne.

---

[1] Misprinted 'thy.'   [2] *Ibid.* 'mote.'   [3] *Ibid.* 'Mahomet.'

Alarum. Scale the walles. Enter *Acomat, Vifir,*
    and *Regan,* with *Mahomet.*   1130

   Acom. Now yoongfter, you that brau'dft vs on
    the walles,
And / fhook your plumed creft againft our fhield,
VVhat wouldft thou giue, or what wouldft thou
    not giue,
That thou wert far inough from *Acomat* ?
How like the villaine is to *Baiazet* !   [Afide.
VVel nephew, for thy father lou'd me well,
I will not deale extreemly with his fonne :
Then heare a briefe compendium of thy death.
Regan go caufe a groue of fteelehead fpeares,
Be pitched thicke vnder the caftle wall,   1140
And on them let this youthful captiue fall.
   Ma. Thou fhalt not fear me *Acomat* with death,
Nor will I beg my pardon at thy hands.
But as thou giu'ft me fuch a monftrous death,
So do I freely leaue to thee my curfe :
             Exit Regan with *Mahomet.*
   Aco. O, that wil ferue to fil my fathers purfe !

Alarum. Enter a fouldier with *Zonara,* fifter to
    Mahomet.

   Zon. Ah pardon me deare vncle, pardon me.   1150
   Aco. No minion, you are too neare a kin to me.
   Zon. If euer pitie entered thy breft,

Or euer thou waſt touch'd with womans loue,
Sweete vncle ſpare wretched *Zonaras* life.
Thou once waſt noted for a quiet prince,
Soft-hearted, mild, and gentle as a lambe ;
Ah do not proue a lyon vnto me !

    Aco. VVhy would'ſt thou liue, when *Mahomet*
        is dead?

    Zon. Ah who ſlew *Mahomet* ? Vncle did you?

    Aco. He thats prepar'd to do as much for you. 1160

    Zon. Doeſt thou not pitie *Alemſhae* in me ?

    Aco. Yes that he wants ſo long thy companie.

    Zon. Thou art not, falſe groome, ſon to *Baiazet* ;
He would relent to heare a woman weepe,
But thou waſt borne in deſart *Caucaſus*,
And the *Hircanian* tygres gaue thee ſucke ;
Knowing thou wert a monſter like themſelues.

    Aco. / Let you her thus to rate vs ? Strangle her.

             They ſtrangle her.

Now ſcoure the ſtreets, and leaue not one aliue   1170
To carry theſe ſad newes to *Baiazet.*
That all the citizens may dearly ſay,
This day was fatall to *Natolia.*

                        Exeunt All.

    Enter *Baiazet, Muſtaffa, and the Ianiſſaries.*

    Ba. Muſtaffa if my minde decciue me not,
Some ſtrange misfortune is not farre from me.

I was not wont to tremble in this fort ;
Me thinkes I feele a cold run through my bones,
As if it haftned to furprize my heart ;   1180
Me thinkes fome voice ftill whifpereth in my eares
And bids me to take heed of *Acomat*.

    Muſt. Tis but your highneffe ouercharged mind
VVhich feareth moft the things it leaft defires.

Enter two fouldiers with the Belierbey of *Natolia
    in a chaire,* and the bodie[s] of *Mahomet* and
    Zonara* in two coffins.

    Ba. Ah fweet *Muſtaffa*, thou art much deceiu'd ;
My minde prefages me fome future harme ;
And loe, what dolefull exequie is here.   1190
Our chiefe commander of *Natolia* ?
VVhat caitiue hand is it hath wounded thee ?
And who are thefe couered in tomb-[b]lack hearfe?
    Bel. Thefe are thy nephewes mightie *Baiazet*,
The fonne and daughter of good *Alemſhae ;*
VVhom cruell *Acomat* hath murdred thus.
Thefe eyes beheld, when from an ayrie toure,
They hurld the bodie of yoong *Mahomet*,
VVhereas a band of armed fouldiers,
Receiued him falling on their fpeares fharp points. 1200
His fifter, poore *Zonara*, [luckleffe maid]
Entreating life and not obtaining it,
VVas ftrangled by his barbarous fouldiers.

Baiazet fals in a fownd and being recouered fay.[1]

Baia. / Oh you difpencers of our haplefle breath,
Why do ye glut your eyes, and take delight
To fee fad pageants of mens miferies ?
Wherefore haue you prolong'd my wretched life,
To fee my fonne my deareft *Acomat*,
To lift his hands againft his fathers life ?   1210
Ah, *Selimus*, now do I pardon thee,
For thou didft fet upon me manfully,
And mou'd by an occafion, though vniuft.
But *Acomat*, iniurious *Acomat*,
Is ten times more vnnaturall to me.
Haplefle *Zonara*, haplefle *Mahomet*,
The poore remainder of my *Alemfhae* ;
Which of you both fhall *Baiazet* moft waile ?
Ah both of you are worthie to be wailde.
Happily dealt the froward fates with thee   1220
Good *Alemfhae*, for thou didft die in field
And fo preuentedft this fad fpectacle ;
Pitifull fpectacle of fad dreeriment,
Pitifull fpectacle of difmall death.
But I haue liu'd to fee thee *Alemfhae*,
By *Tartar* Pirates all in peeces torne.
To fee yoong *Selims* difobedience,
To fee the death of *Alemfhaes* poore feed.

---

[1] At first I was disposed to read 'fays'; but in his other Plays, *e.g.*,
'James IV.,' Greene gives thus the stage directions.

And laſt of all to ſee my *Acomat*
Prooue a rebellious enemie to me.   1230
   Beli. Ah ceaſe your teares, vnhappie Emperour,
And ſhead not all for your poore nephews death.
Six thouſand of true hearted citizens
In faire *Natolia, Acomat* hath ſlaine :
The channels run like riuerets of blood,
And I eſcap'd with this poore companie,
Bemangled and diſmembred as you ſee ;
To be the meſſenger of theſe ſad newes.
And now mine eyes faſt ſwimming in pale death,
Bids me reſigne my breath vnto the hcauens ;   1240
Death / ſtands before readie for to ſtrike.
Farewell deare Emperour and reuenge our loſſe,
As euer thou doeſt hope for happineſſe.   *He dies.*
   Baia. Auernus iawes and loathſome *Tænarus,*
From whence the damned ghoaſts do often creep
Back to the world, to puniſh wicked men.
Black *Demogorgon,* grandfather of night,
Send out thy furies from thy firie hall ;
The pitileſſe *Erynns*[1] arm'd with whippes
And all the damned monſters of black hell ;   1250
To powre their plagues on curſed *Acomat.*
How ſhall I mourne, or which way ſhall I turne
To powre my teares vpon my deareſt friends ?
Couldſt thou endu[r]e falſe-hearted *Acomat*
To kill thy nephew and his[2] ſiſter thus,

---

[1] Misprinted 'Erymnies.'   [2] *Ibid.* 'thy.'

And wound to death fo valiant a Lord ?
And will you not you al beholding heauens,
Dart down on him your piercing lightning
    brand,
Enrold in fulphur, and confuming flames ?
Ah do not *Ioue*, *Acomat* is my fonne,   1260
And may perhaps by counfell be reclaim'd,
And brought to filiall obedience.
Aga thou art a man of peirfant wit ;
Go thou and talke with my fonne *Acomat*,
And fee if he will any way relent ;
Speake him faire *Aga*, leaft he kill thee too.
And we my Lords will in, and mourne a while,
Ouer thefe princes lamentable tombs.
                    Exeunt all.

   Enter Acomat, Vifir, Regan, and their fouldiers. 1270

   Aco. As *Tityus* in the countrie of the dead,
With reftleffe cries doth call vpon high *Ioue*,
The while the vulture tireth on his heart ;
So *Acomat*, reuenge ftill gnawes thy foule.
I thinke my fouldiers hands haue bene too flow,
In / fheading blood, and murthring innocents.
I thinke my wrath hath bene too patient,
Since ciuill blood quencheth not out the flames
Which *Baiazet* hath kindled in my heart.
   Vifir. My gratious Lord, here is a meffenger 1280
Sent from your father the Emperour.

Enter Aga and one with him.

Aco. Let him come in : *Aga* what newes with
    you ?
Aga. Great Prince, thy father mightie *Baiazet*,
Wonders your grace whom he did loue fo much,
And thought to leaue poffeffour of the crowne,
Would thus requite his loue with mortall hate,
To kill thy nephewes with reuenging fword,
And maffacre his fubiects in fuch fort.
    Aco. *Aga*, my father traitrous *Baiazet*,   1290
Detaines the crowne iniurioufly from me ;
Which I will haue if all the world fay nay.
I am not like the vnmanured land,
Which anfweres not his earers[1] greedie mind ;
I fow not feeds vpon the barren fand ;
A thoufand wayes can *Acomat* foon finde,
To gaine my will ; which if I cannot gaine,
Then purple blood my angry hands fhall ftaine.
    Aga. [Ah]*Acomat*, yet learne by *Selimus*
That haftie purpofes haue hated endes.   1300
    Aco. Tufh *Aga*, *Selim* was not wife inough,
To fet vpon the head at the firft brunt;
He fhould haue done as I do meane to do ;
Fill all the confines, with fire, fword, and blood,
Burne vp the fields, and ouerthrow whole townes ;
And when he had endammaged that way,

---

[1] = tillers—misprinted 'honours.'

Thē teare the old man peecemeal with my teeth,
And colour my ſtrong hands with his gore-blood.[1]

Aga. O ſee my Lord, how fell ambition
Deceiues your ſences and bewitcyes you ;   1310
Could you vnkind performe ſo foule a deed,
As / kill the man, that firſt gaue life to you ?
Do you not feare the peoples aduerſe fame ?

Aco. It is the greateſt glorie of a king
When, though his ſubiects hate his wicked deeds,
Yet are they forſt to beare them all with praiſe.

Aga. Whom feare conſtraines to praiſe their
                      princes deeds,
That feare, eternall hatred in them feeds.   [mace,

Aco. He knowes not how to ſway the kingly
That loues to be great in his peoples grace :   1320
The ſureſt ground for kings to build vpon,
Is to be fear'd and curſt of euery one.
What, though the world of nations me hate ?
Hate is peculiar to a princes ſtate.

Aga. Where ther's no ſhame, no care of holy
No faith, no iuſtice, no integritie,   [law,
That ſtate is full of mutabilitie.

Aco. Bare faith, pure vertue, poore integritie,
Are ornaments fit for a priuate man ;
Beſeemes a prince for to do all he can.   1330

Aga. Yet know it is a ſacrilegious will,
To ſlaie thy father, were he nere ſo ill.

---

[1] As usual with Greene, the grammar somewhat mixed here.

Aco. Tis lawfull gray-beard for to do to him,
What ought not to be done vnto a father.
Hath he not wip't me from the Turkiſh crowne?
Preferr'd he not the ſtubborne Ianizaries,
And heard the Baſſaes ſtout petitions,
Before he would giue eare to my requeſt ?
As ſure as day, mine eyes ſhall nere taſt ſleepe,
Before my ſword haue riuen his periur'd breſt.   1340
   Aga. Ah let me neuer liue to ſee that day.
   Aco. Yes thou ſhalt liue, but neuer ſee that
            day ;
Wanting the tapers that ſhould giue thee light :
                              Puls out his eyes.
Thou ſhalt not ſee ſo great felicitie,
When I ſhall rend out *Baiazets* dimme eyes,
And by his death inſtall my ſelfe a king.
   Aga. / Ah cruell tyrant and vnmercifull,
More bloodie then the *Anthropophagi*,
That fill their hungry ſtomachs with mans fleſh.   1350
Thou ſhouldſt haue ſlaine me barbarous *Acomat*,
Not leaue me in ſo comfortleſſe a life ;
To liue on earth, and neuer ſee the ſunne.
   Aco. Nay let him die that liueth at his eaſe,
Death would a wretched caitiue greatly pleaſe.
   Aga. And thinkſt thou then to ſcape vn-
            pu[n]iſhed ?
No *Acomat*, though both mine eyes be gone,
Yet are my hands left on to murther thee.

Aco. T'was wel remembred : *Regan* cut them off.
　They cut off his hands and giue them Acomat.　1360
Now in that fort go tell thy Emperour
That if himfelfe had but bene in thy place,
I would haue vf'd him crueller then thee :
Here take thy hands, I know thou lou'ft them wel.
　　Opens his bofome, and puts them in.
Which hand is this? right? or left? canft thou tell?
　Aga. I know not which it is, but tis my hand.
But oh thou fupreme architect of all,
Firft mouer of thofe tenfold chriftall orbes,
Where all thofe mouing and vnmouing eyes　　1370
Behold thy goodneffe euerlaftingly ;
See, vnto thee I lift thefe bloudie armes :
For hands I haue not for to lift to thee ;
And in thy iuftice, dart thy fmouldring flame
Vpon the head of curfed *Acomat.*
Oh cruell heauens and iniurious fates !
Euen the laft refuge of a wretched man,
Is tooke from me : for how can *Aga* weepe?
Or runne[1] a brinifh fhow'r[2] of pearled teares,
Wanting the watry cefternes of his eyes ?　　1380
Come lead me backe againe to *Baiazet,*
The wofulleft, and fadd'ft Embaffadour
That euer was difpatch'd to any King.
　Aco. / Why fo, this muficke pleafes *Acomat.*
And would I had my doating father here,

---

[1] Mifprinted 'ruine.'　　　　[2] *Ibid.* 'fhewes.'

I would rip vp his breaſt, and rend his heart ;
Into his bowels thruſt my angry hands,
As willingly, and with as good a mind,
As I could be the Turkiſh Emperour.
And by the cleare declining vault of heauen,   1390
Whither the ſoules of dying men do flee,
Either I meane to dye the death my ſelfe,
Or make that old falſe faitour bleed his laſt.
For death, no ſorrow could vnto me bring,
So *Acomat* might die the Turkiſh king.

Exeunt All.

*Enter Baiazet, Muſtaffa, Cali, Hali, and Aga led
        by a ſouldier : who [ſhewn] k[n]eeling before
        Baiazet, and holding his legs, ſhall ſay :*

Aga. Is this the bodie of my ſoueraigne ?   1400
Are theſe the ſacred pillars that ſupport
The image of true magnanimitie ?
Ah *Baiazet*, thy ſonne falſe *Acomat*
Is full reſolued to take thy life from thee ;
Tis true, tis true, witneſſe theſe handleſſe armes,
VVitneſſe theſe emptie lodges of mine eyes,
VVitneſſe the gods that from the higheſt heauen
Beheld the tyrant with remorceleſſe heart,
Pull[1] out mine eyes, and cut off my weake hands.
VVitneſſe that ſun whoſe golden coloured beames   1410

---

[1] Misprinted 'Puld.'

Your eyes do fee, but mine can nere behold ;
VVitneffe the earth, that fucked vp my blood,
Streaming in riuers from my tronked armes.
VVitneffe the prefent that he fends to thee,
Open my bofome, there you fhall it fee.

Muftaffa opens his bofome and takes out his hands.

Thofe are the hands, which *Aga* once did vfe,
To toffe the fpeare, and in a warlike gyre
To / hurtle my fharpe fword about my head ;
Thefe fends he to the wofull Emperour,   1420
With purpofe fo [to] cut thy hands from thee.
Why is my foueraigne filent all this while?
    Ba. Ah *Aga*, *Baiazet* faine would fpeake to thee,
But fodaine forrow eateth vp my words.
Baiazet Aga, faine would weepe for thee,
But cruell forrow drieth vp my teares.
Baiazet Aga, faine would die for thee,
But griefe hath weakned my poore aged hands.
How can he fpeak, whofe tongue forrow hath tide?
How can he mourne, that cannot fhead a teare ?   1430
How fhall he liue, that full of miferie
Calleth for death, which will not let him die ?
    Muft. Let women weep, let children powre
                foorth teares,
And cowards fpend the time in bootleffe mone.
Wee'l load the earth with fuch a mightie hoaſt
Of Ianizaries, fterne-borne fonnes of *Mars,*

That *Phœb* fhall flie and hide him in the cloudes
For feare our iauelins thruft him from his waine.
Old *Aga* was a Prince among your Lords,
His Councels alwaies were true oracles ;   1440
And fhall he thus vnmanly be mifuf'd,
And he vnpunifhed that did the deed ?
Shall *Mahomet* and poore *Zonaras* ghoafts
And the good gouernour of *Natolia*
Wander in *Stygian* meadowes vnreueng'd ?
Good Emperour ftir vp thy manly heart,
And fend forth all thy warlike Ianizaries
To chaftife that rebellious *Acomat*.
Thou knowft we cannot fight without a guide,
And he muft be one of the royall blood,   1450
Sprung from the loines of mightie *Ottoman* ;
And who remaines now, but yoong *Selimus* ?
So pleafe your grace to pardon his offence,
And make him captaine of th'imperiall hoaft.

    Baia. / I, good *Muftaffa*, fend for *Selimus*,
So I may be reueng'd I care not how ;
The worft that can befall me is but death ;
[Tis] that would end my wofull miferie.
Selimus he muft work me this good turne ;
I can not kill my felfe, hee'l do't for me.   1460
Come *Aga*, thou and I will weepe the while :
Thou for thy eyes and loffe of both thy hands,
I for th'vnkindneffe of my *Acomat*.

                      Exeunt All.

Enter *Selimus, and a meſſenger with a letter*
from Baiazet.

Selim. Will fortune fauour me yet once againe?
And will ſhe thruſt the cards into my hands?
VVell if I chance but once to get the decke,
To deale about and ſhuffle as I would ;   1470
Let *Selim* neuer ſee the daylight ſpring,
Vnleſſe I ſhuffle out my ſelfe a king.
Friend, let me ſee thy letter once againe,
That I may read theſe reconciling lines.

Reades the letter.

Thou haſt a pardon *Selim* granted thee.
Muſtaffa and the forward Ianizaries
Haue ſued to thy father *Baiazet,*
That thou maiſt be their captaine generall
Againſt th'attempts of Souldane *Acomat.*   1480
VVhy, thats the thing that I requeſted moſt,
That I might once th'imperiall armie leade ;
And ſince its offred me ſo willingly,
Beſhrew me but ile take their curteſie.
Soft, let me ſee is there no policie
T'entrap poore *Selimus* in this deuice?
It may be that my father feares me yet,
Leaſt I ſhould once againe riſe vp in armes,
And like *Antæus* queld by *Hercules,*
Gather new forces by my ouerthrow :   1490
And / therefore ſends for me vnder pretence

Of this, and that : but when he hath me there,
Hee'll make me ſure for putting him in feare.
Diſtruſt is good when theirs[1] cauſe of diſtruſt.
Read it againe, perchance thou doeſt miſtake.

(Reade.

O, heer's Muſtaffas ſignet ſet thereto :
Then Selim caſt all fooliſh feare aſide,
For hee's a Prince that fauours thy eſtate,
And hateth treaſon worſe then death it ſelfe.   1500
And hardly can I thinke he could be brought
If there were treaſon, to ſubſcribe his name.
Come friend, the cauſe requires we ſhould be gone :
Now once againe haue at the Turkiſh throne.

Exeunt Both.

Enter Baiazet leading Aga, Muſtaffa, Hali, Cali,
Selimus, the Ianizaries.

   Baia. Come mournfull Aga, come and ſit by me,
Thou haſt bene ſorely grieu'd for Baiazet ;
Good reaſon then that he ſhould grieue for thee.   1510
Giue me thy arm; though thou haſtloſt thy hands,
And liu'ſt as a poore exile in this light,
Yet haſt thou wonne the heart of Baiazet.

   Aga. Your graces words are verie comfortable,
And well can Aga beare his grieuous loſſe,
Since it was for ſo good a Princes ſake.

---

[1] — there's.

Seli. Father,—if I may call thee by that name,
Whofe life I aim'd at with rebellious fword,—
In all humilitie thy reformed fonne,
Offers himfelfe into your graces hands,   1520
And at your feete laieth his bloodie fword,
Which he aduanc'd againft your maieftie.
If my offence do feeme fo odious
That I deferue not longer time to liue,
Behold I open vnto you my breft,
Readie prepar'd to die at your command.
But / if repentance in vnfained heart,
And forrow for my grieuous crime forepaft,
May merit pardon at your princely hands ;
Behold where poore inglorious *Selimus*,   1530
Vpon his knees begs pardon of your grace.
    Baia. Stand vp my fon, I ioy to heare thee fpeak ;
But more, to heare thou art fo well reclaim'd.
Thy crime was nere fo odious vnto me,
But thy reformed life and humble thoughts
Are thrice as pleafing to my aged fpirit.
Selim we here pronounce thee by our will,
Chiefe generall of the warlike Ianizaries.
Go lead them out againft falfe *Acomat*,
Which hath fo grieuoufly rebell'd gainft me.   1540
Spare him not *Selim* ; though he be my fonne
Yet do I now cleane difinherit him,
As common enemy to me and mine.
    Seli. May *Selim* liue to fhew how dutifull

And louing he will be to *Baiazet*.
So now doth fortune fmile on me againe,   [*Afide*]
And in regard of former iniuries,
Offers me millions of Diadems :
I fmile to fee how that the good old man,
Thinks *Selims* thoughts are broght to fuch an ebbe 1550
As he hath caft off all ambitious hope.
But foone fhall that opinion be remou'd ;
For if I once get mongft the Ianizars,
Then on my head the golden crowne fhall fit.
Well *Baiazet*, I feare me thou wilt greeue.
That ere thou didft thy faining fonne beleeue.

      Exit *Selim, with all the reft, faue Baiazet*
                      and Aga.

   Ba. Now *Aga*, all the thoughts that troubled me,
Do reft within the center of my heart ;   1560
And thou fhalt fhortly ioy as much with me ;
Then *Acomat* by *Selims* confuming fword,   [fight.
Shall / leefe that ghoaft, which made thee loofe thy
      Aga. Ah *Baiazet*, *Aga* lookes not for reuenge,
But will powre out his praiers to the heauens,
That *Acomat* may learne by *Selimus*,
To yeelde himfelfe vp to his fathers grace.

      Sound within, long liue Selimus Emperour of
                      Turkes.

      Baia. How now, what fodaine triumph haue 1570
            we here ?

Muſt. Ah gratious Lord, the captaines of the
        hoſte,
With one aſſent haue crown'd Prince *Selimus* ;
And here he comes with all the Ianizaries,
To craue his confirmation at thy hands.

Enter Cali Baſſa, Selimus, Hali Baſſa, Sinam,
      and the Ianizaries.

Sinam. *Baiazet,* we the captaines of thy hoaſt,
Knowing thy weake and too vnwildie age,
Vnable is longer to gouerne vs ;
Haue choſen *Selimus* thy yoonger ſonne   1580
That he may be our leader and our guide,
Againſt the *Sophi* and his Perſians ;
Gainſt the victorious Soldane *Tonumbey.*
There wants but thy conſent, which we will haue,
Or hew thy bodie peece-meale with our ſwords.
  Baia. Needs muſt I giue, what is alreadie gone.
                  He takes off his crowne.
Here *Selimus,* thy father *Baiazet*
Weeried with cares that wayt vpon a king,
Reſignes the crowne as willingly to thee,   1590
As ere my father gaue it vnto me.
                  Sets it on his head.
  All. Long liue *Selimus* Emperour of Turkes.
  Baia. Liue thou a long and a victorious raigne,
And be triumpher of thine enemies.

Aga and I will to *Dimoticum*,
And liue in peace the remnant of our dayes.

              Exit Baiazet and Aga.

   Seli. / Now fit I like the arme-ftrong fon of *Ioue*,
When after he had all his monfters quell'd,   1600
He was receiu'd in heauen mongft the gods,
And had faire *Hebe* for his louely bride.
As many labours *Selimus* hath had,
And now at length attained to the crowne ;
This is my *Hebe*, and this is my heauen.
Baiazet goeth to *Dimeticum*,
And there he purpofes to liue at eafe ;
But *Selimus*, as long as he is on earth,
Thou fhalt not fleep in reft without fome broyle ;
For *Baiazet* is vnconftant as the winde :   1610
To make that fure I haue a platforme laid.
Baiazet hath with him a cunning Iew,
Profeffing phyficke[1] ; and fo fkill'd therein,
As if he had pow'r ouer life and death.
Withall, a man fo ftout and refolute,
That he will venture any thing for gold.
This Iew with fome intoxicated drinke,
Shall poyfon *Baiazet* and that blind Lord ;
Then one of *Hydraes* heads is cleane cut off.
Go fome and fetch [here] *Abraham* the Iew.   1620

              Exit one for Abraham.

Corcut, thy pageant next is to be plaied ;

---

[1] Query a sub-reference to Queen Elizabeth's Jew-phyfician ?

For though he be a graue Philofopher,
Giuen to read *Mahomets* dread lawes,
And *Razins* toyes, and *Auicennaes*[1] drugges;
Yet he may haue a longing for the crowne.
Befides, he may by diuellifh Negromancie
Procure my death, or worke my ouerthrow :
The diuell ftill is readie to do harme.
Hali, you and your brother prefently   1630
Shall with an armie to *Magnefia* ;
There you fhall find the fcholler at his booke ;
And hear'ft thou *Hali* ? ftrangle him.
                    Exeunt Hali, and Cali.
Corcut / once dead, then *Acomat* remaines,
Whofe death wil make me certaine of the crowne.
Thefe heads of *Hydra* are the principall ;
When thefe are off, fome other will arife,
As *Amurath* and *Aladin*, fonnes to *Acomat* ;
My fifter *Solyma*, *Muftaffaes* wife ;   1640
All thefe fhall fuffer fhipwrack on a fhelfe,
Rather then *Selim* will be drown'd himfelfe.

          Enter Abraham the Iew.

Iew, thou art welcome vnto *Selimus* ;
I haue a piece of feruice for you fir,
But on your life be fecret in the deed.
Get a ftrong poyfon, whofe enuennom'd tafte

          [1] Misprinted 'm' for 'nn' ; and so in l. 1647.

May take away the life of *Baiazet*,
Before he paſſe forth of *Bizantium*.

  Abra. I warrant you my gratious foueraigne, 1650
He ſhall be quickly ſent vnto his graue ;
For I haue potions of ſo ſtrong a force,
That whoſoeuer touches them ſhall die.
           Speakes aſide.
And wold your grace would once but taſt of them,
I could as willingly affoord them you,
As your aged father *Baiazet.*
My Lord, I am reſolu'd to do the deed.
           Exit Abraham.

  Seli. So this is well : for I am none of thoſe 1660
That make a conſcience for to kill a man.
For nothing is more hurtfull to a Prince,
Then to be ſcrupulous and religious.
I like *Lyſanders* counſell paſſing well ;
' If that I cannot ſpeed with lyons force,
To cloath my complots in a foxes ſkin.'
For th'onely things that wrought our Empirie,
Were open wrongs, and hidden trecherie.
Oh, th'are two wings wherewith I vſe to flie,
And ſoare aboue the common ſort.   1670
If / any ſeeke our wrongs to remedie,
With theſe I take his meditation ſhort ;
And one of theſe ſhall ſtil maintaine my cauſe,
Or foxes ſkin, or lions rending pawes.
           Exeunt All.

Enter *Baiazet, Aga, in mourning clokes, Abraham*
the Iew with a cup.

    Baia. Come *Aga* let vs fit and mourne a while,
For fortune neuer fhew'd her felfe fo croffe
To any Prince as to poore *Baiazet.*   1680
That wofull Emperour firft of my name,
Whom the Tartarians locked in a cage,
To be a fpectacle to all the world,
Was ten times happier then I am.
For *Tamberlaine* the fcourge of nations,
Was he that puld him from his kingdome fo ;
But mine owne fonnes, expell me from the throne.
Ah where fhall I begin to make my mone ?
Or what fhall I firft reckon in my plaint ?
From my youth vp I haue bene drown'd in woe,   1690
And to my lateft houre I fhall be fo.
You fwelling feas of neuer ceafing care,
Whofe waues my weather-beaten fhip do toffe :
Your boyftrous billowes too vnruly are,
And threaten ftill my ruine and my loffe ;
Like hugie mountaines do your waters reare,
Their loftie toppes, and my weake veffell croffe.
Alas at length allaie your ftormie ftrife ;
And cruell wrath within me raging[1] rife.
Or elfe my feeble barke cannot endure,   1700
Your flafhing[2] buffets and outragious blowes ;

     [1] Misprinted 'rages.'   [2] Qy. flafhing ?

But while thy foamie floud doth it immure,
Shall foone be wrackt vpon the fandie fhallowes.
Griefe, my leaud[1] boat-fwaine, ftirreth nothing fure,
But without ftars gainft tide and wind he rowes,
And cares not though vpon fome rock we fplit :
A reftleffe pilot for the charge vnfit.
But out alaffe, the god that rules[2] the feas,[3]
And can alone this raging tempeft ftent,
Will neuer blow a gentle gale of eafe,   1710
But fuffer my poore veffell to be rent.
Then ô thou blind procurer of mifchance,
That ftaift thy felfe vpon a turning wheele,
Thy cruell hand euen when thou wilt, enhance,
And pierce my poore hart with thy thrillant[4] fteele.
    Aga. Ceafe *Baiazet*, now it is *Agas* turne ;
Reft thou awhile and gather vp more teares,
The while poore *Aga* tell[s] his Tragedie.
When firft my mother brought me to the world,
Some blazing Comet ruled in the fkie,   1720
Portending miferable chance to me.
My parents were but men of poore eftate ;
And happie yet had wretched *Aga* bene,
If *Baiazet* had not exalted him.
Poore *Aga*, had it not bene much more faire,
T'haue died among the cruell Perfians,
Then thus at home by barbarous tyrannie

---

[1] = lewd.   [2] Mifprinted 'vales.'   [3] *Ibid.* 'fea.'
          [4] Mifprinted 'chrillant.'   See Gloffarial-Index, *s.v.*

To liue and neuer fee the cheerfull day,
And to want hands wherewith to feele the way.

 Ba. Leaue weeping *Aga*, we haue wept inough ; 1730
Now *Baiazet* will ban another while,
And vtter curfes to the concaue fkie,
Which may infect the regions of the ayre,
And bring a generall plague on all the world.
Night thou moft antient grand-mother of all,
Firft made by *Ioue*, for reft and quiet fleepe,
When cheerful day is gon from th'earths wide
  hall.
Henceforth thy mantle in blak *Lethe* fteepe,
And cloath the world in darkneffe infernall.
Suffer not once the ioyfull dailight peepe,   1740
But let thy pitchie fteeds aye draw thy waine,
And coaleblack filence in the world ftill raigne.
Curfe / on my parents that firft brought me vp,
And on the cradle wherein I was rockt ;
Curfe on the day when firft I was created
The chiefe commander of all *Afia* ;
Curfe on my fonnes that driue me to this griefe,
Curfe on my felfe that can finde no reliefe ;
And curfe on him, an euerlafting curfe,
That quench'd thofe lampes of euer burning light, 1750
And tooke away my *Agas* warlike hands ;
And curfe on all things vnder the wide fkie ;
Ah *Aga*, I haue curft my ftomacke drie.

 Abra. I haue a drinke my Lords of noble worth,

Which foone will calme your ftormie paffions,
And glad your hearte[1] if fo you pleafe to tafte it.
    Baia. And[2] who art thou that thus doeft pitie vs?
    Abra. Your highneffe humble feruant *Abrahā.*
    Baia. Abraham fit downe and drink to *Baiazet.*
    Abra. Faith I am old as well as *Baiazet,*   1760
And haue not many months to liue on earth,
I care not much to end my life with him.
Heer's to you Lordings with a full caroufe.
He drinkes.

    Baia. Here *Aga,* wofull *Baiazet* drinkes to thee:
Abraham, hold the cup to him while he drinkes.
    Abra. Now know old Lords, that you haue
                drank your laft;
This was a potion which I did prepare
To poyfon you, by *Selimus* inftigation,
And now it is difperfed through my bones,   1770
And glad I am that fuch companions
Shall go with me downe to *Proferpina.*
He dies.

    Baia. Ah wicked Iew, ah curfed *Selimus,*
How haue the deftins dealt with *Baiazet,*
That none fhuld caufe my death but mine own fon!
Had *Ifmael* and his warlike Perfians
Pierced my bodie with their iron fpeares,
Or / had the ftrong vnconquer'd *Tonumbey*
With his Ægyptians tooke me prifoner,   1780

---

[1] Misprinted 'hearts.'   [2] *Ibid.* 'For.'

And fent me with his valiant Mammalukes,
To be praie vnto the *Crocodilus* ;
It neuer would haue grieu'd me halfe fo much,
But welcome death, into whofe calmie port,
My forrow-beaten foule ioyes to ariue.
And now farewell my difobedient fonnes ;
Vnnaturall fonnes, vnworthie of that name.
Farewell fweete life, and *Aga* now farewell,
Till we fhall meete in the Elyfian fields.

He dies. 1790

Aga. What greater griefe had mournful *Priamus*
Then that he liu'd to fee his *Hector* die,
His citie burnt downe by reuenging flames,
And poore *Polites* flaine before his face ?
Aga, thy griefe is matchable to his,
For I haue liu'd to fee my foueraignes death ;
Yet glad that I muft breath my laft with him.
And now farewell fweet light, which my poore eyes
Thefe twice fix moneths neuer did behold :
Aga will follow noble *Baiazet*,   1800
And beg a boone of louely *Proferpine*,
That he and I may in the mournfull fields,
Still weepe and waile our ftrange calamities.

He dies.

Enter *Bullithrumble, the fhepheard running in haft,
and laughing to himfelfe.*

Bulli. Ha, ha, ha, married quoth you ?   Marry

and *Bullithrumble* were to begin the world againe,
I would fet a tap abroach, and not liue in daily
feare of the breach of my wiues ten-commande- 1810
mens. Ile tell you what, I thought my felfe as
proper a fellow át wafters, as any in all our village,
and yet when my wife begins to plaie clubbes
trumpe with me, I am faine to fing :

What hap had I to marry a fhrew,[1]
For fhe hath giuen me many a blow,
And / how to pleafe her alas I do not know.
From morne to euen her toong ne'r lies,
Sometime fhe laughs, fometime fhe cries ;
And I can fcarce keep her talēts fro my eies.   1820
When from abroad I do come in,
Sir knaue fhe cries, where haue you bin ?
Thus pleafe, or difpleafe, fhe laies it on my fkin.
Then do I crouch, then do I kneele,
And wifh my cap were furr'd with fteele,
To beare the blows that my poore head doth
But our fir *Iohn* befhrew thy hart,   [feele.
For thou haft ioynd vs, we cannot part,
And I poore foole, muft euer beare the fmart.

Ile tell you what, this morning while I was making 1830
me readie, fhe came with a holly wand, and fo
bleft my fhouldiers that I was faine to runne through
a whole Alphabet of faces : now at the laft feeing

---

[1] = shrow.

fhe was fo cramuk[1] with me, I began to fweare
all the criffe croffe row ouer, beginning at great A,
little a, til I cam to w, x, y. And fnatching vp
my fheephooke, & my bottle and my bag, like a
defperate fellow ranne away, and here now ile fit
downe and eate my meate.

   While he is eating, Enter *Corcut and his Page,*
         difguifed like mourners.   1840

  Cor. O hatefull hellifh fnake of *Tartary,*
That feedeft on the foule of nobleft men,
Damned ambition, caufe of all miferie ;
Why doeft thou creep from out thy loathfome fen,
And with thy poyfon animateft friends,
And gape and long one for the others ends ?
Selimus, could'ft thou not content thy mind,
With the poffeffion of the facred throne,
Which thou didft get by fathers death vnkind,
Whofe poyfon'd ghoft before high God doth grone? 1850
But thou muft feeke poore *Corcuts* ouerthrow,
That neuer iniured thee, fo, nor fo?
Old / *Halies* fonnes with two great companie[s]
Of barded horfe, were fent from *Selimus,*
To take me prifoner in *Magnefia* ;
And death I am fure fhould haue befell to me,
If they had once but fet their eyes on me.
So thus difguifed, my poore Page and I,
Fled faft to *Smirna* ; where in a darke caue   1860

       [1] Qy. cranky?

We meant t'await th'arriuall of fome fhip
That might transfreit vs fafely vnto *Rhodes*.
But fee how fortune croft my enterprife.
Boftangi Baffa, *Selims* fonne in law,
Kept all the fea coafts with his *Brigandines*,
That if we had but ventured on the fea,
I prefently had bene his prifoner.
Thefe two dayes haue we kept vs in the caue,
Eating fuch hearbes as the ground did affoord ;
And now through hunger are we both conftrain'd   187c
Like fearefull fnakes to creep out ftep by ftep,
And fee if we may get vs any food.
And in good time, fee yonder fits a man,
Spreading a hungry dinner on the graffe.

Bullithrumble fpies them, and puts vp his meate.

Bull. Thefe are fome felonians, that feeke to
rob me ; well, ile make my felfe a good deale
valianter then I am indeed, and if they will needes
creep into kindred with me, ile betake me to my
old occupation, and runne away.   188

Corcut. Haile groome.

Bull. Good Lord fir, you are deceiued, my
names mafter *Bullithrumble* : this is fome coufoning
conicatching crofbiter, that would faine perfwade
me he knowes me, and fo vnder a tence of fami-
liaritie and acquaintance, vncle me of victuals.

Corcut. Then *Bullithrumble,* if that be thy
name :——

Bull. My name fir ô Lord yes, and if you wil not beleeue me, I wil bring my godfathers and 1890 godmothers, and they fhal fwear it vpon the font-ftone, and vpon the church booke too, where it is written.—Maffe, I thinke he be fome Iuftice of peace, *ad quorum,* and *omnium populorum,* how he famines me[1]: a chriftian, yes marrie am I fir, yes verely and do beleeue: and it pleafe you ile goe forward in my catechifme.

Corcut. Then *Bullithrumble,* by that bleffed And by the tombe where he was buried, [Chrift, By foueraigne hope which thou conceiu'ft in him, 1900 Whom dead, as euerliuing thou adoreft.

Bull. O Lorde helpe me, I fhall be torne in peeces with diuels and goblins.

Corcut. By all the ioyes thou hop'ft to haue in heauen,
Giue fome meate to poore hunger-ftarued men.

Bulli. Oh, thefe are as a man fhould fay beggars: Now will I be as ftately to them as if I were maifter *Pigwiggen* our conftable: well firs come before me, tell me if I fhould entertain you, would 1910 you not fteale?

Page. If we did meane fo fir, we would not make your worfhip acquainted with it.

Bulli. A good well nutrimented lad: well if

---

[1] Some speech supposed of 'Corcut.' '*Bull*' is placed a second time before 'Maffe' inadvertently.

you will keepe my fheepe truly and honeftly,
keeping your hands from lying and flandering,
and your tongues from picking and ftealing, you
fhall be maifter *Bullithrumbles* feruitures.

Corcut. With all our hearts.

Bulli. Then come on and follow me, we will 1920
haue a hogges cheek, and a difh of tripes, and
a focietie of puddings, & to field : a focietie of
puddings, did you marke that well vfed metaphor?
Another would haue faid, a company of puddings :
if you dwel with me long firs, I fhall make you as
eloquent as our parfon himfelfe.

        Exeunt Corcut, and *Bullithrumble.*

Page. Now is the time when I may be enrich'd :
The brethren that were fent by *Selimus*
To take my Lord, Prince *Corcut* prifoner,   1930
Finding him fled, propofed large rewards
To them that could declare where he remaines :
Faith ile to them and get the portagues,
Though / by the bargain *Corcut* loofe his head.

                Exit Page.

Enter *Selimus, Sinam-Baſſa,* the courfes of *Baiazet*[1]
    and *Aga with funerall pompe, Muſtaffa, and
    the Ianizaries.*

Seli. Why, thus muft *Selim* blind his fubieĉts eies,
And ftraine his owne to weep for *Baiazet.*   1940

           [1] Misprinted ' Muftaffa.'

They will not dreame [that] I made him away
When thus they fee me with religious pompe,
To celebrate his tomb-blacke mort[u]arie.

To himfelfe.

And though my heart caft in an iron mould,
Cannot admit the fmalleft dramme of griefe,
Yet that I may be thought to loue him well,
Ile mourne in fhew, though I reioyce indeed.

To the courfes.

Thus after he has fiue long ages liu'd,   1950
The facred *Phœnix* of *Arabia*,
Loadeth his wings with pretious perfumes,
And on the altar of the golden funne,
Offers himfelfe a gratefull facrifice.
Long didft thou liue triumphant *Baiazet*,
A feare vnto thy greateft enemies ;
And now that death the conquerour of Kings,
Diflodged hath thy neuer dying foule,
To flee vnto the heauens from whence fhe came,
And leaue her fraile, earth[y] pauilion ;   1960
Thy bodie, in this auntient monument,
Where our great predeceffours fleep in reft ;

Suppofe the Temple of Mahomet.

Thy woful fonne *Selimus* thus doth place.
Thou wert the *Phœnix* of this age of ours,
And diedft wrapped in the fweete perfumes
Of thy magnifick deeds ; whofe lafting praife
Mounteth to higheft heauen with golden wings.

Princes come beare your Emperour companie
In, till the dayes of mourning be ore paſt,   197c
And then we meane to rouze falſe *Acomat*,
And / caſt him foorth of *Macedonia*.

          Exeunt All.

   Enter *Hali, Cali, Corcuts Page, and one or*
       two ſouldiers.

 Page. My Lords, if I bring you not where
Corcut is, then let me be hanged, but if I deliuer
him vp into your hands, then let me haue the
reward due to ſo good a deed.

 Hali. Page, if thou ſhew vs where thy maiſter is, 198c
Be ſure thou ſhalt be honoured for the deed,
And high exalted aboue other men.

   Enter Corcut and Bullithrumble.

 Page. That ſame is he, that in diſguiſed robes,
Accompanies yon ſhepheard to the fields.

 Corcut. The ſweet content that country life
    affoords,
Paſſeth the royall pleaſures of a King ;
For there our ioyes are interlaced with feares,
But here no feare nor care is harboured,
But a ſweete calme of a moſt quiet ſtate.   199c
Ah *Corcut*, would thy brother *Selimus*
But let thee liue, here ſhould'ſt thou ſpend thy life ;

Feeding thy sheep among these grassie lands :—
But sure I wonder where my Page is gone.

    Hali. Corcut.

    Corcut. Ay-me, who nameth me ?

    Hali. Hali, the gouernour of *Magnesia.*

Poore prince, thou thogh[t]st in these disguised
    weeds,
To maske vnseene ; and happily thou might'st,
But that thy Page betraid thee to vs.   1200
And be not wrath with vs vnhappie prince,
If we do what our soueraigne commands :
Tis for thy death that *Selim* sends for thee.

    Cor. Thus I like poore *Amph[i]araus*, sought
By hiding my estate in shepheards coate
T'escape the angry wrath of *Selimus.*
But as his wife false *Eriphyle* did
Betray his safetie for a chaine of gold ;
So / my false Page hath vilely dealt with me ;
Pray God that thou maist prosper so as she.   1210
Hali, I know thou sorrowest for my case,
But it is bootlesse ; come and let vs go,
Corcut is readie, since it must be so.

    Cali. Shepheard.

    Bulli. Thats my profession sir.

    Cali. Come, you must go with vs.

    Bulli. Who I ? Alasse sir, I haue a wife and
seuenteene cradles rocking, two ploughs going, two
barnes filling, and a great heard of beasts feeding,

and you fhould vtterly vndo me to take me to 1220
fuch a great charge.

Cali. Well there is no remedie.

> *Exeunt all, but Bullithrumble ftealing*
> *from them clofely* [1] *away.*

Bulli. The mores the pitie. Go with you quoth
he, marrie that had bene the way to preferment,
downe *Holborne* vp *Tiburne* : well ile keepe my
beft ioynt from the ftrappado as well as I can
hereafter, Ile haue no more feruants.

> *Exit running away.* 1230

> Enter *Selimus, Sinam-Baffa, Muftaffa, and the*
> *Ianizaries.*

Seli. *Sinam*, we heare our brother *Acomat*
Is fled away from *Macedonia*,
To afke for aide of Perfian *Ifmael*,
And the Ægyptian Soldane our chiefe foes.

Sinam. Herein my Lord I like his enterprife,
For if they giue him aide as fure they will,
Being your highneffe vowed enemies,
You fhall haue iuft caufe for to warre on them,   1240
For giuing fuccour gainft you, to your foe.
You know they are two mightie Potentates,
And may be hurtfull neighbours to your grace ;
And to enrich the Turkifh Diademe,

[1] — secretly.

With / two fo worthie kingdomes as they are ;
Would be eternall glorie to your name.

   Seli. By heauens *Sinam*, th'art a warriour,
And worthie counceller vnto a King.

Sound within. Enter *Cali and Hali, with Corcut*
          and his Page.

                             1250
How now what newes ?

   Cali. My gratious Lord, we here prefent to you
Your brother *Corcut* ; whom in *Smirna* coafts
Feeding a flocke of fheepe vpon a downe,
His traitrous Page betraied to our hands.

   Seli. Thanks, ye bold brethren ; but for that
          falfe part,
Let the vile Page be famifhed to death.

   Corcut. Selim, in this I fee thou art a Prince,
To punifh treafon with condigne reward.

   Seli. O fir, I loue the fruite that treafon brings,
But thofe that are the traitors, them I hate.   1260
But *Corcut*, could not your Philofophie
Keepe you fafe from my Ianizaries hands.
We thought you had old *Gyges* wondrous ring,
That fo you were inuifible to vs.

   Cor. Selim thou dealft vnkindly with thy brother,
To feeke my death, and make a ieft of me.
Vpbraidft thou me with my philofophie ?
Why this I learn'd by ftudying learned arts,
That I can beare my fortune as it falles,

G. XIV.   18

And that I feare no whit thy crueltie ;　　　　　1270
Since thou wilt deale no otherwife with me,
Then thou haft dealt with aged *Baiazet*.
　　Seli. By heauens *Corcut*, thou fhalt furely die,
For flandring *Selim* with my fathers death.
　　Cor. Thē let me freely fpeak my mind this once,
For thou fhalt neuer heare me fpeake againe.
　　Sel. Nay we can giue fuch loofers leaue to fpeak.
　　Cor. Then *Selim*, heare thy brothers dying words,
And marke them well, for ere thou die thy felfe,
Thou / fhalt perceiue all things will come to paffe, 1280
That *Corcut* doth diuine before his death.
Since my vaine flight from faire *Magnefia*,
Selim, I haue conuerft with Chriftians,
And learn'd of them the way to faue my foule,
And pleafe the anger of the higheft God.
Tis he that made this pure Chriftalline vault
Which hangeth ouer our vnhappie heads ;
From thence he doth behold each finners fault ;
And though our finnes vnder our feete he treads,
And for a while feeme for to winke at vs,　　　　1290
It [1] is to recall vs from our [ill] wayes.
But if we do like head-ftrong fonnes, neglect
To hearken to our louing fathers voyce ;
Then in his anger will he vs reiect,
And giue vs ouer to our wicked choyce.
Selim, before his dreadfull maieftie,

　　　　　　[1] Mifprinted 'But' in original.

There lies a booke written with bloudie lines,
Where our offences all are regiftred.
Which if we do not haftily repent,
We are referu'd to lafting punifhment.   1300
Thou wretched *Selimus* haft greateft need
To ponder thefe things in thy fecret thoughts ;
If thou confider what ftrange maffacres
And cruell murthers thou haft cauf'd be done.
Thinke on the death of wofull *Baiazet* :
Doth not his ghoaft ftil haunt thee for reuenge ?
Selim in *Chiurlu* didft thou fet vpon
Our aged father in his fodaine flight ;
In *Chiurlu* fhalt thou die a greeuous death.
And if thou wilt not change thy greedie mind,   1310
Thy foule fhall be tormented in darke hell ;
Where woe, and woe, and neuer ceafing woe,
Shall found about thy euer-damned foule.
Now *Selim* I haue fpoken, let me die :
I neuer will intreate thee for my life.
Selim / farewell: thou God of Chriftians,
Receiue my dying foule into thy hands.
                              Strangles him.
    Seli. What, is he dead ? then *Selimus* is fafe
And hath no more corriuals in the crowne.   1320
For as for *Acomat* he foone fhall fee
His Perfian aide cannot faue him from me.
Now *Sinam*[1] march to faire *Amafia* walles,

                    [1] Mifprinted 'Sinem.'

—Where *Acomats* ſtout Queene immures her ſelfe,—
And girt the citie with a warlike ſiege ;
For ſince her huſband is my enemy,
I ſee no cauſe why ſhe ſhould be my friend.
They ſay yoong *Amurath* and *Aladin*,
Her baſtard brood, are come to ſuccour her.
But ile preuent this their officiouſneſſe,   1330
And ſend their ſoule downe to their grandfather.
Muſtaffa you ſhall keepe *Bizantium*,
While I and *Sinam* girt *Amaſia*.

   Exit Selimus, Sinam, Ianizaries all ſaue one.

 Muſt. It grieues my ſoule that *Baiazets* faire line,
Should be eclipſed thus by *Selimus* ;
Whoſe cruell ſoule will neuer be at reſt
Till none remaine of *Ottomans* faire race
But he himſelfe ; yet for old *Baiazet*
Loued *Muſtaffa* deare vnto his death,   1340
I will ſhew mercy to his familie.
Go ſirra, poaſt to *Acomats* yoong ſonnes,
And bid them as they meane to ſaue their liues,
To flie in haſte from faire *Amaſia*,
Leaſt cruell *Selim* put them to the ſword.

   Exit one to Amurath and Aladin.

And now *Muſtaffa*, prepare thou thy necke
For thou art next to die by *Selims* hands.
Stearne *Sinam Baſſa* grudgeth ſtill at thee,   1350

And crabbed *Hali* ftormeth at thy life;
All repine that thou art honour'd fo,
To be the brother of their Emperour.

        Enter | Solyma.

But wherefore comes my louely *Solyma* ?
  Soly. *Muftaffa* I am come to feeke thee out ;
If euer thy diftreffed *Solyma*
Found grace and fauour in thy manly heart,
Flie hence with me vnto fome defert land ;
For if we tarry here we are but dead.   1360
This night when faire *Lucinaes* fhining waine,
Was paft the chaire of bright *Caffiopey*,
A fearefull vifion appear'd to me.
Me thought *Muftaffa*, I behelde thy necke
So often folded in my louing armes,
In foule difgrace of Baffaes faire degree,
With a vile haltar bafely compaffed.
And while I powr'd my teares on thy dead corpes,
A greedie lyon with wide gaping throate,
Seaz'd on my trembling bodie with his feete,   1370
And in a moment rent me all to nought :
Flie fweet *Muftaffa*, or we be but dead.
  Muft. Why fhould we flie beauteous *Solyma*,
Mou'd by a vaine and a fantaftique dreame?
Or if we did flie, whither fhould we flie ?
If to the fartheft part of *Afia*,
Know'ft thou not *Solyma*, kings haue long hands?

Come, come, my ioy, returne againe with me,
And banifh hence thefe melancholy thoughts.

Exeunt. 138(

Enter *Aladin,* [*A*]*murath, the meffenger.*

Aladin. Meffenger, is it true that *Selimus*
Is not far hence encamped with his hofte?
And meanes he to difioyne the haplefle fonnes
From helping our diftreffed mothers towne?

Meff. Tis true my Lord, and if you loue your
liues
Flie from the bounds of his dominions;
For he you know is moft vnmercifull.

Amu. Here meffenger take this for thy reward.

Exit meff. 139(

But we fweete *Aladin*, let vs depart,
Now in the quiet filence of the night;
That / ere the windowes of the morne be ope,
We may be far inough from *Selimus*.
Ile to *Aegyptus*.

Aladin.[1] I to *Perfia*.   *Exeunt.*

Enter *Selimus, Sinam, Hali, Cali, Ianizaries.*

Seli. But is it certaine *Hali* they are gone?
And that *Muftaffa* moued them to flie?

Hali. Certaine my Lord; I met the meffenger   140(
As he returned from yoong *Aladin*;

---

[1] Misprinted ' Alinda': and so a little onward.

And learned of them, *Muſtaffa* was the man
That certified the Princes of your will.
  Seli. It is inough : *Muſtaffa* ſhall abie
At a deare price his pitifull intent.
Hali go fetch *Muſtaffa* and his wife ;   *Exit Hali.*
For though ſhe be ſiſter to *Selimus*,
Yet loues ſhe him better then *Selimus*.
So that if he do die at our command,
And ſhe ſhould liue, ſoone wold ſhe worke a mean 1410
To worke reuenge for her *Muſtaffas* death.

      Enter *Hali, Muſtaffa, and Solima.*

Falſe of thy faith, and traitor to thy king,
Did we ſo highly alway honour thee,
And doeſt thou thus requite our loue with treaſon?
For why ſhould'ſt thou ſend to yoong *Aladin*,
And *Amurath*, the ſonnes of *Acomat*,
To giue them notice of our ſecrecies,
Knowing they were my vowed enemies?
  Muſt. I do not ſeeke to leſſon my offence   1420
Great *Selimus*, but truly do proteſt
I did it not for hatred of your grace,
So helpe me God and holy *Mahomet*.
But for I grieu'd to ſee the famous ſtocke
Of worthie *Baiazet* fall to decay ;
Therefore I ſent the Princes both away.
Your highneſſe knowes *Muſtaffa* was the man
That ſau'd you in the battell of *Churlu*,

When / I and all the warlike Ianizaries
Had hedg'd your perfon in a dangerous ring.   1430
Yet I tooke pitie on your daunger there,
And made a way for you to fcape by flight.
But thofe your Baffaes haue incenfed you,
Repining at *Muftaffas* dignitie.
Stearne *Sinam* grindes his angry teeth at me,
Old *Halies* fonnes do bend their browes at me,
And are agrieued that *Muftaffa* hath
Shewed himfelfe a better man then they.
And yet the Ianizar[ie]s mourne for me ;
They know *Muftaffa* neuer proued falfe :   1440
I, I haue bene as true to *Selimus*
As euer fubiect to his foueraigne ;
So helpe me God and holy *Mahomet*.

   Seli. You did it not becaufe you hated vs,
But for you lou'd the fonnes of *Acomat*.
Sinam, I charge thee quickly ftrangle him,
He loues not me that loues mine enemies.
As for your holy proteftation,
It cannot enter into *Selims* eares :
For why *Muftaffa* ? euery marchant man   1450
Will praife his owne ware be it ne'r fo bad.

   Solima. For *Solimas* fake mightie *Selimus*,
Spare my *Muftaffas* life, and let me die ;
Or if thou wilt not be fo gratious,
Yet let me die before I fee his death.

   Seli. Nay *Solima* your felfe fhall alfo die,

Becaufe you may be in the felfefame fault.
Why ftai'ft thou *Sinam*? ftrangle him I fay.

                           Sinam ftrangles him.

    Soli. Ah *Selimus*, he made thee Emperour,   1460
And wilt thou thus requite his benefits ?
Thou art a cruell tygre and no man,
That coul[d]ft endure to fee before thy face,
So braue a man as my *Muftaffa* was,
Cruelly / ftrangled for fo fmall a fault.
    Seli. Thou fhalt not liue after[1] him, *Solima.*
Twere pitie thou fhouldft want the company
Of thy deare hufband : *Sinam* ftrangle her.
And now to faire *Amafia* let vs march.
Acomats wife, and her vnmanly hoaft,   1470
Will not be able to endure our fight,
Much leffe make ftrong refiftance in hard fight.

                               Exeunt.

Enter *Acomat, Tonombeius, Vifir, Regan, and their*
                  fouldiers.

    Aco. Welcome my Lords into my natiue foyle ;
The crowne whereof by right is due to me,
Though *Selim* by the Ianizaries choyce,
Through vfurpation keep the fame from me.
You know contrary to my fathers mind,   1480
He was enthronized by the Baffaes will,
And after his enftalling, wickedly

        [1] Mifprinted 'after liue.'

By poyſon made good *Baiazet* to die.
And ſtrangled *Corcut*, and exiled me.
Theſe iniuries we come for to reuenge,
And raiſe his ſiege from faire *Amaſia* walles.

   Tonom. Prince of *Amaſia*, and the rightful heire
Vnto the mightie Turkiſh Diadem ;
With willing heart great *Tonombey* hath left
Ægyptian *Nilus* and my fathers court,   1490
To aide thee in thy vndertaken warre ;
And by the great *Vſan-caſſanos* ghoaſt,
Companion vnto mightie *Tamberlaine*,
From whom my father lineally deſcends ;
Fortune ſhall ſhew her ſelfe too croſſe to me,
But we will thruſt *Selimus* from his throne,
And reueſt *Acomat* in the Empirie.

   Aco. Thanks to the[e] vncontrolled *Tonombey* !
But let vs haſte vs to *Amaſia*,
To ſuccour my beſieged citizens.   1500
None / but my Queene is ouerſeer there,
And too too weake is all her pollicie,
Againſt ſo great a foe as *Selimus*.

                       Exeunt All.

    Enter *Selimus, Sinam, Hali, Cali, and the*
                Ianizaries.

   Seli. Summon a parley ſirs, that we may know
Whether theſe Muſhroms here will yeeld or no.

*A parley: Queene of Amaſia, and her ſouldiers on
the walles.*   1510

Queen. What craueſt thou bloud-thirſtie parri-
Iſt not inough that thou haſt foulely ſlaine, [cide?
Thy louing father noble *Baiazet* ?
And ſtrangled *Corcut* thine vnhappie brother ?
Slaine braue *Muſtaffa* ? and faire *Solima* ?
Becauſe they fauoured my vnhappie ſonnes,
But thou muſt yet ſeeke for more maſſacres ?
Go, waſh thy guiltie hands in luke-warme blood ;
Enrich thy ſouldiers with robberies ;
Yet do the heauens ſtill beare an equall eye,   1520
And vengeance followes thee euen at the heeles.
    Seli. Queene of *Amaſia,* wilt thou yeeld thy
            ſelfe ?
    Queen. Firſt ſhall the ouer-flowing *Euripus*
Of ſwift *Eubæa* ſtop his reſtleſſe courſe,
And *Phæbs* bright globe bring the day frō the weſt,
And quench his hot flames in the Eſterne ſea.
Thy bloudie ſword vngratious *Selimus*
Sheath'd in the bowels of thy deareſt friend :
Thy wicked gard which ſtill attends on thee,
Fleſhing themſelues in murther, luſt, and rape;   1530
What hope of fauour ? what ſecuritie ?
Rather what death do they not promiſe me ?
Then thinke not *Selimus* that we will yeeld,
But looke for ſtrong reſiſtance at our hands.

Seli. Why then you neuer danted Ianizaries,
Aduance your fhields and vncontrolled fpeares ;
Your / conquering hands in foe-mens blood embay,
For *Selimus* himfelfe will lead the way.

Allarum, beats them off the walles. Allarum.

Enter *Selimus, Sinam, Hali, Cali, Ianizaries with* 1540
Acomats Queene prifoner.

Se. Now fturdie dame, where are your men of
war
To gard your perfon from my angry fword ?
What? though [you] brau'd vs on your citie walles,
Like to that *Amazonian*[1] *Menalip*,
Leauing the bankes of fwift-ftream'd *Thermodon*
To challenge combat with great *Hercules* ;[2]
Yet *Selimus* hath pluckt your haughtie plumes ;
Nor can your fpoufe rebellious *Acomat*,
Nor *Aladin*, [n]or *Amurath* your fonnes,   1550
Deliuer you from our victorious hands.

Queen. Selim, I fcorne thy threatnings as thy
felfe ;
And though ill hap hath giuen me to thy hands,
Yet will I neuer beg my life of thee.
Fortune may chance to frowne as much on thee ;
And *Acomat* whom thou doeft fcorne fo much,
May take thy bafe *Tartarian* concubine,

---

[1] Mifprinted ' Amanenian.'   [2] She didn't.

As well as thou haft tooke his loyall Queene.
Thou haft not fortune tied in a chaine,
Nor doeft thou like a warie pilot fit,   1560
And wifely ftir this all conteining barge.
Thou art a man as thofe whom thou haft flaine,
And fome of them were better far then thou.
   Seli. Strangle her *Hali*, let her fcold no more.
Now let vs march to meet with *Acomat* ;
He brings with him that great Ægyptian bug,
Strong *Tonombey*, *Vfan-Caffanos* fonne.
But we fhall foone with our fine tempered fwords,
Engraue our prowefse on their bu[r]ganets ;
Were they as mightie and as fell of force,   1570
As thofe old earth-bred brethren, which once
Heap[t]e / hill on hill to fcale the ftarrie fkie,
When *Briareus*, arm'd with a hundreth hands,
Flung foorth a hundreth mountaines at great *Ioue* ;
And when the monftrous giant *Monichus*
Hurld mount *Olimpus* at great *Mars*, his targe,
And darted cedars at *Mineruas* fhield.
                            Exeunt All.

Allarum   Enter *Selimus, Sinam, Cali, Hali, and*
     the Ianizaries, at one doore, and *Acomat,*
     Tonombey, Regan, Vifir, and their fouldiers 1580
     at another.

   Seli. What are the vrchins crept out of their dens,
Vnder the conduct of this porcupine ?

Doeſt thou not tremble *Acomat* at vs,
To ſee how courage maſketh in our lookes,
And white-wing'd victorie ſits on our ſwordes?
Captaine of *Ægypt*, thou that vant'ſt thy ſelfe
Sprung from great *Tamberlaine* the *Scythia* theefe;
Who bad the[e] enterpriſe this bold attempt,   1590
To ſet thy feete within the Turkiſh confines,
Or lift thy hands againſt our maieſtie ?

   Aco. Brother of *Trebiſond*, your ſquared words
And broad-mouth'd tearmes, can neuer conquer vs.
We come reſolu'd to pull the Turkiſh crowne,
Which thou doeſt wrongfully detaine from me,
By conquering ſword from of thy coward creſt.

   Seli. Acomat, ſith the quarrell toucheth none
But thee and me, I dare, and challenge thee.

   Tonum. Should he accept the combat of a 1600
               boy?
Whoſe vnripe yeares and farre vnriper wit
Like to the bold foole-hardie *Phæton*
That ſought to rule the chariot of the ſunne,
Hath mou'd thee t'vndertake an Empirie.

   Seli. Thou that reſolueſt in peremptorie tearmes,
To call him boy that ſcornes to cope with thee ;
But thou canſt better vſe thy bragging blade,
Then thou canſt rule thy ouerflowing tongue ;
Soone ſhalt thou know that *Selims* mightie arme
Is / able to ouerthrow poore *Tonombey*.   1610

Allarum. *Tonombey beates Hali* and *Cali in.*
Selim beates Tonombey in. Allarum. Enter[1]
Tonombey.

Tonom. The field is loft, and *Acomat* is taken :
Ah *Tonombey*, how canft thou fhew thy face
To thy victorious fire, thus conquered ?
A matchleffe knight is warlike *Selimus*,
And like a fhepheard mongft a fwarme of gnats,
Dings downe the flying Perfians with their fwords.
Twice I encountred with him hand to hand,   1620
And twice returned foyled and afham'd.
For neuer yet fince I could manage Armes
Could any match with mightie *Tonombey*,
But this heroicke Emperour *Selimus.*
Why ftand I ftill, and rather do not flie
The great occifion which the victors make.

                    Exit Tonombey.

Allarum. Enter *Selimus, Sinam Baſſa with Acomat*
          priſoner, Hali, Cali, Ianizaries.

Seli. Thus when the coward Greeks fled to their 1630
The noble *Hector* all befmear'd in blood,   [fhips,
Return'd in triumph to the walles of *Troy.*
A gallant trophee, Baſſaes haue we wonne,
Beating the neuer-foyled *Tonombey*,
And hewing paffage through the Perfians.

<hr>

[1] Mifprinted 'Exit.'

As when a lyon rau[n]ing for his praie,
Falleth vpon a droaue of horned bulles,[1]
And rends them ſtrongly in his kingly pawes,
Or *Mars* arm'd in his adamantine coate,
Mounted vpon his firie-ſhining waine,   1640
Scatters the troupes of warlike Thracians,
And warmes cold *Hebrus*[2] with hot ſtreams of
    blood.
Braue *Sinam*, for thy noble priſoner,
Thou ſhalt be generall of my Ianizaries ;
And / *Belierbey* of faire *Natolia*.[3]
Now *Acomat*, thou monſter of the world,
Why ſtoup'ſt thou not with reuerence to thy king ?
    Aco. *Selim* if thou haue gotten victorie,
Then vſe it to thy contentation.
If I had conquer'd, know aſſuredly   1650
I would haue ſaid as much and more to thee.
Know I diſdaine them as I do thy ſelfe,
And ſcorne to ſtoupe or bend my Lordly knee,
To ſuch a tyrant as is *Selimus*.
Thou ſlew'ſt my Queene without regard or care,
Of loue or dutie, or thine owne good name.
Then *Selim* take that which thy hap doth giue ;
Diſgra'ſt, diſplai'ſt, I longer loath to liue.
    Seli. Then *Sinam* ſtrangle him : now he is dead,
Who doth remaine to trouble *Selimus*?   1660

Miſprinted 'balles.'   [2] Miſprinted ' Hebras.'
            [3] Miſprinted ' Natalia.'

Now am I King alone, and none but I ;
For fince my fathers death vntill this time,
I neuer wanted fome competitors.
Now as the weerie wandring traueller
That hath his fteppes guided through many
    lands,
Through boiling foile of *Affrica* and *Ind,*
When he returnes vnto his natiue home,
Sits downe among his friends, and with delight
Declares the trauels he hath ouerpaft.
So maift thou *Selimus,* for thou haft trode   1670
The monfter-garden[1] paths, that lead to crownes.
Ha, ha, I fmile to thinke how *Selimus*
Like the Ægyptian *Ibis* hath expelled
Thofe fwarming armies of fwift-winged fnakes,
That fought to ouerrun my territories.
When foultring heat the earths green childrē
    fpoiles ;
From foorth the fennes of venemous *Affrica,*
The generation of thofe flying fnakes
Do band them felues in troupes, and take their
    way
To *Nilus* bounds: but thofe induftrious birds,   1680
Thofe / *Ibides*[2] meete them in fet array,
And eate them vp like to a fwarme of gnats ;
Preuenting fuch a mifchiefe from the land.
But fee, how vnkind nature deales with them ;

[1] Qy. '-garded.'   Qy. 'Ibifes.'

From out their egges rifes the bafilifke,
Whofe onely fight killes millions of men.
When *Acomat* lifted his vngratious hands
Againft my aged father *Baiazet*,
They fent for me, and I like Ægypts bird
Haue rid that monfter, and his fellow mates.   1690

But as from *Ibis* fprings the *Bafilifk*,
Whofe onely touch burneth vp ftones and trees ;
So *Selimus* hath prou'd a Cocatrice,
And cleane confumed all the familie
Of noble *Ottoman*, except himfelfe.
And now to you my neighbour Emperours,
That durft lend ayd to *Selims* enemies,
Sinam thofe Soldanes of the Orient,
Aegipt and *Perfia Selimus* will quell,
Or he himfelfe will fincke to loweft hell.   1700

This winter will we reft and breath our felues,
But foone as *Zephyrus* fweete fmelling blaft
Shall gently[1] creep ouer the flourie meades,
Wee'll haue a fling at the Ægyptian crowne,
And ioyne it vnto ours, or loofe our owne.

                                            Exeunt.

Conclufion.

Thus haue we brought victorious Selimus,
Vnto the Crowne of great Arabia ;

---

[1] Mifprinted 'greatly.'

Next fhall you fee him with triumphant fword,   1710
Diuiding kingdomes into equall fhares,
And giue them to his[1] warlike followers.
If this firft part Gentles, do like you well,
The fecond part, fhall greater murthers tell.

Mifprinted 'their.

FINIS.

VIII.

A MAIDEN'S DREAME,

1591.

NOTE.

For the title-page of the only exemplar known (at Lambeth Palace Library) see opposite. Our collation corrects numerous misprints, etc., etc., of Dyce. It is to be noted that though on the title the name is spelled ' Green,' it has the usual ' e ' at end of Epistle-dedicatory. On this poem and related matters, cf. Storojenko's annotated Biography (in Vol. I.)   G.

A
MAIDENS
DREAME.

VPON THE DEATH OF THE

right Honorable Sir *Christopher Hatton*, Knight, late
Lord Chancelor of ENGLAND.

By Robert Green Master of Arts.

Imprinted at London by Thomas Scarlet for
Thomas Nelſon. 1591.

To the Right VVorſhipfvll, Bovntifvll,

and Vertuous Ladie, the Ladie Elizabeth
Hatton, wife to the Right Worſhip-
full *Sir William Hatton, Knight,*
Increaſe of all Honorable
Vertues.[1]

OURNING as well as many, (right
worſhipfull ladie,) for the late loſſe
of the right honorable your deceaſed
vnckle, whoſe death being the common 10
preiudice of the[2] preſent age, was lamented of

---

[1] " *Wife to the right worſhipful Sir William Hatton.*—'Sir Christopher
Hatton [who died Nov. 20th, 1591] did not leave a Will. He had
settled his estates upon his nephew Sir William Newport, *alias* Hatton,
and the heirs male of his body; failing which, on his god-son and
collateral heir-male Sir Christopher Hatton. Sir William succeeded
accordingly to Holdenby and Kirby, and all the Chancellor's other
property. He married first, in June 1589, Elizabeth, daughter and
heiress of Sir Francis Gawdy, Justice of the King's Bench,' etc.   Sir
H. Nicolas's *Memoirs of Sir C. Hatton,* p. 502."—*Dyce.*

[2] Misprinted 'a.'

moſt (if not all), and I among the reſt ſorrowing
that my Countrie was depriued of him that
liued not for himſelfe but for his Countrie, I
began to call to mind what a ſubiect was
miniſtred to the excellent wits of both Vniuer-
ſities to work vpon, when ſo worthie a knight
and ſo vertuous a Iuſticiarie had by his death
left many memorable actions performed in his
life, deſeruing highly by ſome rare pen[1] to be 20
regiſtred. Paſſing ouer many daies in this
muſe, at laſt I perceiued mens humors ſlept,
that loue of many friends followed[2] no farther
then their graues, that Art was growen idle,
and either choice ſchollers feared to write of ſo
high a ſubiect as his vertues, or elſe they dated
their deuotions no further then his life. While
thus I debated with myſelfe, I might ſee (to the
great diſgrace of the Poets of our time) ſome
Mycanicall wits blow vp mountaines, and bring 30
forth miſe, who with their follies did rather dis-
parage his Honors than decypher his vertues :
beſide, as *Virtutis comes eſt inuidia,* ſo baſe report
who hath her tong bliſtered by ſlanderous enuie
began as farre as ſhe durſt, now after his death,
to murmure, who in his lifetime durſt not once
mutter : whervpon, touched with a Zealous

---

[1] Misprinted 'men.'
[2] Dyce changes wrongly to 'followed friends.'

iealoufie ouer his wonderfull vertues, I could not,
whatfoeuer difcredit I reapt by my prefumption,
although I did *Tenui Auena meditari*, but difcouer 40
the honorable qualities of fo worthie a Counfellor,
not for anie priuat benefit I euer had of him,
which fhould induce me fauorably to flatter his
worthie partes, but onely that I fhame[d] to let
flip with filence the vertues and honors of fo
worthie a knight, whofe deferts had bin fo many
and fo great towards al. Therfore (right worfhip-
ful Ladie) I drewe a fictiō called *A Maidens
Dreame*, which as it is *Enigmatical*, fo it is not
without fome fpeciall and confiderate reafons. 50
Whofe flender *Mufe* I prefent vnto your Ladifhip,
induced therunto, firft, that I know you are par-
taker of your hufbands forrowes, for the death
of his honourable Vncle, and defire to heare his
honors put in memorie after his death, as you
wifhed his aduancement in vertues to be great
in his life : as alfo that I am your Ladifhips poore
Countrimã, and haue long time defired to gratifie
your right worfhipfull father with fomething
worthie of himfelfe. Which becaufe I could not 60
to my content performe, I haue now taken oppor-
tunitie to fhew my dutie to him in his daughter,
although the gift be farre too meane for fo worfhipfull and vertuous a Lady. Yet hoping your
Ladifhippe will with courtefie fauour my prefuming

follies, and in gratious acceptance vouch of my
well-meant labours,

I humbly take my leaue.

Your Ladiſhips humbly at commaund,

R. GREENE, *Nordouicenſis.*   70

A MAIDENS DREAME.

ETHOUGHT in flumber as I lay
    and dreamt,
   I fawe a filent fpring raild in
    with Ieat,
   From funny fhade or murmur
    quite exempt.
The glide whereof gainft weeping flints did beat,
And round about were leaueleffe beeches fet ;
So darke, it feemed nights mantle for to borrow,
And well to be the gloomie den of forrow.

About this fpring, in mourning roabes of blacke,
Were fundrie Nymphs or Goddeffes, me thought,   10
That feemly fate in rankes, iuft backe to backe,
On Moffie benches Nature there had wrought :
And caufe the wind & fpring no murmure brought,
They fild the aire with fuch laments and groanes,
That Eccho fighd out their heart-breaking mones.

Elbow on knee, and head vpon their hand,
As mourners fit, fo fat thefe Ladies all :
Garlands of Eben-bowes, whereon did ftand,
A golden crowne ; their mantles were of pall ;
And from their waterie eies warme teares did fall : 20
With wringing hands they fat and fighd, like thofe,
That had more griefe then well they could difclofe.

I lookt about and by the fount I fpied,
A Knight lie dead, yet all in armour clad,
Booted and fpurd ; a faulchion by his fide,
A Crowne of Oliues on his helme he had,
As if in peace and war he were adrad :
A golden hind was placed at his feet,
Whofe valed ears bewraid her inward greet.

She feemed wounded by her panting breath ;   30
Her beating breaft with fighs did fall and rife ;
Wounds was there none, it was her mafters death,
That drew Electrum from her weeping eies :
Like fcalding fmoake her braying throbs out-flies,
As Deere do mourn when arrow hath them galled
So was this Hinde with Hart-ficke pains enthralled.

Iuft at his head there fate a fumptuous Queene :
I geft her fo, for why, fhe wore a crowne.
Yet were her garments parted white and greene,
Tird like vnto the picture of Renowne
                                                           40

Vpon her lap fhe laid his head adowne :
Vnlike to all fhe fmiled on his face,
Which made me long to know this dead mans cafe.

As thus I lookt gan *Iuftice* to arife ;
I knew the Goddes by her equall beame :
And dewing on his face balme from her eies
She wet his vifage with a yearnfull ftreame ;
Sad mournfull lookes did from her arches gleame,
And like to one, whom forrow deep attaints,
With heaued hands fhe poureth forth thefe plaints. 50

The Complaint of Iuftice.

Vntoward Twins that temper humane fate,
Who from your diftaffe draws the life of man
Parce, impartiall to the higheft ftate,
Too foone you cut what *Clotho* earft began :
Your fatall doomes this prefent age may ban,
For you haue robd the world of fuch a knight,
As beft could fkil to ballance Iuftice right.

His eies were feates for mercy and for law,
Fauour in one, and Iuftice in the other :   60
The poor he fmothd, the proud he kept in aw,
As iuft to ftrangers as vnto his brother ;
Bribes could not make him any wrong to fmother.

For to a Lord, or to the loweſt groome:
Stil conſcience and the cawſe ſet down the doome.

Delaying law that picks the clients purſe
Ne could this Knight abide to heare debated
From day to day (that claimes the poore mans
    curſe)
Nor might the pleas be ouer-long dilated ;
Much ſhifts of law there was by him abated.   70
With conſcience carefully he heard the cauſe :
Then gaue his doome with ſhort deſpatch of lawes.

The poore mans crie, he thought a holy knell:
No ſooner gan their ſuites to pearce his eares
But faire-eyed pitie in his heart did dwell.
And like a father that affection beares
So tendred he the poore with inward teares.
And did redreſſe their wrongs when they did call:
But poore or rich he ſtill was iuſt to all.

Oh wo is me (ſaith Iuſtice) he is dead,   80
The knight is dead that was ſo iuſt a man:
And in *Aſtreas* lap low lies his head,
Who whilom wonders in the world did ſcan.
Iuſtice hath loſt her chiefeſt lim, what than.
At this her ſighes and ſorowes were ſo ſore :
And ſo ſhe wept that ſhe could ſpeak no more.

The complaint of Prudence.

A Wreath of Serpents bout her lilly wrift,
Did feemly *Prudence* wear: who[1] then arofe.
A filuer Doue, fatt mourning on her fift,   90
Teares on her cheeks like dew vpon a rofe.
And thus began the Goddeffe grefe-ful glofe.
Let England mourn, for why? his daies are don
Whom *Prudence* nurced like her deareft fonne.

Hatton,—at that I ftarted in my dreame,
But not awooke : *Hatton* is dead, quoth fhe.
Oh, could I pour out teares like to a ftreame,
A fea of them would not fufficient be,
For why our age had few more wife then he.
Like oracles, as were *Apollos* fawes :   100
So were his words accordant to the lawes.

Wifdom fate watching in his wary eyes,
His infight fubtil, if vnto a foe ;
He could with counfels *commonwelths* comprife ;
No forraine wit could *Hattons* ouergoe ;
Yet to a frend, wife, fimple, and no mo.
His ciuill policie vnto the ftate
Scarce left behind him now a fecond mate.

For countries weale his councel did exceede,
And Eagle-eyed he was to fpie a fault :   110

[1] Misprinted 'fhe.'

For warres or peace right wifely could he
  reed :
Twas hard for trechors fore his lookes to hault.
The fmooth-fac'd traitor could not him affault.
As by his Countries loue his grees did rife :
So to his Countrey was he fimple-wife.

This graue aduifer of the Commonweale,
This prudent Councellor vnto his Prince;
Whofe wit was bufied with his Miftres heale,
Secret confpiracies could wel conuince;
Whofe infight perced the fharp-eyed *Linx*;   120
He is dead,—at this her forowes were fo fore :
And fo fhe wept that fhe could fpeake no more.

The complaint of Fortitude.

Next *Fortitude* arofe vnto this Knight,
And by his fide fate down with ftedfaft eye[s] :
A broken columb twixt her arms was pight :
She could not weep nor pour out yernful cries.
From Fortitude fuch bafe affects nil rife.
Brafs-renting Goddeffe, fhe cannot lament,
Yet thus her plaints with breathing fighs were fpent. 130

Within the Maidens Court, place of all places,
I did aduance a man of high defert[1] :
Whom Nature had made proud with all her graces ;

---

[1] Mifprinted 'degree.'

Inſerting courage in his noble heart,
No perils drad could euer make him ſtart ;
But like to *Scæuola*, for countries good,
He did not value for to ſpend his blood.

His lookes were ſterne, though in a life of peace ;
Though not in warres, yet war hung in his browes :
His honor did by martiall thoughts increaſe ; 140
To martiall men liuing this Knight allowes,
And by his ſword he ſolemnly auowes.[1]
Thogh not in war, yet if that war were here,
As warriors do to value honor deere.

Captens he kept and foſtered them with fee,
Soldiers were ſeruants to this martiall Knight ;
Men might his ſtable full of Courſers ſee,
Trotters, whoſe manag'd lookes would ſom afright.
His armourie was rich and warlike dight ;
And he himſelfe, if any need had craued, 150
Would as ſtout *Hector* haue himſelfe behaued.

I loſt a frend when as I loſt his life :
Thus playned *Fortitude*, and frownd withall.
Curſed be *Atropos*, and curſt her knife,
That made the Capten of my gard to fall ;
Whoſe vertues did his honors high inſtall.
At this ſhe ſtormd, and wrong out ſighes ſo ſore,
That what for grief, her tongue could ſpeak no more.

   [1] Misprinted 'auowed.'

The complaint of Temperance.

Then *Temperance*, with bridle in her hand,   160
Did mildly look vpon this liueleſſe Lord,[1]
And like to weeping *Niobe* did ſtand;
Her ſorrowes and her teares did wei accord;
Their Diapaſon was in ſelfe-ſame Cord.[2]
Here lies the man (quoth ſhe) that breathd out this,—
To ſhun fond pleaſures is the ſweeteſt bliſſe.

No choice delight could draw his eyes awry,
He was not bent to pleaſures fond conceits,
Inueigling pride, nor worlds ſweet vanitie;
Loues luring follies with their ſtrange deceits;   170
Could wrap this Lord within their baleful ſleights.
But he deſpiſing all, ſaid man was graſſe :
His date a ſpan, *et omnia vanitas.*

Temperate he was, and tempered al his deedes ;
He brideled thoſe affects that might offend ;
He gaue his wil no more the raines then needs ;
He meaſured pleaſures euer by the end :
His thoughts on vertue's cenſures did depend.
What booteth pleaſures that ſo quickly paſſe :
When ſuch delights are brickle[3] like to glaſſe ?   180

[1] Misprinted 'Cord.'
[2] *Ibid.* 'Lord'—transposition in each case.
[3] *Ibid.* 'fickle'—though it yield a sense.

First pride of life, that subtil branch of sinne,
And then the lusting humor of the eyes,
And base concupiscence, which plies her gin;
These Sirens, that doe worldlings stil intise,
Could not allure his mind to think of vice.
For he said stil Pleasures delight it is,
That holdeth man from heauens deliteful blisse.

Temperat he was in euery deep extreame,
And could wel bridle his affects with reason :
What I haue lost in loosing him then deeme; 190
Base death, that tooke away a man so geason,
That measur'd euery thought by tyme and seasson.
At this her sighes and sorowes were so sore,
And so she wept that she could speake no more.

The complaint of Bountie.

With open hands, and mourning lockes[1] dependant,
Bounty stept foorth to waile the dead man's losse;
On her were loue and plenty both attendant.
Teares in her eyes, armes folded quite acrosse,
Sitting by him vpon a turfe of mosse, 200
She sighd and said, here lies the knight deceased,
Whose bountie Bounties glorie much increased.

His lookes were liberall, and in his face
Sat frank Magnificence with armes displaid :

[1] Misprinted 'lookes.'

His open hands difcourft his inward grace :
The poore were neuer at their need denaid :
His careles fcorn of gold his deedes bewraid.
And this he craud, no longer for to liue
Then he had power, and mind, and wil to giue.

No man went emptie from his frank difpofe,   210
He was a purfe bearer vnto the poore :
He wel obferud the meaning of this glofe,
None lofe reward that geueth of their ftore :
To all his bounty paft.   Ay me therfore
That he fhould die: with that fhe fighd fo fore,
And fo fhe wept that fhe could fpeak no more.

The complaint of Hofpitality.

Lame of a leg, as fhe had loft a lim
Start vp kind *Hofpitalitie* and wept;
She filent fate awhile and fighd by him.   220
As one half-maymed, to this knight fhe crept,
At laft about his neck, this Nimph, fhe lept,
And with her *Cornucopia* in her fift ;
For very loue his chilly lips fhe kift.

Ay me, quoth fhe, my loue is lorn by death,
My chiefeft ftay is crackt and I am lame :
He that his almes [1] franckly did bequeath,

---

[1] " Is here, as in the sixth line of this stanza, a dissyllable ;—the pelling of the old copy being 'almes' and 'almes *deede.*' "—*Dyce.*

And fed the poore with ftore of food: the fame
Euen he is dead, and vanifht is his name.
Whofe gates were open, and whofe almes-deede   230
Supplied the fatherleffe and widowes need.

He kept no Chriftmas-houfe for once a yeere,
Each day his boards were fild with Lordly fare :
He fed a rout of yeomen with his cheare,
Nor was his bread and beefe kept in with care;
His wine and beere to ftrangers were not fpare.
And yet befide to al that hunger greued,
His gates were ope, and they were there releued.

Wel could the poore tel where to fetch their bread,
As *Baufis* and *Philemon* were i-bleft :   240
For feafting *Iupiter* in ftrangers ftead,
So happy be his high immortal reft,
That was to hofpitalitie addreft.
For few fuch liue, and then fhe fighd fo fore,
And fo fhe wept that fhe could fpeake no more.

Then Courtefie whofe face was full of fmiles
And frendfhip, with her hand vpon her hart,
And tender Charitie that loues no wiles,
And Clemencie, ther[1] paffions did impart ;
A thoufand vertues there did ftraight vp-ftart,   250

[1] Mifprinted 'her'; yet each taken separately would justify 'her' by
Elizabethan verse. But it is 'ther' = 'their,' onward a little.

And with ther teares and fighes they did difclofe:
For *Hattons* death their harts were ful of woes.

The complaint of Religion.

Next from the fartheft nooke of all the place,
Weeping full fore, there rofe a nimph in black;
Seemelie and fober with an Angels face,
And fighd as if her heart-ftrings ftraight fhould crak.
Hir outward woes bewraid her inward wracke.
A golden booke fhe caried in her hand,
It was *Religion* that thus meeke did ftand.   260

God wot her garments were full loofelie tucked,
As one that carelesse was in fome defpaire;
To tatters were her roabes and veftures pluckt,
Her naked lims were open to the aire;
Yet for all this her lookes were blith and faire:
And wondring how Religion grew forlorne,
I fpied her roabes by Herefie was torne.

This holy creature fate her by this knight,
And fighd out this, Oh here he lies (quoth fhe)
Liuelefs, that did religions lampe ftill light;   270
Deuout without diffembling, meeke and free
To fuch whofe words and liuings did agree;
Lip-holy Clergie men [1] he could not brooke,
Ne fuch as counted gold aboue their booke.

---

[1] Mifprinted 'Lip holinefs in clergymen'—Dyce's reading accepted.

Vpright he liud as holy writ him lead;
His faith was not in ceremonies old,
Nor had he new-found toies within his head,
Ne was he luke-warme, neither hot nor colde :
But in religion he was conftant bold,
And ftill a fworne profeffed fo to all, 280
Whofe lookes were fmooth, harts pharefaicall.

The brainficke and illiterate furmifers,
That like to Saints would holy be in lookes,
Of fond religions fabulous deuifers
Who fcornd the Académies and their bookes,
And yet could fin as others in clofe nookes.
To fuch wild-headed mates he was a foe :
That rent her robes and wrongd Religion fo.

Ne was his faith in mens traditions,
He hated Antichrift and all his trafh ; 290
He was not led away by fuperftitions,
Nor was he in religion ouer-rafh ;
His hands from herefie he loud to wafh.
Then bafe report, ware what thy tongue doth fpred,
Tis fin and fhame for to bely the dead.

Hart-holy men he ftill kept at his table,
Doctors that wel could doom of holie writ ;
By them he knew to feuer faith from fable,

And how the text with iudgement for to hit:
For Pharifees in Mofes chaire did fit.   300
At this *Religion* fighd, and greeu[d] fo fore:
And fo fhe wept that fhe could fpeak no more.

Primate[s].

Next might I fee a rowt of Noble-men,
Earles, Barons, Lords, in mourning weedes attir'd :
I cannot paint their paffions with my pen,
Nor write fo queintly as their woes requir'd :
Their teares and fighs fome *Homer's* quil defir'd.
But this I know their grief was for his death :
That there had yeelded nature, life and breath :   310

Milites.

Then came by Souldiers trailing of their pikes,
Like men difmaid their beuers were adown,
Their warlike hearts his death with forrow ftrikes,
Yea War himfelfe was in a fable gowne;
For griefe you might perceiue his vifage frowne.
And Scholers came by, with lamenting cries :
Wetting their bookes with teares fel from their eies.

Plebs.

The common people they did throng in flocks,   320
Dewing their bofomes with their yernfull tears ;
Their fighs were fuch as would haue rent the rocks,

Their faces ful of griefe, difmay and feares ;
Their cries ftroke pittie in my liftning eares.
For why ? the groanes are leffe at hels black gate,
Then Eccho there did then reuerberate.

Some came with fcrolles and papers in their hand,
I gheft them fuetors that did rue his loffe :
Some with their children in their hand did ftand,
Some poore and hungrie with their hands acroffe :   330
A thoufand there fate wayling on the moffe.
O pater Patriæ ! ftil they crièd thus :
Hatton is dead, what fhal become of vs ?

At all thefe cries my heart was fore amoued,
Which made me long to fee the dead man's face :
What he fhould be that was fo deare beloued.
Whofe worth fo deepe had won the people's grace.
As I came preffing neere vnto the place,
I lookt, and though his face were pale and wan,
Yet by his vifage I did know the man.   340

No fooner did I caft mine eie on him
But in his face there flafht a ruddie hue ;
And though before his lookes by death were grim,
Yet feemd he fmiling to my gazing view :
(As if, though dead, my prefence ftill he knew :)
Seeing this change within a dead mans face,
I could not ftop my tears, but wept apace.

I cald to mind how that it was a knight,
That whilome liu'd in England's happie foile ;
I thought vpon his care and deepe infight,   350
For Countries weale, his labour and his toile
He tooke, leaft that the Englifh ftate might foile ;
And how his watchfull thought from firft had been
Vowed to the honor of the maiden Queene.

I cald to minde againe he was my friend,
And held my quiet as his hearts content ;
What was fo deare, for me he would not fpend,
Then thoght I ftraight, fuch friends are feldom hent.
Thus ftill from loue to loue my humor went
That pondering of his loyaltie fo free,   360
I wept him dead that liuing honord me.

At this *Aftræa* feeing me fo fad
Gan blithly comfort me with this replie :
Virgin (quoth fhe) no boote by teares is had,
Nor doth laments ought pleafure them that die,
Soules muft haue change from this mortalitie ;
For liuing long finne hath the larger fpace,
And dying well they find the greater grace.

And fith thy teares bewraies thy loue (quoth fhe)
His foule with me fhall wend vnto the fkies ;   370
His liueleffe bodie I will leaue to thee,
Let that be earthed and tombed in gorgeous wife ;

I place his ghoſt among the Hierarchies :
For as one ſtarre another far exceeds,
So ſoules in heauen are placed by their deeds.

With that methought within her golden lap,
(This ſun-bright Goddeſſe ſmiling with her eie,)
The ſoule of *Hatton* curiouſly did wrap,
And in a cloud was taken vp on hie.
Vaine Dreames are fond, but thus as then dreamt I, 380
And more, methought I heard the Angels ſing[1]
An Alleluia for to welcome him.

As thus attendant[2] fair *Aſtræa* flew,
The Nobles, Commons, yea and euerie wight,
That liuing in his life-time *Hatton* knew,
Did deepe lament the loſſe of that good Knight :
But when *Aſtræa* was quite out of ſight,
For griefe the people ſhouted ſuch a ſcreame :
That I awooke and ſtart out of my dreame.

[1] Dyce suggests 'hymn.'   [2] *Ibid.* prints 'ascendant.'

FINIS.

390

END OF VOL. XIV.